OTHER BOOKS BY ROBERT HUNTER

To Save a Whale
Warriors of the Rainbow
On the Sky
Occupied Canada (with Robert Calihoo)

Red Blood

Red Blood

One (Mostly) White Guy's Encounters with the Native World

ROBERT HUNTER

SIERRA CLUB BOOKS
San Francisco

The Sierra Club, founded in 1892 by John Muir, has devoted itself to the study and protection of the earth's scenic and ecological resources—mountains, wetlands, woodlands, wild shores and rivers, deserts and plains. The publishing program of the Sierra Club offers books to the public as a nonprofit educational service in the hope that they may enlarge the public's understanding of the Club's basic concerns. The point of view expressed in each book, however, does not necessarily represent that of the Club. The Sierra Club has some sixty chapters coast to coast, in Canada, Hawaii, and Alaska. For information about how you may participate in its programs to preserve wilderness and the quality of life, please address inquiries to Sierra Club, 85 Second Street, San Francisco, CA 94105.

www.sierraclub.org/books

Originally published in Canada by McClelland & Stewart Inc.
481 University Avenue
Toronto, Ontario
M5G 2E9
A Douglas Gibson Book

Published by Sierra Club Books, in conjunction with Random House, Inc.

Library of Congress Cataloging-in-Publication Data

Hunter, Robert
Red blood : one (mostly) white guy's encounters with the Native
world / Robert Hunter.
p.   cm.
ISBN   1-57805-048-0   (alk. paper)
1. Indians of North America—Canada.   2. Hunter, Robert, 1941– .
3. Environmentalists—Canada—Biography.
E78.C2H84   2000   363.7'0092—dc21[B]   99-39577

1   3   5   7   9   8   6   4   2

To Will
Who said, "I'm proud of what you used to do, Dad.
Are you ever going to do anything again?"

"There's no longer any context for redemption."

Gentleman Death
by Graeme Gibson

Contents

1. The Huron in the Forest   3

2. An Indian in the Family   8

3. Bow Rider   14

4. The High of Battle   25

5. The Honorary Kwakiutl Shuffle   33

6. Sweat Lodge at My Door   48

7. Indian Time   60

8. *Occupied Canada* and the Governor-General   68

9. Flying South with Grizzly Bear Tracks   79

10. "Not Traditional Seafarers"   93

11. "Columbus, Make My Day!"   101

12. Native Trappers v. Saintly Vegans   112

13. Behind Enemy Lines in San Juan   121

14. Bring Me the Head of Inspector Garcia   130

15. Playing Chicken with a Frigate   145

16. Warbonnet Time   160

17. Storming the *Santa María*   169

18. Counting Coup   190

19. To the Powwow, with Expenses   206

20. Passing the Eagle Feather   218

21. "Willing to Pick Up a Gun Right Now"   230

22. The Talking Stick Descends   243

23. The Fall of the Medicine Man   252

24. Discussion by the Sacred Fire   258

25. Good Hunting at Gustafsen Lake   263

26. What Side Are You On?   271

Acknowledgments   273

Red Blood

I

The Huron in the Forest

Every journey is a test of your karma. In 1959, when I was eighteen years old, I had taken a Greyhound bus a couple of hours east of Winnipeg in the middle of January, equipped only with a summer sleeping bag and some cheap Boy Scout camping gear. I had been in Scouts years before, and had gone "winter camping," but in fact only for daytime trips. This was to be my first overnighter, and I was doing it solo. I had just moved out of home, leaving Mom, and was living by myself for the first time. Nobody could tell me what to do or not to do. The ecstasy of independence was upon me, and, on the spur of the moment, I decided to step out into the breathless purity of a winter forest, with only my wits to keep me alive.

I got the driver to let me off shortly after crossing the border into Ontario. As the bus disappeared down the highway, a ringing silence closed in, broken only by the cawing of crows. Just like that, I was alone in the second-largest boreal forest in the world, surrounded by dark coniferous trees stooped under huge cones of snow. There was nobody within fifty miles.

This is what I wanted: independence, adventure.

I snowshoed maybe half a mile into the woods, checking my compass and chipping the bark of every third or fourth tree so I would be able to find my way back, standard Scouting procedure. But when I decided to stop and make a fire, I discovered that my hatchet wasn't biting very far into the frozen wood. Only the thinnest branches could be broken off.

This was going to be a more daunting task than I'd thought. There wasn't a group of us, as there had been during day trips in

Scouts, to forage for wood. Just me. And I was getting exhausted fast. I had counted on a big fire to stay alive. And the light seemed to be going.

Darkness fell early and swiftly. I could feel the lethal sub-zero atmosphere closing in around me like a fist. It was too late to try to find my way back to the highway, and my pathetic stash of wood, acquired at the cost of more sweat than was good for me in the cold, was barely more than kindling.

The possibility of freezing to death was suddenly in the cards. Just like that. My God, it could be all over by morning. The thought kept me stumbling around in the snow, struggling to break off other little branches, anything to keep the cold at bay. But I was starting to get so overwhelmingly sleepy . . .

It was almost completely dark when a voice boomed at me out of the shadows: "You're on my property!"

When my heart stopped pounding enough for me to focus, I made out a man wearing thick furs and real moccasins, snowshoeing into view from between the trees, cradling a three-ought-three in one arm. How he had got that close without me hearing, in the extreme silence, was a question that left me feeling almost a superstitious rush of fear. A forest demon? Half-man, half-animal. A ghost? But as he moved closer he seemed real enough, with a long black ponytail coiling out from his parka hood.

I stammered out an explanation about how I didn't know it was anybody's property. No signs! And how it was too late to go back now, and, as a matter of fact, it was getting awfully cold, and I was having trouble gathering enough wood to keep me warm through the night.

His eyes took in my gear.

"No tent?" he asked.

"I didn't think I'd need it."

"It's gonna get plenty cold," he observed, and then, with a shrug, leaned his gun against a tree, unslung a saw from somewhere, and started taking down branches. Within minutes, he had a big pile ready. A few minutes more and a near-bonfire was crackling. Oh, thank God.

As I unpacked my cooking gear, he snowshoed off into the bush, returning some ten minutes later with a freshly snared rabbit. He skinned it, gutted it, and soon had it turning on a spit. He showed me how to cook it until you could break a bone and the marrow would bubble.

"That's when it's ready," he said.

It so happened I had brought along a bottle of port that I'd gotten my older cousin to pick up for me. The moon had sailed clear of the treetops by then, as we sat by the fire and ate and drank.

My rescuer told me he was a pure-blood Huron. Not just Huron, but pure blood. He made a point about the purity. At first, I shook my head, smiling, feeling superior due to my education compared to this poor primitive hunter, still doing what his ancestors were doing for thousands of years. Very clearly, back in whatever grade it was, probably 10, the textbook had stated that the Hurons were extinct, felled by a deadly combination of smallpox and Iroquois. Those few that survived were adopted and assimilated, so now their descendants would be mostly Iroquois. No, definitely, I explained, the Hurons were gone. Kaput. Exterminated. Left behind in history. I didn't put it quite that crudely, but crudely enough so that he stopped talking. A long silence followed. And who was I, it suddenly occurred to me, to argue with this very real Indian gentleman squatting across the fire from me who had just saved my life? What did I know anyway? I quickly apologized for my youthful arrogance. And he seemed to accept that. We finished the rabbit, cleaned out a can of beans and another of fruit, and polished off the port.

The air seemed to have drained from the sky and stuck to the snowdrifts around us, and the deadly chill of space pressed down. It was only a reflection of the moon, but a light seemed to be coming out of the ground itself, a blue-green light shining up through the moulded ice-glass glazing everything.

Before he glided away on his snowshoes into the night, my Huron saviour showed me what to do to stay alive until dawn. First, we heaped the fire up until it was roaring, and spread it out over the flat rock we had been sitting on. He instructed me to wait for the flames to burn down completely, then place my sleeping bag in the ashes.

It wouldn't be very comfortable, but the rock would hold the heat of the fire, releasing it as the hours went by into my sleeping bag. As long as I remembered to keep turning over, I should be okay.

It went down to something like fourteen below zero Celsius that night. By rights, morning should have found me in a sleeping bag turned body bag, my molecules adhering to the rock, fusing me to the planet until spring. Instead, I had been saved by a man whose almost-extinct tribe had been surviving on this scoured rockface since the last glacier melted away. Who could calculate what the odds were of him stumbling across me exactly when he did in the midst of the vast winter Canadian Shield? Ridiculous.

Come dawn, I was giddy from exhaustion and numb from the knees down, but nothing was seriously frozen. I made it back to the highway. It started to snow, huge flakes. I took off my snowshoes and started hitchhiking along the road. The world seemed new. I trembled with ecstasy, so beautiful was the sight of the snow falling hugely, slowly, silently, eternally. Except for this strange frozen canal of asphalt winding through the forest, this could be any moment in the last few million years. That's what I sought! To get out of my moment in time. To feel timelessness, or at least to get a sense of what it might be like to experience existence in terms of epochs and eras and ages, instead of insignificant hours and days.

Was this another lifetime begun? Each time you come that close, does it represent passing a previous high point in a string of existences? Crazy thoughts. The snow padding down. My mind sank into the Ecstasy of the Forest, even if I *was* walking on a highway, and I hiked for the longest time, blissed. Born again. Rapturous. Saved!

I suppose this experience changed me. Gave me a different take on Indians. They weren't just people drunk on the street, begging. One had saved my life when I was floundering in a hostile, alien world where I couldn't figure out what to do, either. He had basically given me a new life. For if my life had ended that night at fourteen below on the forest floor, everything that has happened to me since wouldn't have happened, which would change other people's lives, eliminate some in fact, as well as cancelling a few media events here and there. It gets too complicated too quickly to bear much thinking about.

It's not that I went through my life thinking I owe these guys because one of their boys saved my ass way back when. Rather, it was that I always felt comfortable around them. My first meeting with an Indian had been as equal citizens, though even that was downplaying the role of my life-saving friend, in my humbled opinion. In fact, it had been very similar to the experience of the early French colonists who plunged into a Canadian winter even more ill-prepared than me, and who also had to be saved by the local inhabitants. The Huron, whose name I have never been able to remember, finished the port with me on the frozen forest floor around a fire, under the moon. The memory could hardly be more archetypal: young white guy saved by a Native with whom he has absolutely nothing in common. Or so I thought at the time . . .

2

An Indian in the Family

It was only after my mother had died that my stepfather, Fred, got around to telling me about what Uncle Charlie had told them many years before, and which my mother had decided should not be made public, "since it was just Uncle Charlie talking." Still, she was gone now, and so was Uncle Charlie, my mother's last uncle on her father's side, and if Fred didn't tell us now, he reasoned, soon he'd be gone, and the story would be lost forever. As Fred talked about the visit to Uncle Charlie's side just before the old fellow died, I felt my neck hairs tingling. I knew, by then, about the Oral Tradition. Here I was, being let in on my own tiny, fragmented tribe's remembered history.

Uncle Charlie had said, "The Indian only showed up in Augustine, Noella, and Jeanne." That would be my mother and two of her sisters, my aunts.

"What Indian?" my mother had demanded.

And Uncle Charlie's reply had been that *his* great-grandfather had married a Huron, but that nobody ever talked about it, and nobody in the family had "looked Indian" for two generations, until his brother's three girls had come along. It wasn't so noticeable anybody ever said anything, but once you did notice, it was unmistakably there. The moment Fred mentioned the three names, it made perfect sense to me. Indeed, my mother and those two particular sisters, my closest aunts, stood out from their other six siblings by virtue of high cheekbones and the oval shape of their faces. And in her final weeks, as my mother lay dying, she looked more and more like an Indian.

Knowing how desperately ill she was, in the final stage of inoperable lung cancer, I had left the ship I was on in Seattle and driven up to Vancouver, to visit her one last time before she passed away.

She was supposed to be staying in the house Roberta and I had lived in for nearly a decade, across Burrard Inlet, north of Port Moody. It stood in a two-and-a-half-acre clearing in a second-growth coniferous forest where the Douglas fir had climbed back up to eighty feet tall. After we moved to Toronto, a string of caretakers had let the place fall apart until my brother Don decided to rent it, with the idea of moving Mom and Fred in with him so she could enjoy her final years in the countryside instead of an apartment. We all knew what was coming. But there was one delay after another, so that by the time Mom and Fred were finally ready to move, she was close to the end. The cancer had spread faster than predicted.

Just days before the move, Tony, the Medicine Man, arrived, along with four other Indians, to let my brother know that they were planning to use the Sweat Lodge on the weekend, and how would Don like it if they had a feast in the house, as they'd done before? Don gulped. I had explained to him about the Sweat Lodge. The rule was, any time the Indians wanted to use it, they were welcome. In fact, the circle of land down by the creek at the bottom of the yard where the Sweat Lodge stood was to be considered Sacred Ground, and nobody was supposed to desecrate it, i.e., leave cigarette butts or beer bottles. It had been built probably seven years before by a group of Natives who had been directed to me after they had been refused permission to build a Sweat Lodge on nearby parkland. No problem, I assured them, although, since I wanted to build a cabin for writing somewhere down by the stream when I could afford it, maybe the Lodge could be set up just a couple of yards downstream? The result had been the odd sight of a cedar-shake cabin with lots of big windows and skylights, hunkered down on the bank of the stream, with a low-slung Sweat Lodge, draped in used office carpet instead of buffalo hides, squatting beside it, and a fire pit in front of the entrance. My brother had, in fact, been waiting eagerly for the Indians to arrive, not knowing when it would be, but expecting it sooner or later. The timing, though, couldn't have been worse, what with our mother, on the verge of dying, about to move in, and needing peace and quiet. Tony promised to confine all activities to the lower yard. There'd be smoke and a bit of drums, that was all . . .

Mom was moved in to the house on a Saturday. On Sunday morning, Tony's truck arrived along with several station wagons and pickups filled with Indians, who filed down to the back acre, where soon you could hear the sound of axes, and then see smoke billowing up from behind the trees along the lower stream. Tony invited my brother down to join the ceremony, which, after only a moment's hesitation, he did.

I've done it a couple of times before, so I knew the routine, even before he described it to me. He was handed a bundle of red cloth and a traditional tobacco pouch and instructed to strip down to his underwear and climb inside the Sweat Lodge, with the cover pulled shut behind him. Then he and the others squatted on cedar boughs in total darkness, while water was splashed on heated rocks. Sensory deprivation and a sauna, combined with church: no matter how unimpressive it might look from outside, like a pile of old rugs, it was a Native temple perched lightly on the land. In the pitch darkness, the voice of an Elder told Don that he would call the spirits so our mother would pass easily beyond, and we would understand, and it would lessen the grief. After the Sweat was over and he staggered into the cool air, Don was invited to join a circle around the fire pit. The Elder cut the red cloth into ten pieces and packed each with tobacco. He lit five of them on fire, and after they had smoked for a while, buried them in front of the Lodge. Then he took the other five and hung them from trees near the stream, giving Don instructions about what to do after Mom passed away. The spirits would help her and help us. Don't worry when they come for her. They will only be helping her.

My brother walked back up the hill in tears. The sky had the biggest rolling and towering clouds he'd seen since he left the prairies. He could see beyond everything on Earth, as he put it, and he is not normally prone to poetry. When Tony left that evening, he stopped by the house to thank Don for the use of the Sweat Lodge, and to say that the way was clear for our old mother. All was ready for her. The Elder had seen a feather falling, turning as if it was flying as it fell, and that was a Sign that all was ready.

She was so far gone when I reached her side that I wasn't certain she even knew I was there. I wanted to get through to her, but the morphine doses were so heavy she was lost in a pharmacological fog. When the nurse came in, I asked if there was any way to make her hear me. She said the only way was to hold off on the morphine. That way, she might come to the surface. Okay, would she do that? The nurse shrugged and left without giving Mom a shot. I laid my head on her pillow, held her thin, translucent hands, and started singing songs from the Thirties and Forties to her, the songs she had played all through the war years on the piano to ease the loneliness, and then again later after Dad had run away.

I sensed her stirring. Though she didn't open her eyes, her head turned ever so slightly toward me. And as I was singing the words from "Lilli Marlene," tears finally welled out from between her eyelids and I knew she had heard. I held her as tightly as I dared and never had she been more precious, and I bathed in the memory of all the love she had given me, waves of it washing over and over me. Whether she knew it was me or not singing to her, I didn't know. But she had heard. She remembered the pain and the joy. I hoped that they were tears at the memory of the beauty, not tears at the loss of it. But it was emotion. She was aware.

And then she started twitching. Her mouth opened as though in a scream, but only a tortured rasping came out. Spasms ran through the thin cords of her muscles. It was as if she were being given electric shocks. Panicky, I ran out into the hall, yelling for the nurse. By the time she finally came and administered more morphine, I was nearly hysterical. To my horror, the twitching didn't stop immediately.

"How long before it takes effect?" I demanded.

"Fifteen minutes."

I was furious. Why hadn't she *told* me?

So for fifteen awful moments, I held my twitching, soundlessly screaming mother in my arms while the cancer tore her cells apart at the very core of her being. I knew what I *should* do. I had the pillow in both hands and I was holding it over her face. How could I let her go on suffering like this? My duty was so clear: I should be putting her out of her misery. But I couldn't do it. I couldn't smother the life in that body I had once inhabited. The last person I could kill even though her agony was in extremis and I wanted desperately to be able to release her. It was a long, long fifteen minutes before the morphine took hold.

That afternoon, the doctor conferred with Fred, Don, and me in a low, confidential voice. Did we want her taken off the intravenous? We all looked at each other and answered at once: "Yes, for God's sake, do it!"

And even at that, without any liquid coming into her body at all, it took three whole days before that tough old heart of hers would finally stop beating.

From the hospital, Don, Fred, and I went back to the house. My oldest son, Conan, showed up. By mutual consent, not having any church of our own, we drifted down to the Sweat Lodge, and sat around in silence in bright sunlight for a long time, grieving. I don't know about the others, but I certainly expected a Sign. I wasn't sure what. Something that said, Don't worry, this is all as it should be. Some little mystical blip on the radar. But nothing happened. A few ravens calling, but that was too common. The noon whistle from a distant refinery. All that told me was that I was running out of time and had to get back to my ship, which was supposed to be ready to go, maybe that evening. If not, certainly the next day.

By mid-afternoon, I was on my way back to Seattle.

After taking care of all the red tape at the hospital, my brother and stepfather eventually found their way to a pub, and stayed for a few rounds. It didn't seem that long, yet by the time they emerged into the parking lot, it had grown dark. My brother checked his watch, astonished. A storm had come in out of nowhere, crashing on top of the mountains, stirring up a ferocious wind and adding something you don't get too often on the Coast: broken-plate-glass cracks of lightning shattering across the whole sky. As Fred and Don drove up the slopes of Eagle Mountain to the empty house, the wind turned into a gale. By the time they climbed out of the van in the front yard, the creaking of the giant trees in the wind was so loud they had to yell to hear each other. Rain came in slanting fusillades and the bursts of lightning silhouetted the surrounding forest. Don suddenly remembered he hadn't followed the Elder's instructions about the tobacco pouches hanging down by the stream. The last thing he wanted to do in the middle of a storm when a tree might blow down on him any moment was splash all the way down to the Sweat Lodge and try to burn some soggy tobacco. But that's what he did. The lightning was so spectacular he didn't need a flash-light. He brought a butane lighter and managed to coax a smudge of smoke out of each of the five wet pouches hanging in the branches. There was a shovel and the ground was so thoroughly soaked it was no problem digging holes in front of the Lodge and burying them. Racing through the storm, Don got back to the house and he poured himself and Fred a drink. There was a lull in the rain. They stepped out onto the balcony overlooking the backyard to admire the swirl-ing tide of clouds overhead, its underbelly lit by the orange glare of Vancouver over beyond the tossing trees.

Just then, a ragged and immense bolt of lightning came blasting down into the yard, hitting the ground no more than twenty-five feet away from where Don and Fred were standing, so close that the hair on their arms was singed.

Tony, the Medicine Man, showed up at the front door the next morning, returning to pick up some stuff he'd forgotten down at the Lodge. Fred and Don babbled to him excitedly about what had hap-pened. He listened, then said to Don, almost casually: "Sounds like your mother went into the Great Sweat Lodge in the Sky and slammed the door behind her."

3

Bow Rider

·

The ship I sailed on from Seattle just after that was called the *Sea Shepherd II*, and her captain was my old eco-war buddy Paul Watson, famous for sinking and ramming any number of whaling, sealing, and drift-netting boats. I was onboard as a reporter for a television station, along with my cameraman, Jamie Tumulty.

I didn't talk about it to anybody, but as I prowled the clanking corridors of the ship and crawled out to the bow, I felt Mom's ghost beside me. It was as though she had timed her departure so that I would be close by physically, and when I left, she could attach herself to me and follow along. Rather than fighting the idea, I let myself talk to her—silently, of course. Hand in hand, we rambled back through the course of our life together. I wasn't afraid of the idea of her ghost being there. She was coming with me, for some reason. Maybe her presence was only like the feeling one has after a limb has been amputated: you close your eyes and you're certain it's there. But it was something more, I was sure. There was something she wanted so badly to tell me . . . about what I was doing, and why I had to do it.

At the very end, I could hardly recognize her. The face I remembered so well had been transformed into that of an ancient Indian woman. It was as though the cancer had acted as a sculptor, chiselling away at her features until a face behind the face could be seen; another layer, let's say, a long-hidden identity emerging in the fading days of this lifetime. Rather than looking ravaged, the old Indian woman's face had enormous dignity, wisdom, beauty. It was both my mother and not my mother. I was seeing the grand-mother within, the great-grandmother, the great-great-grandmother. It wasn't actually such a long genetic road back to *her*: the Huron. It was her I was seeing in the ruins of my mother's body on the hospi-tal bed. And if this was true, it meant there *was* some great incarna-tional mystery unfolding before my eyes. It had never occurred to me before that I might be making decisions in this life that were dic-tated by my mother's soul-imprint, as it were, let alone my mother's soul three generations removed. But this was a distinctly Indian thing we were doing on the *Sea Shepherd II*. Paul Watson had had a vision during an Oglala Sioux sweat ceremony at Wounded Knee, no less, in 1973, in which a huge buffalo appeared. He wasn't quite sure what it meant, but two years later, after I had enlisted him to join the campaign to end the slaughter of the great whales, it all sud-denly made sense to him. The whales were to the sea what the bison had been to the Great Plains. And the Sioux, under Sitting Bull, had gone to war to stop the White Man from wiping the buffalo out completely. After our anti-whaling campaigns had run their course, Watson took his buffalo vision a step further, and started working to save seals, dolphins, sea lions, tortoises, you name it.

This drift-net campaign is the ultimate extension of all those pre-vious actions. The drift-nets (some stretching a zillion miles and even more kilometres, strangling everything that swam into them) were a threat to nearly every living creature in the ocean, and Paul meant to "neutralize" as many drift-net ships as he could: a very "Sioux" warrior-brother vision. The old Indian woman who had ap-peared in my mother's death bed approved—of this I was passion-ately certain.

The first day out on the open sea, we ran into a typhoon big enough to deserve a name: Winona. This meant twenty-foot seas and forty-knot winds. The radio and chart rooms were quickly flooded. The forward head had to be shut down after water exploded from its throat and cascaded into the engine room, blowing a fuse. Between a quarter and a third of the crew went down immediately, including my cameraman, Jamie, who became a legend in the course of the voyage for generating more vomit than any of us would have believed it was possible for a single human being to produce. One time, he staggered out onto the deck just as the boat was plunging downhill. Too weak to resist gravity, he did a nice barefoot hippity-hop ballet down to a position parallel the wheelhouse, then, as the bow began to rise, stopped in his tracks, turned sideways, flung himself to the railing, opened his mouth as wide as it would go, and let loose a faucet of vomit that became a levitating green snake riding the wind down toward where half a dozen of us were hanging out by the starboard stern doorway, trying to get away from the diesel fumes inside the ship. As the snake undulated toward us (it was an *Exorcist*-thing come alive, I swore!) we adopted different strategies to escape being hosed. Some people ducked, some dodged. Miraculously, the apparition coiled by at chest level without splattering a single one of us before disintegrating into the fog behind.

At least once every day, the engine broke down. In the galley, somebody Scotch-taped up a sign saying WORRY, DON'T BE HAPPY. As the barometer dropped, tensions naturally rose.

Happy Hour at Marc Gaede's cabin was the big social event of the day, and there was a definite pecking order. Marc, Paul, Peter Brown, and I were the Old Warriors, spinning old war yarns as the old ship lurched across Old Man Sea. Marc, actually, was the oldest old-dog eco-guerrilla of the lot, having been around in the days when Edward Abbey's "Monkeywrench Gang" was first doing their thing, and he had been involved in a standoff with the Indians against a mining project at Black Mesa, a kind of early environmental Wounded Knee. He was one of the original Earth Firsters! And damned proud of his gun collection back home in L.A., when he wasn't at his ranch in Montana. He was rich enough through inheritance and marriage that he didn't have to work, although he was an accomplished photographer with several books out. Mainly, these days, he went off to war, accompanying Watson on *Sea Shepherd* expeditions.

A few evenings we clambered up to the captain's cabin and watched videotapes of earlier *Sea Shepherd* adventures. The television was lashed by rope to a table with the VCR wedged in beside it so they wouldn't fall over when the boat rolled. Here we were in the midst of the infinite kalumping blackness of the North Pacific, watching reruns of Paul's earlier escapades—or were they episodes, as in a series? A media-warp moment. A little box with yesterday's adventures captured on a glowing screen, while we splash toward our conclusion, camera batteries plugged in, tapes at the ready, shooting the next instalment as we go. Life as a sequel! A wave finally hit that was so big it sent the television set flying, and that was the end of the home movies.

There was something to be learned about Paul here, I thought, watching him watch himself. Kerouac said: Live your life as a legend! Certainly, Watson was doing this. And not only as a legend, but as the star of a Wagnerian epic broadcast from a planetary studio. Some people live for their clippings. Paul, I suspected, lived for whole sections in a tape library. And I realize my old buddy has metamorphosed since the days when I was his mentor, even his leader. Most obviously, his thick black hair has turned into thick silver hair. This is no stress-free line of work he has taken up. I remember how responsibility for more than my own life scared the crap out of me. Still does. Paul is ultimately responsible for the lives of everyone on board—and, let us not forget, the lives of the working men on the drift-net boats somewhere ahead that we plan to ram. How does he bear this?

Paul's photographic memory allows him to burst forth in song, remembering all the lyrics for almost any Fifties rock 'n' roll song you can name, effortlessly calling forth jokes from decades ago, which means, in a group, he easily overwhelms those still groping in the fog of their brains for something witty to say. If he is in the mood, he can hold court for hours, dispensing quotes from books, lines from movies, poetry, statistics, profound sayings; dipping effortlessly into the bulging grab-bag of info-goodies in his head, enjoying it when he makes people laugh, enjoying it equally when he makes them squirm. And getting bored quickly with any single line of discussion. When bored, he retreats into the lecturing mode. I think I have it now, the difference: Paul has been giving lectures at UCLA for years. He gets paid to do it. He lives in airports en route to lectures at colleges and universities, where he commands the microphone. He has an office and staff. He has contributors who worship him. He appears on talk shows. He has written his own books. And otherwise, he is captain of his own ship. He has grown slightly jaded about communication. I sympathize with him. You get used to talking from a stage to students or giving sound bite to a reporter or bellowing orders to a crew, and the niggliness of most conversation, in which you have to patiently wait for the interruptions of other people to end, grows . . . boring. Also, it's just verbiage. Above all, Paul is an action junkie. He lives for that moment on the highwire, with the eyes of as much of the world as we can make watch fixed upon him. It is a performance, sure—but possibly for God. Gaia, at least. If mere mortals don't like his act, it doesn't matter. And that's a gift: to be able to shut out all the whines and groans and catcalls and shouts and hoots of derision, for they do grow into a cacophony once you start to make an impact. The trick is to acquire the necessary density so that it all bounces off.

Come to think of it, that's probably why none of the dozen-odd film scripts that have been written about him, including his own, have so far succeeded in making it to the screen. The modern protagonist must have doubts about himself and what he is doing. He must be at war with himself. He must embody the contradictions of our dysfunctional civilization. But Paul doesn't have any doubts. He's perfectly straight-ahead. He isn't at war with himself. Au contraire. In fact, he is enormously at peace with himself. As for personifying anything, it would be a figure more familiar to mythology than contemporary Hollywood. How can you possibly make a commercially viable formula movie with a main character as out of synch with modern ennui as Watson? Nobody in the urban mass audience would be able to relate.

Few would be able to relate, either, to our actual life on board the *Sea Shepherd*. To flush a toilet, you had to throw a bucket over the side (regardless of weather), haul it aboard, slog along a slippery deck, clamber over hatchway bottoms all the way to the stern, where the head was, and pour it into the toilet tank. If one flush didn't work, you had a real moral dilemma. As for the showers, they were salt-water and so cold that if you didn't get in and out within a minute, hypothermia began to set in. Such fresh water as could be had from the sink taps was rust-coloured. It had to be boiled to drink. Throw a tea bag in, it wasn't too bad.

One night, Jamie and I and a writer named Chuck Bowden, who was sharing the cabin with us, were kept awake for hours by a new irritating sound on top of all the old irritating sounds. It was impossible to figure out what it was. Some rather large, heavily armoured insects making love or fighting? But no, it must be inanimate, its maddening *clackity-click-fitz-squeak* sound linked to the rolling of the ship, something moving maybe in the hull itself. Exhausted from the daily effort of moving about in the pounding sea (and having stayed late at Marc Gaede's open bar), neither Chuck nor I had the strength to climb out of our bunks, and Jamie was just a feeble, twitching thing dying horribly in his sleeping bag. We prayed weakly that, whatever it was, it would just move away to another section of the boat. But it persisted until I finally heroically hoisted myself to my feet, got a flashlight, and fumbled out into the corridor, expecting to find little robot rats crawling out of the engine room. It took half an hour to track down the source of the noise: two transistor batteries, which one of the younger Walkman-generation crewpersons had tossed aside. They must have slid down through a broken grill into the air vent. I was in such a heart-hammering rage at whoever had done such a stupid thing that by the time I got back in my bunk I couldn't sleep for hours. I awoke the next morning to the drip-drip-drip of tepid liquid on the side of my head, and discovered that Jamie had recovered enough to dry his socks by hanging them on the curtain string along the upper bunk, so that as the moisture drained out of them it found its way down in droplet form (the distilled essence of filthy feet) onto my face.

Tensions. Stress. Cabin fever. All the inevitable stuff. At the beginning of the trip, uncertain I would be able to get through the drama to come without breaking down and smoking, I had purchased two cartons of cigarettes. Since, as usual, I was trying desperately to quit, I had my plastic smoke and an emergency supply of Valiums. Thank God for the Valiums. Jesus was a pharmacologist, I always say. I entrusted the cartons of death-sticks to an honest-looking crewperson named Lisa, asking her to hide them away somewhere safe so that they would be available in the unlikely event that, despite my famous willpower, I broke. If I didn't use them by the end of the trip, they were hers. When I did break, about a week into the trip, and went to Lisa, asking for my smokes, she looked at me as though I was the village idiot. "Shit, Bob," she said matter-of-factly, "I sold them. Haven't you noticed all those people smoking your brand? None left, I'm afraid."

And then there were the inevitable philosophical confrontations with the Vegans. The cook could warm up rice without burning it, but she had a mean streak. I made the mistake of poking a bit of good-humoured—oh, all right, sarcastic—fun at her. Worse, I joined conspicuously in a plot to force her to cook a salmon that Watson had bought before we left port. The scheme was little more than a raw power play. Several of us low-born Meaties egged the captain on until he threatened to bust the cook down to being just an oiler, the lowest of crew positions, unless she did the deed. Cooking, particularly in bad weather, was a nightmare, for sure, but the hours were much better. Oilers were the poor souls who crouched in the engine room, sweating and covered with grease, trying not to tangle hair in the machinery or get zapped by any loose wires. If the boat sank, they'd be the first to drown. Apart from the noise and the heat and the fact that you couldn't see what was going on in the outside world, there was the constant state of emergency down there that you had to cope with. The chief engineer was a skeleton-thin Vegan named David Howitt, who had jumped on the boat at the last minute, but had done previous eco-work like helping to scuttle the Icelandic whaling fleet and smash the computers in their processing plant, inflicting a total of five-million-dollars' worth of damage. David was so shy and tongue-tied that I could barely coax ten words at a time out of him during an interview, yet his eyes sparkled with an inner frenzy, and no matter how often the engine failed him, he just smiled and shook his head, and plunged his arms back into its innards, performing what seemed like nothing less than open-heart surgery. A saint, I would have to say. And that was the point: you had to be a saint to work down in the engine room, and our cook was definitely no saint. Faced, basically, with the threat of being cast from Purgatory (the galley) down into Hell (the engine room), she wisely bowed to Watson's cruel demand, and cooked up a salmon stew.

To preserve her Vegan purity during this disgusting ritual, she strapped on a gas mask. Inhaling the fumes of a dead sentient being was apparently almost as bad as actually ripping off the flesh with your fangs. The meal was fantastic, as I recall, and I didn't take the icy glare of the cook as anything to worry about. So she hated us, so what? It wasn't until I climbed into my sleeping bag after a few glasses of Scotch-and-water that night that I realized my paranoia had failed me. I should have been on guard. My feet and legs were slashed—bitten, was what it felt like—by the spiky bones and spine of the skeleton of the salmon, which had been stuffed into my bag. In the utter blackness of the cabin, still being brutally heaved around by the typhoon, I banged my head on the bunk above and flopped onto the floor, smashing my elbow as I struggled convulsively to escape the jaws of whatever nameless monster had gotten hold of me. In the dark, in a storm, as you thrash about on the deck, a sleeping bag with teeth is much like a boa constrictor.

One for the Vegans!

It was probably no surprise that I spent a lot of time out on deck, if for no other reason than to get away from the saintly folk I was liable to meet in the galley. Apart from that, I am a compulsive bow rider. There is one thing about a big steel boat that beats smaller, more ecologically sensitive vessels like sailboats hands down: when you come to the top of a swell or wave, you are, to begin with, a good twenty feet above the water. By the time the bow reaches its highest point, the sea has begun to drop beneath you. With luck, you can be rearing maybe forty feet above the surface, hanging on to the V-shaped railing like a biker to handlebars, your feet apart, straddling the deck, with gravity grabbing you from behind and trying to haul you backwards as the seven-hundred-ton beast comes up like a killer whale snapping for something in the air. There is probably more of a parallel with riding a bronco than a bike. But as a bike, it was vastly bigger than the biggest old Harley-Davidson: a Hog of Hogs! There is always the trembling in the floor plates of the pistons, and the underground-train sound of the engine muttering when the wind pauses for breath. Otherwise, blasted by minuscule salt pellets, the tops of the waves sliced and blown into smoky foam, with the sky pulled down around my head, I can't hear anything mechanical at all, just a moaning in my ears coming from out there in space. No wonder sailors thought they heard spirits whispering to them; how could they not? The banshee wind!

Then riding down, down, down. Into a small valley. Like a truck leaping in slow motion off a cliff. This is like flying, except that now there is a forty-foot-high wall rearing ahead of us. Looking back, I see the wheelhouse towering like a great black chess piece alone above the grey-green hissing surge of ocean. We wallow horribly. The ocean fizzes like a cold cauldron into which I am about to be plunged. The North Pacific trumpets and thrashes around us and boils up in the form of house-sized green pyramids. And I am up again, clinging to the point of a steel iceberg before it crashes, the tops of the rolling, sloshing hills breaking through the smoke, air blasting beneath the forward hull, and I am looking around for miles at the storm, right out here about as close to the edge as you can get and still be alive. And then: the descent. Will we torpedo into the racing flank of the sea? If the bow bites deep enough, tons of white water will sweep me from the deck like a rag doll. A burst of authentic terror, and I would probably run for the wheelhouse, but it is too late. The explosion, as steel *ka-chunks* into ponderous sea, and the whole boat shudders, leaves me feeling weak and small in the midst of gigantic forces. And then, agonizingly, the bow begins to lift, scuppers spouting white, and the tons of water which have flash-flooded across the deck miraculously drain away.

Repeatedly, wimps in the wheelhouse (not Paul) would yell at me to come back in on the grounds that it was too dangerous out there, but of course I'd turn my back on them and pretend not to hear, until they got so agitated they'd sound the horn. One time they did this over and over again, until I reluctantly obeyed, galloping back across the high foredeck so that I was on the ladder, shielded by the bulkhead, when the biggest wave yet hit, and the *Sea Shepherd's* forward deck looked like nothing so much as a submarine sounding. If I'd stayed at the bow, I would have been washed away, no doubt about it. Why had I listened? Was it because, seeing from their vantage point what was coming, they sounded the horn so urgently? Or was it because my mother's ghost, with perhaps some Guardian Angels, was present, invisibly ushering me across the deck?

The feeling that something was going on—so much more than met the eye that it was beyond calculating—was as thick in the air as the fumes from the poor old diesel. What with the engine dying every day in the midst of the typhoon, there was a basic, grateful feeling that it was a miracle we were alive. Well, at least those of us who weren't seasick felt that way. I looked at poor Jamie in his bunk, his face like lime, and wondered whether he was going to make it. Good Irish-stock Ontario lad that he was, he felt guilty because he wasn't out there in the maelstrom rolling tape, and struggled to his feet to groggily shoot interviews even as the world seemed to be falling apart around us, pots and pans clashing, seemingly animate chairs squeaking on their own across the floor, then falling over as though shot. I kept him whacked out on Gravol as much as possible. It was too late to fend off the seasickness, but at least he could fade out of his awful state of consciousness. Yet I wasn't really worried about him. We still had work to do in the world. He would be spared, just as we would all be spared, at least until we had done it. Hard to stay rational, at sea.

Harder still when extremely weird shit happens. Like, after a week of taking a pounding that by rights should have shaken the old boat apart, the wheel suddenly jammed. It would not respond to attempts to turn it. In a panic, the helmsperson on duty that night ran down to wake the captain. Paul clambered up to the wheelhouse and grabbed the wheel. It wasn't just that it was jammed, he discovered. It had swung fifteen degrees to starboard, and was locked there, taking us off on a new heading. He was quiet for several minutes, then stepped back and said calmly: "Okay, we've got a new heading."

There was much shaking of heads among the crew for the next couple of days. Watson had lost it, was the buzz. The challenge of trying to find the drift-net fleet somewhere out in the middle of the planet's largest ocean, with no more special equipment than a radar with a mere fifteen-mile range, had been described as like looking for a convoy of Winnebagos somewhere in continental North America, and doing it at roughly the speed of a bicycle. A couple of years before, Watson had spent a whole summer hunting the drift-netters in the Gulf of Alaska, and had missed them by one day. Now we're a week out, going straight into the deeps of the Pacific, and the steering wheel mechanism has broken down, and what does the captain do but say, "What's the problem? The ship wants to go that way. That's the way we'll go." Worse than his abdication of rationality is the fact that we are now taking a pounding on the port side more brutal than anything we'd experienced when we were going straight into the waves. I can see in the eyes of people around me the dawning fear that Watson is, indeed, a mad captain, and we are all therefore going to our doom.

4

The High of Battle

Two days later somebody spots two blips on the radar. By this time, the wheel has been fixed, so we have manoeuvrability, although we have stayed with the new ship-inspired heading. And it is well, it turns out, that we did. The ships ahead prove to be Russian warships, one of them equipped with the Russian equivalent of Cruise missiles. Good God, a nuke! They are belching smoke so badly we think at first they must be on fire, but no, one of them breaks off from the war games they must be playing, and charges toward us, rumbling past, and swinging around so that they are coming up on us from behind, their foredeck guns pointed straight at us.

In the wheelhouse, Paul and I get to play old warriors, rattling off a few searing anecdotes about Ye Olden Days when we were fighting the Soviet whaling fleet, or when Watson took the *Sea Shepherd* right up to the shore of Siberia to expose a secret whaling operation, and only escaped because he ignored the Soviet helicopters and warships thundering around him, ordering him to stop. They finally did position themselves right next to him, and were aiming their cannons, when—*shazam!*—a grey whale surfaced between the two racing ships, blowing, and a rainbow formed. The Russians were so astounded they forgot to pull the triggers—or this was a clear-cut case of some kind of divine intervention, and there was nothing they could have done anyway. In the extra few minutes given to him by the whale, Paul shot across the line into American waters, and the Russians settled back like snarling guard dogs.

Little wonder he is unfazed now, despite those guns aimed at us.

He gets on the radio and explains to the Russians what the *Sea Shepherd* is all about. The Russian radio operator, to our astonishment, says: "We salute your noble cause." Of course! They have been watching their own fisheries vanish into the monstrous spider webs of drift-net, as apparently helpless as any other country to stop the rapacious Asian fleets. Why shouldn't they help us? The Russians go one step further. Since our Loran gear seems to be wonky, they do us the favour of giving us an exact navigational fix. They even crank up their own superior radar, but can report seeing nothing. They do tell us one critical thing, though: Yes, they did see drift-netters a few days ago. Thataway. Watson alters course just slightly. The *Sea Shepherd* had been on the right trail, after all. This is duly noted by all on board. I touch her metal skin, and think: "You are alive, aren't you, old tub?" Either that or she is a sword being wielded by a Higher Power. At this point, I am too far into the trip to resist insanity any longer. Go with it.

Two days later, a cluster of six blips! As we lumber toward them in waning late-afternoon light, we find ourselves in seas that have calmed nicely. There is still the eternal deep-sea swell, but the typhoon has spent itself. The surface of the water is the colour of aluminum with glittering bronze hammered along the horizon, the sun a pale orange orb in the lingering silken fog. We all move, and it is all relative, scattered ships riding different swells, bows pointed in different directions, superstructures moving like . . . cattle! They move in a herd pattern, each chomping at its own pace in its own patch of field. If you were from another planet, you might mistake these rusting, off-white hulks for mechanoid dinosaurs overgrazing a vast, once-fertile plain. The appalling spectacle comes into focus as though on grainy paper. There is silence except for the mewling of the wind and the cries of sea gulls and puffins as they dive around the antennaed buoys with the silver-blue sheen of monofilament webs coming out of them like silk from Styrofoam spiders. What planet? At what awful hour? A lot of those birds will die as they try to extract the fish and squid already snared, thrashing just below the

surface. And they are the *only* birds we have seen so far, after thir-
teen days at sea.

I prowled the decks as we closed. We all did, of course. The sea
made a slicing sound like the most fantastic knife being sharpened.
Watson himself had taken the wheel. He had come into his own.
There was much power and circumstance attached to this taking of
direct personal command by the captain. Not once before, except to
check when the wheel had responded to the command from the
ship to alter course, had he actually taken the helm. My God, this
must be some kind of archetypal moment. More than just another
moment in time: some kind of history coming down here. Be alert!
You will not experience the electrifying buzz of the next few minutes
and hours often in this lifetime! I realized, for the first time, that
physical might was okay, too. All along, in the Olden Days, I had
bought into passivism. It was a tactical thing, to be honest: outnumbered and outgunned, what are you going to do? But Paul had
gone ahead and armed himself. And rather than agonizing any
longer (as I had agonized for years) over the correctness, the moral
as well as the political correctness, of putting a big steel-tipped boot
to some mass-biocide jerk's head, I was savouring every second, urg-
ing Watson on. Fuck Gandhi! Let's clobber these bastards! The
blood-lust took over amazingly fast. Of course, I was primed. From
the moment the *Sea Shepherd* catapulted from the dock she had
been a seagoing missile, whether I wanted to acknowledge it openly
or not. There was no kidding myself I was here to do anything other
than help commit an act of pure violence. Momma's Boy/Nice Guy
was gonna get to hit somebody hard—finally!

The loveliness, the sweetness, of brute steel power; a maybe-
genetic memory surfaces of running across a field swinging a broad-
sword, roaring; I am not sure I had ever felt this good before. This
sure beat standing on ice or bobbing in a Zodiac in front of one of
these suckers! Watson was on to something here. God, what admiral until this century wouldn't have given his left ball to command
a weapon such as the *Sea Shepherd*? For that's what this is, this vibrating deck, this thing of rivets and bolts and flywheels and gener-
ators and pumps and pistons: a metal-shielded fortress driven by a

mighty prop with a giant battle-axe/battering-ram bow. I remember the pale gold light reflecting in the washes of spray across the *Sea Shepherd*'s huge black wheelhouse as we charged, and the singing of the wind . . .

The high of battle!

I was in the wheelhouse, braced against the port wall, my Hi-8 camera rolling, while Paul worked the wheel, licking his lips as he aimed. I had a life jacket wedged between my back and the wall, hoping my spine wouldn't snap when we hit. Jamie was lashed to the railing on top of the wheelhouse on the starboard side with his camera aimed exactly where Watson was pointing our bow. It was an interception with us coming in at a thirty-degree angle on their port, targeting the huge winches hauling the nets in from amidships. There were dozens of tiny men down there, one of whom stayed crouched over his net, oblivious. Watson sounded our horn no fewer than five times before the fellow looked up in horror and sprang backwards across the deck, where the rest of the Japanese crew were already retreating. We came in at full throttle, somewhere around ten knots. My sense of reality was no doubt impaired by the fact I had the Hi-8 poked against my eye half the time, the other eye shut, making sure I had a good picture framed up on the little black-and-white viewscreen. Mainly I stayed on Paul, but with as many back-and-forth pans as I could squeeze off. Amateur that I was, I couldn't help forgetting my main mission and looking up now and then to see what else was going on.

If we'd have been coming in this fast against a fixed object, we'd have been meat. The bow stayed aimed for the winch until we got in close and then the weight of water crushed between the ships tried to pry us apart. Paul had to swing her hard to starboard, otherwise we'd have simply slid in against their side, our hit cushioned by Archimedes' Principle. There was a certain chopping effect Watson wanted, and so the whole front body of the *Sea Shepherd* lurched to the right to get that bow-edge back in position. When we hit, it was dead on. The winch folded like a bug, our bow splayed back the railing and tore open a hole along the deck's edge, then glanced off and shouldered the drift-netter hard over on her starboard side while we rolled back to port, kept plunging ahead, and finally swept across their bow, trailing tendrils of shredded drift-net.

The collision was enough to stagger us all, but no one was knocked over. The most terrifying part was the noise as the metal hulls scraped against each other: rather than being a shriek or a clang, it sounded like high symphonic orchestral strings, varying in pitch and rhythm, but providing something so much like an actual scored sound track that people listening to the tape on dry land would forever assume we had dubbed that in. The weirdest, most unexpected thing of all: it was music, for God's sake! I heard it. I have the tape!

One of the Japanese crewmen was so incensed he threw not one but two knives at us. I had run out on deck by then and climbed up beside Jamie. The first one flew over our heads into the ocean. The second one clattered at my feet. I was glad we were quickly out of range.

The second drift-netter was just puttering along, showing no sign of being aware what had just happened to its sister ship. Obviously, these guys didn't communicate among themselves a whole hell of a lot. Same deal. We came up behind and hit them in the same place. An armoured elbow in the gut. This time, everybody in the wheelhouse, including me, was wearing Kevlar flak jackets and helmets, in case, having been warned, these guys were just playing dumb, while secretly uncocking their rifles. Ever the student of imagery, I noticed that now, instead of looking like the good guys, scruffy but brave, we looked like Darth Vader clones. The helmets, in fact, were reminiscent of German World War One helmets. Oh God. I wanted to tell everyone to take them off, but then I remembered this was reality, not a location shoot. Well, maybe both. This is gonzo media, *sí?*

Jamie stood up well to the beating he took up on top of the wheelhouse, where, of course, when the boat sways, everything is magnified. You get heaved further to the side each time. Luckily, he had been lashed in tight. The ropes hurt, but the nightmare was hanging on to the camera as it tried to levitate off on its own orbit; not to mention the hard sleet whipping down; or the electronic horn going off unexpectedly three feet from his ear, then again, and again, and again, and again. Unlike me, he kept his stuff in frame, and though he staggered each time he was hit by another blast of sound, he didn't lose his footing—just his temper. Why hadn't someone warned him that would happen? Not the way things work around here, was the answer. After the second ramming, Jamie had had just about enough of being strapped atop the big kamikaze contender in a demolition derby with thousands of fathoms of ocean underneath and no land for a thousand miles. We had torn our own hull open after the first hit and simply enlarged it on the second. Above the water-line. Shrug. By now it was pouring. We retreated below to dry the cameras.

A party is about to start in the wheelhouse, but Watson wants to go after a third boat. We are feeling the urge to beat our chests.

Sensing a chance to do something completely new in life, I volunteer to have myself lashed to the anchor winch right up at the bow, where I will roll with the Hi-8 and get possibly some of the greatest sea-collision footage ever recorded, or possibly just get shot or knifed or crushed. It is fun for a while, huddled in a rain slicker, tied to the winch. I can slide to the right or the left, but not right around. So I look back at the Sea Shepherd's wheelhouse, the windows fogged with condensation, rain lashing across them, wipers thumping, and ahead to the next target, a drift-netter materializing out of the squalls. I swing the camera, practising. Check helmet. Tighten flak jacket. Ready.

I feel so calm I scare myself. Hold up my hand, palm flat. Steady as it's ever been. Squatting on the foredeck with the rain pattering down, bow-riding, body sweating inside the raingear, steam coming off my hands, clutching the Hi-8, waiting for the moment when I will ride this sea-ram right into a steel wall, just feet away from the coming together of molecules at the instant of collision, a sensation I imagine will be something like being on a ferris wheel thrown at the side of a train, except on a bigger scale; and then there's all that stuff about knives and guns. Hope we don't get stuck and they board us and slice me into little pieces because I'm tied up and can't get away. Yoga breathe. Enjoy. Expect surprises. This could be the dumbest thing. I might just be pushing my luck. Or it could be that revelatory moment I've been waiting for.

Surprise: the ship ahead has dropped its nets, smoke is belching from its stack, and the water is churning up at its stern. It is out of here. And they seem to be just slightly faster than us. Revelatory moment? I am wet and chilled, the Hi-8 is soaked, water dribbles down my plastic cigarette onto my chin, and I am left to ponder. Did something come along and move that boat?

That night, after several miles of abandoned drift-net had been sunk with old engine parts to the bottom, and the area of ocean visible on radar cleared of any trace of ships, we turned south toward Hawaii in triumph. Late that night I staggered from Marc's open bar out to the bow under a glinting giant moon and rode for a while and then said aloud, marshalling all my tumultuous thoughts: "Okay, God, give me your best shot!" Nothing happened for a few moments. I waited some more. And then I looked down, and saw written on the deck in black paint the words: *Fuck Off, Bob.*

For several moments I hovered on the edge of a nervous breakdown. Then I realized that the Vegans had struck again. This time they got me right in the middle of the head. I hauled my mattress up on the stern deck, and lay down under the universe. After a while, Myra Finklestein came up and asked if I'd mind if she put her sleeping bag down beside me. Sure. This seemed strange, since Myra had been careful to avoid romantic relationships, so far as I could see, and had coined the term eco-dinosaur to describe my kind. Youthful enough to be my daughter, and all that. But after a while I noticed several young guys had also moved silently up onto the deck, and had bedded down in a restless circle around us. It finally registered on me that Myra was just looking for a safe old married bull, even if he was a meat-eater, to lie beside in order to keep the young bucks at bay so she could sleep unmolested under the stars.

About an hour before dawn I awoke to find my buttocks gone numb from lying on a thin mattress on a steel deck. I sat up and looked around. The moon was gone. The black helmet shape of the ship hunched along contentedly. Yet I felt emptied to the drain of my soul. And frightened. It wasn't exactly a vision. I didn't *see* anything. Rather, I felt something. It ran a fingernail across my soul.

The genes never really divide, you see. They just take up residence in the bodies of the offspring, even after the progenitor expires. She might be disembodied now, my mother, but she was still incarnate in me and my children. Part of me was her. And that was true of everyone. The genes of men and women, commingled, formed the basic human entity, something more than the mere sum of their organs.

I *am* my mother. She lives!

And she has thoroughly enjoyed this ride.

5

The Honorary Kwakiutl Shuffle

Paul and I had known each other since the late Sixties, although I can't remember where exactly we met. Probably at a rally, a march, a picket line, a meeting hall, a Be-In, a concert. We were both on hand when Jerry Rubin, the original Yippie, liberated the Faculty Club at the University of British Columbia, although we didn't actually know each other yet. Times were lively and radical in Vancouver at the height of the Vietnam Era, the counterculture hangouts filling up with draft dodgers, Armageddon aglow on the horizon, nuclear bombs being tested along geological fault-lines, high-grade weirdness all around, Timothy Leary, Marshall McLuhan, John Lilly, R. D. Laing, The Moody Blues, student uprisings, early Space Age, mid-Cold War, all that stuff. I will never forget listening to humpback whales singing pleadingly as the shadow of the end of all sentient life fell across Planet Earth; just a generation ago, to be sure—but that means at least an entire epoch.

If for no other reason than the physical fact that Paul and I were both living on the West Coast at the time, the Native influence on us was strong from the very beginning. The totems in Stanley Park loomed over our minds in some ways even more impressively than the Coastal Mountains themselves, because they spoke of reincarnation, transmigration of souls, of men, fish, birds, and animals being equally possessed of a spirit; children of a common Earth Mother.

At about the same time, because it was on the bestseller list, Paul and I both read Dee Brown's *Bury My Heart at Wounded Knee*, which was pretty much required reading for anybody of an activist mindset then, the first popular account of the massacre of some two hundred Oglala Sioux men, women, and children by the U.S. Army in 1890.

When armed American Indian Movement militants seized the trading post and church at Wounded Knee in February 1973, and the U.S. government responded by ringing the village with marshals, troops, and FBI agents equipped with armoured personnel carriers, Paul walked off the landscaping job he was doing, jumped in an old truck, and drove straight from Vancouver to South Dakota, where he found himself in a war zone. Stopped by FBI agents when he tried to drive into the Pine Ridge Reservation, he was charged with being an alien in the United States during a time of emergency, and locked up for eight hours. A second attempt to reach the Indian side ended after he had crawled and clawed his way through several miles of snowdrifts straight into the hands of an FBI patrol. Upon release this time, facing a court order to be out of the country in twenty-four hours, he used his brains and lied to a bureaucrat at the Bureau of Indian Affairs, claiming to be a reporter from the Vancouver *Sun*, the paper I happened to be working for at the time. Thus equipped with a press pass, he got through the FBI lines on the pretence of doing interviews with the besieged Indians. Once inside the encampment, he dropped his fake identity and volunteered to help in any way, ending up serving as a medic. This was a real job, since about fifteen hundred marshals, FBI agents, and members of the U.S. Army's 82nd Airborne Division were directing as many as twenty thousand rounds of ammo a night at the village, while at least sixty armoured personnel carriers lumbered along the perimeter, and parachute flares kept the night skies bright. It was, of course, the first time he had been under fire, inevitably a defining experience—although not quite as much of an epiphany as the final hours of his month-long stay at Wounded Knee, when he was rewarded for his solidarity with the Brothers by being initiated as a full-fledged member of the Oglala Sioux tribe. The ceremony involved going naked into a sacred Sweat Lodge, where he was given an Indian name by two medicine men. He went in as Paul Watson and emerged as Grey Wolf Clear Water.

God, how I envied him that name!

I had had a few transcendent experiences of my own with Indians by that time, in addition to being saved from freezing to death by the pure-blood Huron. But nothing I had done had been deemed worthy of giving me an actual name.

In 1971, I had sailed with eleven other guys on an old fish boat, the *Phyllis Cormack*, in a futile attempt to blockade an American nuclear test in the Aleutian Islands. The trip was a flop because we failed to stop the test, but a year later all further testing at the site was cancelled, and as a result of the voyage an eco-organization was formed that eventually became world-famous, but the whole Greenpeace thing is another story.

On the way up the coast from Vancouver we had stopped in at the village of Alert Bay on Cormorant Island, where we were given fresh salmon by the local Indians, the Kwakiutl, who supported our anti-nuclear stand. I don't suppose I'd even heard of the Kwakiutl before, but I was impressed when a middle-aged Native woman named Daisy Seweid, a hereditary princess, corrected one of our crew who made a bad joke about scalping: "We never scalped anybody," she said icily. "We took the whole head." Indeed, these were the famous headhunters of the Northwest Coast. Fortunately, we were on the same side. In fact, they were in the process of erecting the world's tallest totem pole, and somebody, a councillor, promised that if we came back alive from our mission (to park next to an island where a hydrogen bomb was being tested) our names would be carved in the totem.

As things worked out, a combination of bad weather, tactical delays by the Americans, and our getting busted by the U.S. Coast Guard resulted, after much yelling and screaming, in our boat turning around and heading home before we reached our objective. A second protest ship was sent out from Vancouver to carry the torch, and Paul Watson was onboard. Arguably, Paul might never have come to command his own ship, except for that failure of ours. He had wanted badly to be onboard the first anti-nuclear voyage, but had been rejected as a crew member, even though he had practical experience as a sailor, simply because other people, like me, had more political clout. I was writing a column at the *Sun*, which was the biggest newspaper in British Columbia, for instance. Anyway, the moment our little fish boat turned back from the Aleutians, the drive was on back home to find a bigger, faster ship to replace us. This time, Watson had no trouble winning a berth. Briefly, the two of us met in a chaotic scene at sea as the newer, bigger ship rendezvoused with us, and we all exchanged Revolutionary Handshakes, before the minesweeper sped northward, and we, the burned-out original crew, limped on down the coast, feeling like miserable failures. That was why it seemed so important when we got an invitation over the radiophone to stop back in at Alert Bay for a special ceremony.

It was *not* the carving of our names in the totem. That proposal had quietly been dropped. (After all . . .) Instead, we were herded up to the Big House, and there, in the smoke, under the great wooden wings of the totems that held up the roof, while the drums vibrated through our bones, dancing around the fire amid sprinklings of dove feathers, we were adopted as honorary Brothers of the Kwakiutl. An Elder explained that this was a dance to men "letting go of their egos."

Later I would stare at the black-and-white photos of the ceremony for hours at a time, convincing myself that it hadn't been a hallucination. There we were, members of the *Phyllis Cormack*'s crew, covered with feathers, in our button-blanket robes, like ghosts in the haze from the fire, with the eyes of the thunderbirds carved in the mighty cedar beams staring down at us. And the Kwakiutl Elders dancing. I danced too. We all did, I think. Shuffled, at least.

Yes, it did happen, which meant that everything leading up to that moment, including the nightmarish voyage, must have been real too, even if I'd had my doubts along the way, thinking maybe I was just losing my grip on sanity. Which, of course, was completely possible. Even likely.

Of course, it could all be written off as coincidence and selective perception. But, as I danced, feeling as though I were still at sea, but floating through inner space, too, the term *Rainbow Warrior* swirled through my mind, admittedly my "sea-mind," because my "land-mind" had long since lost control over my perceptions. This was an actual initiation into a secret Native society, I was convinced. And the evidence of my senses (and the camera) seemed to testify to it.

We were being anointed as Warriors of the Rainbow. It was absolutely clear to me.

It was not that anybody said anything to that effect. It was just my conclusion, based on first-hand observation. At the very least, it certainly *seemed* as though a prophecy was coming true before my wondering eyes. One moment, a myth. The next moment, an event! Here! Now!

As it happened, I had a book of strange and prophetic dreams with me. By mere coincidence? From my particular vantage point, in the blue smoke of the Big House, under the wings of the totems, the coincidence argument didn't make sense. There was something fucking mysterious going on here. There was virtually no chance that anybody on that boat would ever have heard of the Rainbow Warrior if I hadn't had that little book along with me, and as for how I happened to have a copy, it was weird enough to keep your voice low if you talked about it, but utterly true . . .

I could vividly remember the arrival of the dulcimer-maker on my doorstep a couple of years before, in 1969. He had driven an old Chevy pickup down the driveway of the farm I was renting in Richmond, just south of Vancouver. The vehicle had a cedar-shake Hobbit house mounted on the back, complete with a crooked stove pipe and a macramé God's Eye in the window. He was full-bearded, long-haired, hook-nosed, wearing a black frock coat and a skull cap, pants with buttons instead of a zipper, and beaded moccasins. He marched over to me, glowering, as I lounged on the front porch under the greengage tree, and handed me a frayed lithographed booklet—his manner as brusque and impersonal as a cop delivering a parking ticket. Whether he had read some of my newspaper columns and tracked me down, or simply appeared out of the blue, I never did find out.

He said his name, which I didn't catch, and immediately launched into an explanation that he was an Orthodox Jew *and* a gypsy, although there was no trace of an accent. He made it clear he was not to be mistaken for a mere hippie. Okay.

"Here," he said, "this is for you. It will reveal a path that will affect your life." Exact words.

As soon as I had accepted the book, he asked if he could cut down the old fence posts out in the field. The dry wood made excellent dulcimers. No argument. Go ahead, man.

The booklet was titled *The Warriors of the Rainbow, Strange and Prophetic Dreams of the Indian Peoples,* by William Willoya and Vinson Brown, a collection of peyote visions and cautionary Native tales.

Onto the bookshelf went the mystical text, unread any further, soon to be forgotten among all the other spiritual exotica of the Sixties, from *The Teachings of Don Juan* and *Light on the Path* to *I Ching* and *The Tibetan Book of the Dead.* It wasn't until I was hurriedly packing my duffel bag the night before I was to depart on the *Phyllis Cormack* that it re-entered my sphere of consciousness. I was pulling books out at random, thinking all I was going to have to do was lie around in my bunk, killing time by reading, while somebody steered the boat toward Amchitka. *The Warriors of the Rainbow* booklet fell off the shelf by accident, a normal person would think, but true to the countercultural spirit of the times, alert always for cosmic connections, I thought: "Far out, this wants to come with me!"

During the forty-four nights I lay in my bunk, wedged tight against the battering of storms in the Gulf of Alaska or riding the astral plane of dreams in the surges and upwellings of some of the deepest waters on the planet, I found myself reading in the little *Warriors of the Rainbow* booklet about Eyes of Fire, a Native grandmother, not identified by tribe, whose grandson finally asked, "Why did the Grandfather In The Sky allow the White Men to take our lands, Oldest Mother?"

In the tale that followed, the boy was sent on a quest, and along the way he learned to "help protect and bring back to the earth the animals that the White Man had almost destroyed," and that "one day, when the Indians got the old spirit back again, they would teach the White Men how to really love one another and to love all mankind," and that "just when the Indians seemed to be all becoming like the more foolish White Men, just when everyone thought they had forgotten about the ancient days, at that time a great light would come from the east." The rainbow "is a sign from Him who is in all things."

It was time for Eyes of Fire's grandson to become a Warrior of the Rainbow "by spreading love and joy to others." Indeed, more specifically, the task of the Warrior of the Rainbow was to work toward a "new, spiritual civilization that is coming [which] will create beauty by its very breath, turning the waters of rivers clear, building forests and parks where there are now deserts and slums, and bringing back the flowers to the hillsides. What a glorious fight to change the world to beauty!"

The text went on: ". . . so the Indians of today will brighten the understanding of the ignorant destroyers. They will soften the hearts of would-be killers so the animals will once more replenish the earth, and the trees shall once more rise to hold the precious soil. In that day all peoples will be able to walk in wilderness flowing with life, and the children will see around them the young fawns, the antelope and the wildlife as of old. Conservation of all that is beautiful and good is a cry woven into the very heart of the new age."

Reading passages like this aloud to various fellow crewmembers produced dramatically different reactions. The older, mature chaps looked at me as though I was the village idiot. The younger long-haired bearded types grooved on the poetry of it, but that was about all—until our first allies turned out to be, well, Indians. It was a highly polarized situation on the West Coast then, because John Wayne was still alive, and he happened to be in British Columbia waters on his converted minesweeper. His message to us protesters— "Commies," he called us—had been: "Mind yer own bizniz, boys." Immediately afterwards, Dan George, the famous Coast Salish actor, declared himself on our side. Then came the gift of salmon in Alert Bay, and shortly after that we stopped for repairs in the little Kitasoo village of Klemtu, where children gathered on the dock at night and began singing to us, and we—amazingly enough, for a bunch of aspiring and/or established alpha males—serenaded them back before chugging away into the darkness, me thinking: Is this reality or an opera?

Out at sea for a couple of months, tied up in little redneck Alaskan ports, caught out in the open in Gale Force Eight, but miraculously spared, we played mind-games with each other, spotted a few rainbows at auspicious moments, encountered a few dolphins and an even more rare fin whale, and had our consciousnesses expanded, you could say, about the true condition of the devastated, over-fished, nearly birdless, polluted North Pacific. By the time we got back down to Alert Bay for the dance in the Big House, and our adoption as Kwakiutl Brothers, I'd say that about half of us were thinking *There may be something to this Rainbow Warrior thing, after all.* Maybe, if nothing else, we white-folk environmentalists and anti-nukers *needed* a defining myth. Something bigger than just headlines or even books. Here was one that sure seemed to fit the specs. During the voyage we had climbed a small mountain in the fog on Akutan Island, overlooking Unalaska Pass, and even though I had no authority whatsoever, I had made a unilateral declaration that we *were* the Warriors of the Rainbow. I also founded a Church of Ecology, all in the spirit of a Merry Prankster-type mindfuck, you understand, but also to test the waters of the group mind. The mystic faction flowed with it. The mechanical types (captain, engineer, scientist, public relations man) were convinced that it was a stoner's fantasy, period. If you want to make a big deal out of somebody's delusional system, including the Kwakiutl or some mythical Rainbow Warrior, they snorted, go ahead. But don't expect to be taken seriously.

Yet here I was, just having been *adopted* as an Indian. And fresh (so to speak) from having seen abandoned whaling stations on the bone-strewn shores of North Pacific islands, the ocean and sky almost empty, nuclear bombs being tested whose shock waves killed sea mammals en masse, not to mention being arrested by the U.S. Coast Guard—and now here were these Indians, who spoke of animals as their brothers, if I understood this stuff properly, welcoming us into their tribal embrace, teaching us to let go of our egos. This was not your routine coastwise cruise, surely.

After the ceremony in the Big House, I wandered around outside by myself, staring through the blazing new eyes of somebody who has been through a transformative experience, even if I didn't know what I had transformed from, exactly, or into, for that matter. But I was a changeling, of that much I was sure.

The totems out there spoke to me. Some lay in meadows, disintegrating into mulch. Broken-winged, they still tried to snarl their warnings like skeletal guard dogs. Moss had blurred the hawk features. Their eyes were blinded by pale mustard fungus, their mouths like open sores. But on their faces the expression was somehow less defiant than horrified, as if, standing or fallen, they were aware of their own decay. And it was the decay of the world I was seeing now. Happening all around. I could see it. Why couldn't everyone else?

By the time we left Alert Bay and the totem poles behind and headed down to Vancouver in pelting snow that late November in 1971, my head definitely felt *different*. Slightly alien. I was still *me*, but looking out through a different slit in the wall separating me from the real universe. Indeed, maybe my whole head had been taken by Daisy Seweid, a princess who was a witch in disguise, at some psychic level, and I was a Kwakiutl of some kind now, a mutant Kwakiutl, to be sure, starting to actually *think* differently.

Like, looking for signs. And, of course, seeing them just about everywhere.

I wasn't quite at the stage of getting messages from licence plates, but I was highly sensitive—attuned, I liked to think—to the play of synchronicity upon events, or from underneath them, let's say, like reflections on a ceiling from water rippling. I was convinced this was what they called a "higher level of consciousness," and I was stuck there, beached like a little glowing jewel of self-awareness in a strange Power Zone where what you willed to happen *could* happen (if you willed it hard enough, persistently enough, purely enough) and ideas got transmogrified into media events, marches, rallies, concerts, actions, almost at the mere flicker of a few impatient phone calls, a few meetings, a fund-raiser or two. It was a glorious, insane state of mind, where, for a while, it seemed I could actually shape events. It was impossible to distinguish between what an occult power would be and this strange new ability I seemed to have to make things happen. If I really needed something—like a landing craft at a very particular moment or a paper bag full of money—it would appear. Right on schedule. I knew this all had to be an illusion, but there would be the very thing, or person, I needed. And we were photographing and filming it all.

Clinically insane, I think is the term. But documented.

In any event, it was contagious. En route from Alert Bay to Vancouver, we decided around the galley table to set up a permanent international non-violent environmental "strike force." It was just a matter of signing some documents under the B.C. Societies Act—but within just a couple of years, there was a whole gang of us, all believing that we were, indeed, moulding reality. We had other names for ourselves besides Warriors of the Rainbow, of course; other corporate, organizational, political, copyrighted labels, but it wasn't long after our little crusade got rolling full blast that all eco-ships going to sea, to save whales or seals or to stop bombs, had rainbows painted on their bows. From 1975 onward, these ships—a fleet of seven of them at one point—also displayed a Kwakiutl whale family-crest, a sea serpent on the outside, containing a soul inside. The soul was replaced by our peace-and-ecology symbols. Just because I was an adopted Brother of the Kwakiutl, I made the enormous presumption that I could employ one of their ancient clan crests without asking permission. The symbol subsequently showed up from the Antarctic to the Bering Sea. We also had tee-shirts, called Warrior Skins. There were maybe over a thousand of us at various times, and who knows what the numbers are now? On the tee-shirts, as on the thousands of buttons that were printed in a dozen different languages and sold throughout Europe in the 1980s, a Plains Indian squatted in a full lotus position, his hand held palm upward and open with a rainbow between thumb and forefinger. The caption read: *When the earth is sick the animals will begin to disappear: When that happens the Warriors of the Rainbow will come to save them.*

What had happened here?

It depends on where the paraphrasing begins. In my summary of Willoya and Brown's little booklet in a book of my own, after the fact, I wrote:

"It contained one particular prophecy made two hundred years ago by an old Cree grandmother named Eyes of Fire, who saw a time coming when the birds would fall out of the skies, the fish would be poisoned in their streams, the deer would drop in their tracks in the forest, and the sea would be 'blackened'—all thanks to the White

Man's greed and technology. At that time the Indian people would have all but completely lost their spirit. They would find it again, and they would begin to teach the White Man how to have reverence for Mother Earth. Together, using the symbol of the rainbow, all the races of the world would band together to spread the great Indian teaching and go forth—Warriors of the Rainbow—to bring an end to the destruction and desecration of sacred Earth."

This was the story everyone ran with afterwards, getting it honed down to button and tee-shirt perfection over the years. It was a rewrite, sure. But the raw material was there. I simply spun it a certain way. Was this evil and revisionist, or could I claim I was just peeling back another layer from the onion of truth? I could play any cute little verbal games I wanted, the fact remained that I was playing with either eco-Elmer Gantryism or spiritual theft. It was one thing to act as a self-appointed flack and part-time candidate martyr for the biosphere, it was another to appropriate a religion and hook it up to an otherwise purely political movement, without consulting anybody, and sending it lumbering off into global mythos.

It might have been that I just missed it, prone as I was in my bunk on the *Phyllis Cormack* some nights, exhausted after a watch, simply scanning the pages of *The Warriors of the Rainbow*, looking for wisdom, but my published summary neglected to mention the authors' Note at the beginning of the tale about Eyes of Fire and her grandson, the first aspiring Rainbow Warrior, which stated:

"The story below we believe actually happened, though not in these exact details. We have deliberately named no tribe in this story because we want it to mean the same to all tribes, to all the Indians, for a wise old woman anywhere and a boy who had curiosity and spirit anywhere could find together this same miracle. This story makes live for us the heart of the message given us in all great Indian prophetic visions told about in this book."

Oops! That was some qualifier.

By the time it got down to tee-shirts and slogans on buttons, the nuances were inevitably lost. Scholars would not be impressed, however, and I knew this, and fretted, fearing an exposé of how I had taken a generic Indian yarn and bent it to suit my eco-agenda—my

God, what could be more shameless? As it began to become clear that my version of the vision was the one with legs, I began to squirm privately with New Age guilt.

Then, one afternoon in June of 1976, at a United Nations conference in Vancouver, with the flags of nearly one hundred nations flying dockside, as we were preparing to launch not one but two rainbow-hued ships in pursuit of the Soviet whaling fleet in the Pacific, with thousands of people gathered to wave us off, just as I was about to speak to our supporters, a Native fellow walked up to me, wearing a blanket over his shirt, and introduced himself as Fred Mosquito, a Cree Medicine Man from Saskatchewan. My heart thumped. I was about to be busted for a myth-heist! But au contraire, the prophecy of the coming of the Rainbow Warrior had been a major feature of Cree legends and stories for hundreds of years, he said. "I'm surprised you heard about it," he added, offering to speak to the crowd. It was from the High—meaning ancient—Cree culture, it turned out, that Willoya and Brown had pinched the original story of Eyes of Fire.

"You *are* the Warriors of the Rainbow," the Medicine Man declared, his voice booming through the microphone. Nearly everyone's head was bowed. Nearly everyone was wearing a whale button with a rainbow-coloured strip of cloth underneath. It was a benediction, a mass ordination. Thousands of Rainbow Warriors assembled.

No one had known Fred Mosquito was going to show up. He had just *appeared* . . . like the dulcimer-maker had appeared so long ago . . . like the Kwakiutl Elders had appeared . . . like so many rainbows had appeared along the way . . . If the Medicine Man said so, it wasn't just me playing games, after all. You mean, it was *really* real? I was just midwifing a legitimate prophecy? Boy, that was big, archetypal stuff to be messing with!

A few more years were to pass before we could afford to buy our own ship, a British-registered out-of-work North Sea trawler which was immediately renamed the *Rainbow Warrior*. With its rainbow bow and its Kwakiutl symbols painted on the wheelhouse and stern it became a very famous ship, indeed—especially after it was sunk with limpet mines by French commandoes in Auckland, New

Zealand, at midnight on July 10, 1985, resulting in an international uproar over the death of a photographer and, eventually, causing the cessation of nuclear testing by France in the South Pacific. Big stuff, yes.

From its origins in the Alert Bay Big House, the little West Coast Canadian idea of an organization that would send ships out to sea to blockade nukes or whalers or sealers or waste-dumpers rapidly metamorphosed into a true eco-multinational. Of course, depending on your frame of reference, it could also be seen as a long drawn-out struggle, but within a couple of decades (a blink of history's eye) the biggest offices of the little organization we started in the wake of the experience in Alert Bay were to be found in Europe, with the strongest membership in Germany and Holland, and for a while the United States. Millions of supporters. Dozens of offices around the world.

Along the way (especially at the beginning) our little band of Rainbow Warriors, having taken flight, crashed back repeatedly to earth, caught up in the unpleasant realities of power and the difficulties of sharing it. "Letting go of egos" proved not to be as easy as it had seemed in the ecstasy of dancing around the fire in the Big House, not at all. Soon, within days of our return from the Amchitka campaign—in other words, from Day One-and-a-bit— we "veterans" were arguing among ourselves about what to do next, how to deploy precious resources, how to use the fame of the thing we had created to achieve a vaguely agreed-upon goal of "saving the planet." Nothing less! The term "power struggle" emerged darkly from within and soon became the central business of our lives: people struggling over which way to steer. Absolutely convinced that I knew which direction was best, I made a bid in 1974 to take over the group, which had gotten bogged down in internal bickering, even though there were only a few dozen people involved on a regular basis. It took a few months of manoeuvring, but I eventually managed to grab control—with the backing of, among others, a young Paul Watson. This wonderful, not-quite-self-fulfilling prophecy of Rainbow Warriors rising up everywhere was spreading around the world, true enough, but the closer you got to the centre of the transcendent image we were projecting out there, the messier and more obstinately human things got—everybody involved being flawed human beings, after all.

At first, it was deceptively easy.

Having hit upon the bizarre but original and media-savvy idea of trying to position an inflated high-speed rubber Zodiac in between a harpoon boat and a hunted whale, I needed someone to drive the vessel, but I didn't trust my physical reflexes. I needed someone strong, fearless, and crazy enough to risk his life. If I could have done it by myself, I would have. But the scheme called for at least two people—one to watch for whales ahead and the other to watch the harpoon ship as it bore down on us when we interfered. I knew exactly who to call upon. The problem was, I was asking Paul to risk being blown apart by a 250-pound explosive harpoon, and to ask anyone to die with you had to entail an outrageous karmic debt, I was certain.

Indeed. As it happened, our outboard engine died out in the Pacific in front of the harpoon boat, but a bow-wave lifted us aside at the last second, as though an angel had reached down. We saw rainbows at night, and were guided to the whaling fleet by what can only be called a string of miraculous coincidences. And a year after that, when Paul and I stood shoulder to shoulder on the ice off the Labrador Coast to block the passage of a sealing ship, the bow came within four or five feet of crushing us. We had our backs to the ship. The idea was not to look back so the onus was on the captain not to kill us. Chunks of ice the size of small cars were popping up around us. I will never forget the sound of that steel hull crunching nearer and nearer and the ice starting to move like an escalator under our boots. It had been my bright idea to stand in front of the ship. The moment I did it, Paul did it too. As the boat smashed toward us, he did say: "This is a lousy way to die." I told him to jump if he wanted, but I wasn't moving. I was, in fact, in the grip of an insane fantasy that I would hold back a ship weighing many tons by sheer force of will—at least so long as we had cameras rolling.

The fact that I wasn't going to move meant that Paul wasn't going to move either, even if it meant being grated. This was a high plateau for individuals to climb onto together, the sort of thing normally only done in combat, the sort of thing that binds guys together for life, long after the war is over. At one point, we clasped hands, which is probably how we would have died if the ship hadn't stopped. The closer we got to death, the closer it seemed we got to each other.

Alas, we got swept away in the avalanche of energy we had unleashed. I went slightly nutzoid with power, carrying a loud-hailer everywhere to harangue crowds (it worked!), using a gavel to nail down control of board meetings (that worked, too). Paul and I eventually clashed over the fundamental issue of which way to do things: guerrilla warfare or the Gandhi route? At the end of a brutish power struggle, Paul was out of the organization, on his own. Shortly thereafter, I threw myself on my sword and resigned. And there were now two new radical eco-outfits loose in the world.

When he decided to buy a ship of his own, the first *Sea Shepherd*, Paul couldn't quite scratch together enough money, so he called me and asked if Roberta and I would put up the house and property we had just bought as collateral for part of the bank loan to purchase an old North Sea trawler.

A long, deep breath. And somewhere, the Wheel was turning. Time to pay for my sins.

I knew, by then, that I had, indeed, committed the paramount sin of failing to hit the bull's-eye by quitting when I had quit, by doing what I had done for the sake of revenge as opposed to the sake of the planet. A hole of guilt had opened in my soul that was slowly draining away my will to live. And here, now, was Paul offering me a chance to throw away the hard-earned home and farm that sheltered the two children Roberta and I had spawned since going off to do our own thing. Putting your property up as collateral for a madman who wants to smash head-on into a whaling ship somewhere out in the middle of the ocean hardly ranks as a prudent fiscal manoeuvre, but it made perfect sense in every other respect.

Roberta saw that right away. "Of course we'll do it," she said.

And off Paul went into history. On his own. Hauling a great shell of a ship on his shoulders.

6

Sweat Lodge at My Door

The call from Paul came almost exactly a year after we had moved into our house some five hundred feet above sea level on the slopes of Eagle Mountain, east of Indian Arm, surrounded by coniferous forest, with a mountain stream running through the back acre. Two and a half acres had been cleared single-handedly by Roberta's father. Otherwise, although we were less than an hour east of the centre of Vancouver, we were surrounded by sound-absorbing Douglas fir and cedar, and in any place where the forest was open, glades of alders and tangles of impenetrable blackberries. Amidst the salal lushness, following the trails left by coyotes, mule deer, black bear, racoons, rabbits, and at least one mountain lion, you could quickly find stumps the size of small houses. It slowly dawned on you that as massive as this cathedral grove of rain forest was, the biggest trees standing seventy or eighty feet, it was a *baby* forest compared to what it had been at the turn of the century before the loggers came and took out the giants that had been growing since the arrival of the Europeans. The property butted against a six-thousand-acre greenbelt around an oil refinery down at the water-front, the entire area completely untouched, not even turned into a park.

The forest became "our" backyard, and I'd brag that we were actually the laird and lady of 6,002-and-one-half acres, making us the biggest property holders in the Lower Mainland. On cloudy nights the lights of Vancouver silhouetted the ramparts of trees flanking us to the southwest. There were neighbours on one side of us, but, again because of the foliage, we couldn't see their lights. We were surrounded by primeval blackness, like life before electricity. If I drew a line straight north from the front door, it wouldn't encounter a single village or town on its way to the North Pole. Three or four or five times a year, I'd see an eagle. Our pet rabbit, I noticed, would immediately play dead, knowing somehow that eagles weren't carrion-eaters.

When I went for hikes in the forest, I carried a three-ought-three, not for hunting purposes but because bears and mountain lions scared the crap out of me, and my Saint Bernard, while lovable, was a wanderer who seldom stayed at my side. In fact, I had silver-tipped bullets because they do the most damage. It was not lost on me that here I was, a fallen Rainbow Warrior, reduced to carrying a gun to protect myself from my animal brothers.

Reduced. Fallen. Former. Retired. Ex. As in exile, even if self-imposed.

It was around the time Paul called seeking collateral to buy the *Sea Shepherd* that Tony, the Cree Medicine Man, showed up at the front door, wanting to know if he and his brothers could set up a Sweat Lodge on our property, since they were being refused permission to do so in any of the nearby public parks. I was a guy, by then, who was trying hard *not* to notice miracles or coincidences or synchronicity. I knew I had fucked up in my moment of planetary duty. All I could hope for now was to mend my head, go through power-junkie withdrawal, come back to Earth, literally. I had set up a huge vegetable garden behind the house and started raising sheep, chickens, ducks, turkeys, and geese. I was in my psycho-Humpty-Dumpty recovery mode. Enough with rainbows, thanks. Stay calm. Walk around in the forest a lot with my fickle dog and my gun.

And now, damn it, here was one of those bloody Rainbow Warrior-type Medicine Men at the front door, wanting a place to set up a Sweat Lodge, by which, I knew full well, he meant nothing less than a Cree temple. Were these guys stalking me? There was a slightly cosmic thread connecting things here, too, of course. Tony had first been drawn to the West Coast from the Prairies by the United Nations convention where we had launched our anti-whaling campaign in 1976, when Fred Mosquito had spoken. Tony had been involved in Sweat Lodge ceremonies featuring prayers for

Mother Earth (to which I had received an invitation, but caught up in too many other last-minute things to do, had declined). It was there that Tony had networked with other Natives, the long-term result of which had been this return to the coast at their request—only to run into bureaucrats who would not let him set up a Lodge anywhere on public lands.

I felt trapped. I wanted to say, "Go away!" But of course I couldn't. With every appearance of the utmost politeness and respect—but inside just plain numb—I escorted him down to the back acre, on the other side of the stream, where he inevitably picked out exactly the spot I had reserved in my mind for my writing cabin as the one location that would be perfect for a Sweat Lodge. It took all my feeble burned-out will to resist him, but I mustered the strength somehow. "Sorry, man. You'll have to be down there. I've got this picked out." Irked by my white property-owner capitalist nation-state oppressor attitude, he nevertheless reluctantly agreed to build on the second-best spot, just a few yards downstream. So we had our primal and ancient land-claims struggle one-on-one standing in the drizzle, right off the bat, just like that. As far as I knew there was no evidence that *anyone* had ever lived on this particular tract of coastline until after the loggers came.

But I would have to understand, he stated firmly, the land *surrounding* the Lodge was to be considered Sacred Ground for all time.

Right. Hope we can keep the mortgage payments up, I thought mean-spiritedly. Hope Watson doesn't sink us along with his ship. But I let all those little niggling fiscal and legal matters go unspoken. Instead, I mentioned the bears, having spotted one just the day before, hoping it might frighten him off.

He smiled. "Ah, Brother Bear. A good sign."

My heart sank.

The truth was, by then I was *afraid* of these Native guys. Just like I was afraid of magic. Afraid of inexplicable coincidences that suggested a higher level of order at work in the universe than one could directly perceive. I didn't want to hear from old eco-war buddies. Roberta and I had a pact: no talking about miracles or the past unless it was the remote past. Be Here Now became the mantra, à la

Baba Ram Dass. We talked resolutely about kids and chickens and plugged water drains, which are disastrous if you live in a rain forest on a cleared-out section of mountain slope.

A couple of weekends later, the pickups and station wagons arrived, and about three dozen Natives, including women and children and one very old woman, clambered out and began hauling bags and baskets and axes and saws down to the back. They crossed the pasture single file and followed the sheep trail down to the creek, waded across, and disappeared behind the veil of young alders. Soon there was the sound of axes, the creaking of trees falling, a plume of smoke.

I was invited to take part in the Sweat, naturally. And naturally accepted.

Utter blackness inside, two layers of carpet pulled down over the doorway, just the pink glow of the hot ash-powdered stones. There are seven of us, unbelievably, squatting inside on the cedar boughs. No room to stand up, and to get out, I would have to crawl on my hands and knees over the laps of three guys to avoid dragging myself through the coals. I am stressed at first because of my claustrophobia. Get in a thing that small? With that many guys? In our underwear, or wrapped in towels? It only stands three feet tall at its cone. And now, sensory deprivation. Great. I am having to concentrate very intensely on stilling the *whap-whap-whapping* of my heart. Is this going to be a Big Moment or am I simply going to have to shame myself by bolting? I know where Tony is and I hear his voice. Rather than focusing on myself, I focus on that terrific disembodied baritone, much deeper than his normal speaking voice. He is chanting, sing-songing, keening in High Cree. And the others come back as a choir. It *is* church!

Unfortunately, Tony dips into a steel bucket with a ladle and splashes water on the stones. With a hiss, the Lodge becomes a sauna, and soon I am having trouble breathing. Starting to lose it. Tony pauses in his ritual to say: "Press your face into Mother Earth. Breathe through Mother Earth." Which I do, having to shift out of my squatting position onto all fours, nose burrowing through the cedar boughs until it is pressed against the damp cool muck below and my mouth is open, and I am sucking air through the needles of the boughs. And, yes, I *can* breathe. I stay like this, thinking, my God, am I being born again? This is what it would be like, wouldn't it? In the darkness and the steam, on my knees and elbows, head down, listening intensely as Tony switches to English out of politeness to me, and breathing as though through a spaceman's mask, maybe taking more oxygen than usual because I'm breathing through my mouth too, I start to feel like the whole Sweat Lodge is spinning. Up. I'm clinging to the boughs now, like a bat hanging on. Are we upside down? How fast are we moving? And I realize that the Medicine Man is calling out to Mother Earth and the other guys are calling out to Mother Earth. All of this is a group prayer ritual designed to communicate with their *God*, an entity known as Mother Earth. And for a moment, high on oxygen or lack of it (maybe pine needles emit psychoactive triggers) *I got it!* This was Mother Earth, the Loved One, the Real Living God, The God I Could Touch and Who Could Feel Me. The ground felt *personal.* It was flesh. Earth Was Flesh.

Afterwards, ecstatically lowering myself into the down-from-the-icecaps cold waters of the stream and being able to remain there for minutes instead of seconds, looking around, at the softly breathing living forest-entity and the even more softly breathing lovemaking clouds of the sky, I realized I was high. Way high. This was how these guys did it. A natural high. Wonderful. And I saw God! Not bad.

Still, it was a matter of tinkering with the chemicals in the brain, wasn't it?

Wasn't everything?

My daughter Justine had tried to sneak down to watch the ceremony, but had been shooed away since females weren't allowed to watch. "Sexist pigs!" she railed. The women, having nothing else to do, drifted up toward the house, and Roberta invited everyone in. By the time we men emerged from our mystic experience, a feast was in the works. There were jokes about how I had become a "Redskin" because my flesh was parboiled bright pink. A "cleansing," Tony called the ceremony. The kids were great, including our kids. Nobody drank. Everybody laughed a lot. There was a lot of cigarette-smoking. It was a gentle, easy afternoon and evening with our newfound friends, who left early in the evening. I don't remember any-thing profound having been said, just a lot of joking and bantering and bouncing off each other; men, women, and children treating each other with mutual affection and respect, in a raincoast para-dise. And, *of course*, around four p.m., a rainbow came unlocked above the treetops north of the house. The sun had punched its way through the cloud cover in the last hour, allowing us to spill out onto the damp, steaming patio deck over the carport, so that every-body witnessed it. By the time they all left Roberta and I were *almost* willing to talk abut a mini-miracle having possibly happened—like, my faith having been restored.

But even that—a legitimate Sweat, a plausible New Age vision, a reputable guru, and a verified rainbow in one afternoon—wasn't enough.

Rainbows happened a lot, after all. One of the reasons no Natives had settled here on this particular mountain slope in the past was that they knew better. The clouds driven from off the Pacific piled up against the Coastal Range and stayed piled up overhead, like a giant-scale ice jam. It rained, children. Lord, it rained! All you needed was a few minutes of sunlight, a single beam of cosmic rays, and the soggy atmosphere was bound to flare into a rainbow some-where. How much of a miracle did that really count for? Nada, prob-ably. We were just in a rainbow-prone area.

The lapse into old-style eco-era magical thinking was short-lived. In no time, I was back to brooding darkly over my failings as a leader, a man, and a sentient being. Maybe the battle for Planet Earth was critical, when you looked at the whole continuum, and maybe the fate of this entire quadrant of the galaxy pivoted on what happened here, and by abdicating, I had blown the gig for zillions of living be-ings on tens of thousands of planets, maybe millions of zillions of planets, who knew? How could you prove that you *hadn't* fucked up at a key moment just as a galaxy-wide or maybe even intergalactic paradigm shift was taking place, and your failure would mean the de-feat of the entire new, superior paradigm! You *couldn't*!

Aha! I had me.

Technically, it was a nervous breakdown. In my own mind, it was cast-iron logic. I no longer had a purpose. I couldn't go back. I didn't want to go forward. There was no forward I could see to go to. I couldn't stand leaders and detested followers. That left out almost the entire human race. Every function I had performed was now being performed by someone else. My Brothers had betrayed me. I had betrayed them. It was like the final scene of 1984. It was time for someone to escort me away. Thoughts like this. I obviously wasn't enjoying obscurity as much as I thought I would. The rain might have been a factor, the nearly endless cloud cover, sloshing about in the sheep poop and hauling bales of hay from the pickup down to the barn, always wearing rubber boots and a hooded rain-slick. I didn't have a job for the longest while. Couldn't go back. Burned too many bridges. Roberta was supporting us.

One afternoon, under a fairly low-level cloud cover, out trekking in the forest, I decide I am, indeed, washed up. And why don't I just do something honourable for once? Get out of the picture entirely. I think I am sane at a spiritual level. I'm not going to ever be anything more than pond scum in this lifetime, anyway. Move on, move on! Quit cluttering the stage.

In a small clearing, in the midst of a salmonberry patch where an animal trail ran, I leaned my three-ought-three against the trunk of a fallen branch, took off my rubber boots, peeled off my socks, wiggled my toes in the wet cold slime of the mud, removed my farmer's coveralls (didn't wear underwear), my old felt hat, and finally my tee-shirt, and lay down naked (didn't wear a watch, kept my wedding ring on) on a bed of pine needles, picked up the rifle, took it off safety, cocked it, put my thumb rather than my forefinger on the trigger. I would have to squeeze the other way. Holding the thing awkwardly, starting to shiver from the damp air. Open my mouth. But I will not stick the muzzle into my mouth, as Hemingway did, because that will be taken as subconscious homosexuality. No, I will fire with the gun resting on my chin just outside my wide-open lips so the bullet goes through the roof of my mouth and splatters my brain instantaneously. I am hidden far enough from the house so that it will be the police or a search party who will find me. Nothing more to say. Take a slow, deep, yoga breath.

A high-fidelity silence.

I don't know what people mean when they say they heard "a voice from within." All voices are from within to start with. So that doesn't help me describe it. How about: a voice from *deeper* within? *more* within? Or maybe the same old voice—me—just thinking in a deeper-sounding voice as a desperate tactic in order to wield more influence over my disintegrating will to survive, or risk-taking gene run amok.

But a voice definitely said, clear as a phone call in the middle of my brain:

Wait. See if there's a sign. Give it a minute.

If this is a game, it's a really stupid game, I am realizing. But even though my heart is pattering at what seems like twice its normal speed and my hands are shaking slightly, my right thumb is still steady on the trigger, for how much longer I don't know.

I listen. I open my eyes to look around, scan the sky. Maybe an eagle. No. Silence. A squirrel somewhere. Not enough. The creaking of a huge old tree. No. Heartbeat. Shaking. *Chicken! Do it!* I wouldn't even see the puff of smoke. The click of the trigger would have barely begun and it would be over. The wrestling with myself goes on beyond the minute, but despite a cresting wave of panic there is something inside that is remorselessly angry with myself, that is really *pissed*, in fact. And while this might just be some neurotic/psychotic event, it might also be a paranormal thing. How would you know?

But . . . okay, okay . . . there *is* something. Just beyond hearing, at first, but enough to trip a tiny advance-warning vibration mechanism in the ear. A deep, deep vibe. Something huge coming. From *behind* my head, the direction the bullet would have headed after tearing through my skull. It is this detail more even than the great-throated voice gathering at the edge of hearing, that sends the goosebumps rippling.

It *is* a roaring. It is the roaring of a jet, or rather, several jet engines. But it can't be! This side of Eagle Mountain is well out of the flight paths of any of the jetliners using the Vancouver airport, far across the peninsula. Around 7:00 p.m., we often see the passage of several craft, already at a tremendous altitude, streaking northward on a polar route for Europe. But this was coming from the north, and it was flying low, especially considering it was skimming over the Coastal Range and coming down over the crowded Lower Main- land, and it was the middle of the day. In the year we had been liv- ing there, I had never once seen a jet take this particular low-flying route right over the forest adjacent to our property, right over where I happened to be naked on my back in a clearing, open-mouthed, gun to head, thumb on trigger. The sound preceded it, building in volume until I began to think it might be coming down for a crash landing and would smash right into me, meaning I would have taken a whole pile of people out with me. I might just have been strung- out, but it felt to me like the trees were vibrating and that there was even a discernible tremble in the hard ground under the pine nee- dles, and slowly, partially veiled by the clouds so that it was at least part-phantom, the 747 came thunderbirding down over the lower southern slope of Eagle Mountain, sound cascading in an avalanche that drowned out absolutely everything else. Its incredible wings were folded back as wings should be, like an opening Swiss Army knife, but it still managed to look like some kind of Eastern Ortho- dox broken-cross-from-space. It seemed so huge and low, it was as though a brontosaurus had walked across me without stepping on me. Then it was gone, the forest trembling and flickering and crack- ling, the molecules of everything from the great trunks of the Doug- las fir to my heart left still resonating.

Very cautiously, very firmly, I pulled the gun barrel away from my face with my left hand, removed my right thumb from the trigger, clicked the safety back on, set the whole heavy thing aside on the ground beside me, and sat slowly up.

Buzzed.

Timing, I thought. Miracles are in the timing. They do happen. You just have to be there to *see* them. If a miracle occurs in the for- est and nobody sees it, did it really happen? Of course not. Miracles need us, just as we need them.

That was it. The inquiry was over. I dressed calmly, knowing that my life was indeed blessed, that there *was* magic, that I would never be fully rational again, and I would never stupidly aspire to be. I bowed Hindu-style with a ragged, blissed grin to the sky and the forest and the ground. Thought: *Okay. That's good enough for me. Something going on here, even if I'm blind and insane. Thank you, Whoever/Whatever. Great Spirit sounds good.* And, lo! Doing myself in has never been an issue since. A few months after that, on the insistence of an old buddy, I started a ten-year career as a travel writer, flying (frequently, yes, on 747s) around the world . . . *that's* what it had meant. I should go check out the world instead of checking *out* of the world, yeah!

Gradually, my life redefined itself. In addition to travel writing I took on a job teaching journalism, did some public relations for a friend who was trying to set up a fake space station, and got handed a job writing a column in a twice-weekly suburban handout tabloid. Soon I was cranking out a near-record number of magazine articles each month, bopping around the world, recovering nicely from my bummed-out suicidal phase.

One day I came home from a two-week trip through Norway, Denmark, and Sweden, and marched down to the back acre to inspect the writing cabin that had been finished in my absence. It was a fresh cedar-shake thing with skylights and huge windows and a porch. Alas, the two fellows who had built the place had spent the last night after the job was done getting drunk and stoned down around the fire pit in front of the Sweat Lodge. They had left the Sacred Ground littered with broken booze bottles, beer caps, empties, cigarette butts, roaches, bent nails, sawdust, bits of two-by-fours, unfinished pizza and two encrusted pizza boxes. Some of this sacrilegious mess was INSIDE the Sweat Lodge! I cringed, but thought: "At least I'll be able to clean it up before Tony sees this."

Too late. Jammed into my typewriter on the fresh new desk in the new cabin was a neatly typed message from Tony, saying that I, Custodian of the Sacred Ground, had allowed it to be treated with contempt. I had failed in my duty to protect it. I wasn't worthy of being called a brother any longer, and that if I didn't get it together I would no longer even be considered a friend.

Oh, great! I finally buy in to a religion and the first thing that happens, I get excommunicated! It was like a Woody Allen scenario.

Nevertheless, I thought, let's act as though this all has some meaning. So I decided to behave *as if* magic was at work. I climbed back up to the house, grabbed a bunch of garbage bags, pounded downhill across the pasture, over the new bridge, and started picking up the garbage around the Sweat Lodge. It took a couple of hours, but I picked up *everything*, down to the last fleck of sawdust, and replaced the floor of the Lodge itself with fresh new cedar boughs, took the cigarette-butt-stained stones from the fire pit down to the creek and scrubbed them clean, returned them to the pit. This was the most humble thing I had done since I was an altar boy, unimaginably long ago in the past history of the world. I got very sincere about it.

You could no doubt call this a nervous breakdown, too. This white guy sifting through ashes to pluck cigarette filters and load them into his bag, using a tablespoon to pick up tiny shards of glass, a hand-held broom and a dustbin to remove the upper layer of soil from the floor of the Lodge, splash buckets of water on the ground where ants had gathered to feast on the pizza, washing them not-too-violently away.

I hauled the loaded garbage bags back up to the altitude of the house, struggled into the forest along the narrow path through the salmonberries to our private garbage dump, obsessed with the idea that I HAD to do this. It was important. It was a cleaning and purifying and reverence-displaying ritual. More goddamn Indian craziness, to be sure. When was I going to get free of it?

But anyway, I've done it. I've atoned as best I can. I have played by the rules of the Brotherhood. The only question now is, will they ever come back? I decide to march uphill a little further to the front-road mailbox, having heard the Post Office Jeep stop and start. I squeak open the little door of the corrugated metal mailbox and pull out several letters and a parcel. The parcel is from the United Kingdom. It comes from an another old eco-war buddy, a Rainbow Warrior who is still out there in the front lines. I have no inkling as I open it what will be inside. Out spill two tee-shirts: Rainbow Warrior tee-shirts, with the beatific Plains Indian in a Hindu position, the rainbow arching about his yogic hand, and the 7070 inscription about saving the animals.

This is, like, mere minutes after I've cleaned up the mess on the

Sacred Ground. *Mere minutes!* And I received out of the blue not one but *two* Warrior Skins.

It means . . . I have been forgiven. I have been doubly forgiven. Standing there alone among the gigantic trees in the wet West Coast air, clutching two tee-shirts, I think: *It's all true at some level. Insane but true. And what do you do if reality turns out to be mad?*

7

Indian Time

It was shortly after *that* when the phone call came from Bob Royer (aka Robert Calihoo), the new band manager for the Kwakiutl Nation, asking if I would consider doing some "media advising" for the Nimpkish Band Council at Alert Bay.

Royer wasn't Kwakiutl himself.

"I'm part Cree, eh?" he said.

"Ever hear of the Rainbow Warrior?" I asked, testing him.

A pause and a grunt. "Not many goddamn white men've heard about *that*. We don't advertise it, eh? Where'd you . . ."

"Long story," I muttered.

I was already flashing back to dancing in the blue smoke in the Big House in 1971, the Elders in their bead blankets, the eyes of the thunderbirds carved in the beams looking down. All the rainbows and miracles I'd seen since then scrolled at high speed across my mind. I remembered the sound of Fred Mosquito's amplified voice.

"You . . . are . . . the . . ."

Well, this was not quite in the league of saving entire species or ecosystems at a time, and what Royer was talking about was hiring me as a PR man, for God's sake. This could be construed as low. Actual flacking. But then, on the evidence, there was a good damned chance this was a genuine Warrior thing, anarchistic, out-of-control, on the cusp between absurdity and eco-occultism, sheer Indian weirdness . . .

I liked to think I was being summoned. At the very least, I was being hired for my spin-doctor skills. Spin-doctoring *could* be seen as answering a call to arms, too. No need to be ashamed of it. It wasn't like I would be flacking for a CFC manufacturer. These were the Brothers. I was a trusted radical comrade. Right on! Wasn't this what I always wanted to be?

Besides, I could always use the money.

I'm not sure where Royer and I first encountered one another, but it was in the bar of either the Harbour Inn or the Nimpkish Inn, both overlooking Johnstone Strait, and it must have been during a trip I took to Cormorant Island in February 1973, when a freighter named the *Irish Stardust* went up on the rocks in the mouth of the strait, and huge bonfires of oil-soaked driftwood were lit on the beaches to burn the blackened kelp and sea grass. Blooms of black smoke billowed as crews threw more gasoline on the flames. The totem poles in the cemetery looked with stern expressions of disapproval across the oil-slicked water. There were gusts of cold rain. It seemed like an End-Time.

But, then, one way or another, I had always gotten a whiff of End-Timeness every time I went near Alert Bay. It was the totems, mostly, that spoke to me.

The expression carved into their features made me think what it must have been like for the thousands of Natives who fell to small-pox and rubella. I knew that plagues had struck everywhere in the world, but this was the first place where I could see the faces of the fallen staring like grey cedar ghosts—and of course it wasn't just humans whose images had been carved into the long-dead trees. The Beaver. The Killer Whale. The Frog. The Sea Otter. The Eagle. The Raven. The Thunderbird.

The sight of the oil on the beaches, lapping at the feet of the totems, was a dark apocalyptic scenario come true. It was all the more horrifying because, on previous visits, I had been able to achieve a state of beatific near-oneness simply by walking along the pure crushed-seashell sands, just sucking in the salt air. Everywhere I turned my eyes were treated to an ecstasy of form and light: the river mouth where a heron stood daintily, its beak poised like a surgical instrument to pluck a ling cod from a silver tray; a beam of golden light falling between two peaks, boring into the dark turquoise depths of the underwater canyons between the cliffs. If there was no cloud cover, the Coastal Range could be seen in its tiered majesty, arrowhead peaks throwing off sheets of blinding light, an Ice Age fallen over the wreckage of castles. Between the paws of the mountains, streams fell like undone necklaces, conjuring small rainbows. The lower slopes wore the forest like an unbroken skirt of cedar and hemlock and fir. Trees that had grown too fast and had been punished by lightning pierced the canopy like ivory needles: Spiketop country. The water slapped against the rickety legs of a wharf beside an abandoned cannery, its hundred little windows broken. Reeds grew up on all sides. Ramshackle houses stood in a row, thin wedges of light driving down through cracks in delicately rusted, corrugated sheet-metal roofs. Tarpaper walls, cedarshakes carpeted with jewelled moss, grains of grass sticking up from plugged eaves troughs . . . It is as though not just one but two civilizations had clung precariously to a foothold here in the dark green vastness for a time, and were now both disappearing, eaten away by rain and wind and the arrival of seeds.

The deal Bob Royer offered was two hundred bucks a day plus travel expenses for me to come up and be available to advise the band council on media strategies when they wanted to get something done. My job description also required me to write press releases, speeches, and letters, contact news organizations, and generally try to line up any coverage I could. The spokesman I'd mainly be working with would be the elected chief, in this case Patrick Alfred. Bob Royer was his primary adviser. I was the hired media gunslinger. But I couldn't just take orders from Chief Patrick and Royer. We had to get the majority of council onside before doing anything.

The first thing I suggested to them was that they copyright all their names and totems and songs and dances and emblems and crests. There were wry smiles when I mentioned it. Yes, I was the guy who—never mind!

Was this, too, some kind of atonement?

One characteristic this job did share with my idea of atonement, it involved rather a lot of work. Slow work, too. Tedious. Sitting through entire band council meetings. Taking notes. Looking attentive. Sitting on committees. Since we were operating in a highly localized situation—which is to say, you couldn't cross a street without someone spotting you, and word getting around when it wanted to get around—we had to spend a lot of time drinking coffee when it would have been far more creatively productive to slip in through the back door of the Nimpkish Inn for a little libation. This was the trouble with a tribal scene, I realized. With a thousand eyes out there, at least one pair, just by the law of random averages, was on your every move. Since I was actually being paid out of band funds, and so was my fellow employee, Band Manager Royer, it behoved us not to start drinking in public, let alone doing anything else, until working hours were over, which was generally conceded to be any time after three o'clock or so. Unless, like Pat Alfred, you were chief and facing election, and you had to hang out at the band council office, looking busy, until at least five. Besides, if the chief's wife found out he was goofing off with the guys down at one of the inns during the day, there'd be hell to pay. That applied to most of the other married guys as well.

It was a grinding line of work, being an Indian Chief. It required, I quickly realized, the patience of a saint. Hours spent on the phone with bureaucrats. More hours spent puzzling over letters sent by bureaucrats. Days spent in meetings with bureaucrats. Years spent in consultation with bureaucrats. At every turn, another bureaucrat. The political entity known as Canada had come up with a Stamplicker's Wall as a way to fence the Natives in. Every time they tried to make a move, another little bureaucrat was blocking the way, wanting to communicate earnestly. Of course, if anybody tried to push past the bureaucrat without him having had his way, a whistle would be blown and the Mounties would pop into view. And if *they* couldn't handle it (i.e., a gun appeared), the Armed Forces would soon be revving up the armoured personnel carriers. Trying to launch a media campaign from *inside* a reserve was a matter of lobbing telexes over the heads of the encircling civil servant hordes, armed with their memos and agendas and flow charts and stamp pads and guns. We *were* surrounded.

My media doctrine in this situation was: break through and attack them on the high ground, retreat before they can muster force, lure them back into a trap, and then finish them off.

The classic campaign employing this doctrine was the Battle of the Nimpkish River, in 1982.

A hotshot developer had showed up from out of the blue at a zoning subcommittee meeting of some kind in the town of Port McNeill. This was across the strait from Alert Bay on the northeast shore of Vancouver Island, well within the range of traditional Kwakiutl hunting and fishing grounds. He had talked the half-dozen local white fellow-businessmen present at the meeting into giving him the go-ahead to develop a fabulous sports fishing project north of the town—on Nimpkish River shoreline property that was expected to be the subject of a land claim, when the day came for such a reckoning. The Kwakiutl could prove through archaeological digs that they had been fishing and hunting along the Nimpkish for four thousand years. When confronted with these details, the developer argued that it didn't matter in the least. There was no legal or technical reason why the project could not proceed until such time as a claim was actually filed, possibly in the unimaginably distant future.

Thus, without so much as a letter of notice of meeting to the Nimpkish Band Council just three miles away on Cormorant Island, the Port McNeill Development Subcommittee unilaterally, behind closed doors, handed over control of a large tract of ancient Kwakiutl hunting grounds—a very old trick, by the way.

My mission: get this land-grab reversed.

With just a few hours' notice by phone from Bob Royer, I was hopping on a plane to Cormorant Island, lugging along my thirty-pound steel-shelled Kaypro II word processor, a book-sized metal modem, and a cumbersome old pre-laser printer. This was the late Seventies. The equipment was actually fairly cutting edge, the Kaypro having been designed to fit under the seat of an airplane. The Sherman tank of prototypal portable word processors, it lost its market niche and went extinct when the airlines changed the regulations about carry-ons. I wound up, at the end of that particular era, having to pay a half-fare and strap the damned thing into a seat beside me on a flight back from a script-writing assignment in New

Zealand, or risk having its circuitry jogged loose while being bumped along the baggage conveyer belt.

The Kaypro and the printer are mounted on the old wooden table in the middle of the living room at the band manager's place on the reserve, just down the hill from the Big House. I am sitting there, ashtray overflowing, empty beer bottles arrayed on the table, poking one finger at a time at the keyboard, squinting at the screen, writing something like "Welcome to the Land of the Kwakiutl." That was a good start, we'd all agree. The numbers would vary, but sometimes there might be a dozen people in the room, standing in a semi-circle, watching over my shoulder as the letters sail silently across the screen, and the computer makes its occasional *ka-chug* as something turns over inside. Sometimes, the advisory panel would get down to Bob Royer and Pat Alfred, and quite often Pat's son, George, who was a councillor already, and had his father's ear. He was being groomed for the top job. They'd still be haggling over my wording of the chief's words, or yapping on about some local or federal issue I really didn't give a shit about, when I'd hit the sofa with the earplugs in and airline blinders on, and would apparently start snoring so loudly that nobody else could get to sleep. They were, of course, too polite to manhandle me, but it meant that long after I woke up the next day, which wouldn't be until noon, anyway, Chief Pat and his closest advisers would still be catching up on the shut-eye, and if we weren't careful, closing time at the post office might come, and that inspired message for the Prime Minister of Canada which we fine-tuned so beautifully so late last night might not get sent off for another full *day*, which would take us to the weekend before the Prime Minister's Office could possibly respond, which would delay *everything* for probably another full *week . . .*

After screaming "Foul!" from Victoria to Ottawa to New York via a new wire service where you paid for your releases to be carried verbatim into every major newsroom in the world, the campaign called for the entire Nimpkish Band council to take the ferry over to Port McNeill to catch the next development subcommittee meeting. It was the first time in history that the Nimpkish council members had crossed Johnstone Strait en masse, at least without bearing weapons. There is much joking about "taking the whole head" as the councillors and me, their adviser, fill up the chairs surrounding the three Port McNeill councillors in their white shirts and ties. The dozen Kwakiutl interlopers are wearing mostly black leather jackets, jeans, and cowboy boots; almost all have long black hair and baseball hats, more than a few have scars on their faces and hands from fishing accidents. At a glance, it would be forgivable to mistake Chief Patrick for the leader of a biker gang. Over by the clerk, I am startled to see the Man from Glad sitting, hugging his briefcase.

Indeed, the marina developer looks exactly like the TV commercial character: dazzling white hair, bushy white eyebrows, gleaming white teeth, black polished shoes that twinkle, a flashy wristwatch. When Chief Pat finally rises to read from his speech, I almost expect a spotlight to fall upon him. The role-reversal imagery could not be more compellingly symmetrical. Great, deep voice, the chief has. Nice cadences. Sonorous. Instead of calling the councillors names, which is what they deserve, Chief Pat surprises them by inviting the entire Port McNeill council over to Alert Bay for a salmon barbecue and a festival of Kwakiutl song and dance. What can they do but accept?

On the day the ferry pulls in, bearing nearly a dozen nervous Port McNeill town councillors and their spouses, none of whom has ever crossed over to "the reserve" in their lives, they are greeted by children singing a haunting, unfamiliar refrain. It is, in fact, the Kwakiutl Death Chant, originally intended as a curse upon enemies, but it sounds great.

At the barbecue, after the dances and the displays of masks, the visitors are hustled into a classroom where they are shown several large coloured maps and a white biologist explains in painstakingly scientific detail how well the ten-year ecological restoration program the Nimpkish Band has been paying for out of its own pockets (money that could have gone into badly needed housing) is doing, how fragile this nearly restored ecological prize is, and how the proposed marina is far too big to go in without devastating the results of a decade's labour of love. Back the councillors go, wined, dined, and propagandized (a "dialogue," we call it), heading happily home to Port McNeill, where the marina project on the Nimpkish River dies on the vine of the next development subcommittee agenda.

A breeze! But it takes me maybe three visits of varying duration to put this all together. And the debates behind the scenes have been interminable. My patience isn't up for it.

I get out of this line of work after about three years of on-and-off shuttling back and forth to Alert Bay. The all-night creative sessions at Bob Royer's place were hard on the lungs and guts and head. My colleague and I, approaching midlife, were both under a lot of stress—the stress of holding one's act together, for instance—so we tended toward a hairy-chested, last-to-pass-out imbibing style. I'd need to "taper" the last day before heading back to my less politically charged existence on my farm just outside of Vancouver.

And then there was the question of "Indian Time."

Working with hippies had been hard enough, but at least you could sometimes browbeat and guilt them into immediate action. It didn't work with my employers. They had to talk things through. They had to chew the bone over and over again until every last participant was satisfied. Consensus may be the great alternative to hierarchical power structures, and in theory I'm all for it. I tried hard to gear myself down to this slower, more democratic, and, indeed, nobler way of getting things done, I really did, but I was too full of other, more hustling-along genes. I *envied* the mellower approach, but it was as unattainable as Yoga calmness or Zen serenity or any of the other systems of attaining peace of mind I had tried along the way. My Kwakiutl employers/brothers were just more beatific than me. Not knowing at the time that I had any Native blood in me at all, I started to see myself as that most pathetic of creatures, a *failed* wannabe Indian.

One morning I found myself dragging Chief Patrick and Councillor George from their hotel room in downtown Vancouver, herding them into the elevator and pushing them into my car in order to get them on time, goddammit, to a press conference I'd organized at great expenditure of energy at the University of British Columbia. By now the novelty of their pattern of time-insensitivity or indifference had worn off. I was so furious with them I roared and screeched down the worst potholed back lanes I could find through Kitsilano just to give them both a good physical pounding . . .

Oops! Time to re-assign myself.

8

Occupied Canada *and the Governor-General*

W hile I was still doing my PR gig for the Kwakiutl, over the course of several late-night sessions with Band Manager Bob Royer, he got to telling me the story of his life, which was virtually a Canadian saga.

It cried out movie to me. A TV series. At least a book. . . . Raised by his white grandmother in a middle-class section of Edmonton, he'd thought he was white, and was treated as though he was white until the old woman died and he got dumped on the street. After a brief stint with his estranged white mother, he tracked down his biological father, an Indian with the name Calihoo, and moved on to the Calihoo reserve, where the boy found himself experiencing literally Third World living conditions. "This is what it means to be an Indian," his grandfather told him. But he grew up feeling neither Indian nor white. He fell through the cracks of the Indian Act, was arrested young, bounced in and out of prison and a life of crime, with his crimes getting progressively more serious until it looked like he could be permanently incarcerated. Wising up, the angry young halfbreed put his mind to studying, trying to find a way out of the corner he'd got himself into. In a few years, he earned a degree in sociology, and when he was finally released, started working for Native Rights organizations, quickly finding himself in Ottawa, lobbying at the highest levels in the land. It was while working in Ottawa that he discovered what had happened to his reserve back in Alberta while he was in prison. It had been—very much against the law— sold out from under the Natives. A few sharp operators had managed to detach it from the usual provisions of the Indian Act. As a result, he was forever disenfranchised. Poverty-stricken as it had been, it had at least been a permanent home. Now he had no place to go back to, and without a reserve, he didn't have an identity as an Indian, and therefore no rights.

Whether the brutal punishment he took along the way simply left him too angry for a career as a bureaucrat, or natural impatience got in the way, he lost his lofty perch in Ottawa. With nowhere to go, he tapped into the network he'd established, and managed to land on his feet with his wife and two kids, hired as band manager at Alert Bay. Streetsmart, hip to the bureaucratic mode, eyes darting, always sizing up the situation, playing it like a game, infinitely wary, one of those guys who can never forget how alone he really is. He had done a lot of time, hard time. He had been in riots and solitary and had been badly beaten more than once. He had the scars to show it. He was short, but you didn't fuck with him. He had a blurred, ragged edge. He chain-smoked, drank, hankered after women, and had a late-night kind of energy that would get angry near the end. Wild. Exploding. He was coughing already, the years on the reserve and the prisons and street taking an early toll. But he sure liked to laugh, and what we did mostly together was laugh.

Also: we sat enough nights in my little cabin down by the stream in the back acre beside the Sweat Lodge, tape recorder going, because I had decided he *was* worth a book, while he told me his story in detail. Sometimes (very late in the taping sessions, admittedly) he seemed to change before my eyes as he spoke, for a while looking like a pool shark with a butt in his mouth, a shifty cabby, a street hustler, then suddenly a noble warrior, back to being a battered thug, switching to being a philosopher, a chief, then a cheat, then wise, high, clear, then tricky and elusive. Tribeless, I think.

I got more deeply involved than I expected one January when Royer, too sick to travel, called me from Alert Bay to ask if I would go back east for him to attend a meeting of the Native Council of Canada in Ottawa in a bid to have his "extinguished" reserve granted recognition, so that he might file a land claim. I agreed. I had the time . . . and the sense of, gee, I guess I've got to do this. So I flew, at the expense of the Indian Affairs Department, as the representative of Bob Royer's "lost tribe," meaning his disenfranchised fellow Calihoos, whose land had been illegally wrested from them. Once in Ottawa, I found myself attending a meeting of some two hundred Natives, the only white guy in sight. When I was allowed a turn, in the very last minutes of the meeting, to explain Bob Royer's request on behalf of the scattered and dispersed Calihoos, dead silence followed—until Grand Chief Joseph Norton of the Iroquois Six Nations Confederacy stood up and said: "We should claim that land ourselves." It turned out the "Calihoos" were descendants of a handful of Iroquois, named Karhiio, who had fled from Caughnawaga in 1793, establishing a foothold in unpopulated land just west of Fort of the Prairies, now Edmonton, on the slopes of the Rockies.

Natives who had migrated west, too!

Aha! It seemed to me that I had blundered across a lost piece of Canadiana—a piece that, when examined, revealed a whole lot about the country's inner skeleton. The book I had intended to write, telling Bob Royer's dramatic story of self-discovery, suddenly exploded in my mind into something far more staggeringly ambitious, never mind a mere TV series or movie: a revised history of Canada, no less! From the *Native* point of view!

Out of this inspiration was to come a book titled *Occupied Canada*, co-authored by Bob Royer (under the name Robert Calihoo) and me, which, to the astonishment of everyone involved, won the Governor-General's Award for Non-Fiction in 1991. Most reviewers seemed to like it. The Regina *Leader Post* called it "A compelling book." Canadian Press wrote: "Rarely has so much information about Canada's treatment of its aboriginals been put together so cogently, and with such great value to the average reader . . . Devastating." *The Calgary Sun* said: "*Occupied Canada* is among the best books ever written about the problem facing Natives . . . It is readable, factual, honest." I had now actually *done* something for the Brothers. I felt proud. And winning a G-G! This was quite amazing. I would now enter the Pantheon of CanLit, my name carved for all the ages alongside the likes of Margaret Laurence, Hugh MacLennan, and Robertson Davies.

But of course it wouldn't do to let the vastness of one's secret ego show, so the point to remember was that the winning of this oh-socoveted award was more than just an ego-wallow in glory, it was a way of bringing public attention to bear on a lingering Canadian injustice, to wit, the illegal disenfranchisement of the Calihoo people. In other words, I played it straight. This was a serious political issue. And as an award-winning author/historian, I would henceforth have to be listened to in the great struggle to correct the injustices to Native people in Canada, and not just Canada but the entire hemisphere, Turtle island itself. . . . Yadda yadda. I had, after all, written dozens of speeches for my chief back in Alert Bay, and knew the buzzwords and numbers and plenty enough of the history to talk the talk. Moreover, in the period between the time I handed the manuscript in and the day it came out (while several real historians went over the stuff, and the Oka Crisis flared), I had learned about my Huron blood connection. I had actually written the book in complete ignorance of my own genetic link to the people I was writing about. To have been saved by an Indian, to have worked for the Indians, to have researched and written a history of Canada's Indians, and only *afterwards* to find out you have an Indian ancestor, surely this is the stuff of mystical experiences! At the very least, as a mere coincidence, it was spectacular. It left me shaking my head, I'll tell you. Like being tapped on the shoulder by a giant invisible finger, and when you look around there's nothing there, but you *know* you have been zapped by something cosmic, inexplicable and ineffable. Proof, as if I needed any more, that there is more going on in life than meets the conscious eye. The truth was, I was starting to see a virtually mystical (let's say) relationship between myself and the Aboriginals.

The book was not a stunning commercial success and vanished into the void. Not even my best friends could bear to read it, it was such an appalling tale: imperialism, land theft, disease, genocide. And it cast the expanding Canadian "empire" as being every bit as evil as its British parent. My dedication had said: "Vive l'Oka Libre." How much more radical could you get? This was fairly high-grade giving-of-the-finger. Too bad about nobody reading the thing . . . Too depressing, said one friend, who normally read every word I wrote. It made her feel (for a little while anyway) not quite as thrilled to be a Canadian. And who wanted that? There was enough grief in the world, why dredge up the past? Even the Mounties came out as bad guys. Well, especially the Mounties . . .

It's strange what thinking you have a reputation does to your logic. The book had come out, although it hadn't won any prize yet, when Good Captain Watson called up again. It was a year after our Pacific drift-net adventure. He had something different to offer. No chasing after drift-netters or whalers or sealers (ho hum). This time he was going to do something a little more political. He had had a beer with a West Coast writer, Terry Glavin, who did the same work for the Gitksan Nation as I had done for the Kwakiutl. Paul had commented how he would love to see someone go out and confront the Columbus caravels, which everyone knew were being readied to sail across the Atlantic Blue in '92 to celebrate the five-hundredth anniversary of The Landing, which of course was the precise point when the North American Holocaust began. Glavin took the suggestion to *his* chief, a fellow named Wii Seeks, who said: "Hmmmm. Sounds like a good idea." The next thing Paul knew he was getting a phone call telling him that representatives of "several" British Columbian tribes were willing to sail with him into the Atlantic to confront Columbus.

So there it was. Paul knew *Occupied Canada* had just been published, and I had told him about my Huron link. "I thought of you right away," he rumbled. Would I like to grab a cameraman and come along? More to the point, could I convince the station that such a voyage was even remotely relevant to my beat, which was supposed to be the environment. Well . . . When I pitched the idea to the news director, I argued that the Indians were the original environmentalists. Witness the Oglala Sioux War to Save the Buffalo, which led to Custer's Last Stand (overlooking a few other mass slaughters by Natives of bison and otters and beaver). And furthermore, Spanish colonization opened the door that led to the eventual ecological pillaging of the continent. It was a thin connection, God and the news director knew, but the power upstairs at the station, executive-producer Moses Znaimer, had actually *liked* the previous year's drift-net footage, and was up for me doing more action stuff. It looked like I was at last actually going to go into battle with my warrior-brothers. It did not occur to me that I might *not* go. After all, wasn't I a radical Native rights activist now?

What an anguish, then, when news of winning the Governor-General's Award came, and it turned out the ceremony would be on December 11—two days *after* the *Sea Shepherd* was scheduled to depart from Nassau. Okay. What was I going to do? Forfeit the opportunity to go off to battle with the Brothers in order to bask in the spotlight at home? A clear hard choice between ego gratification and dedication to a higher duty. And an ethical question was posed, too. Would I seriously consider accepting an award, plus $10,000, from the same neo-colonial Canadian government whose historical guilt for crimes against the Native population I had just finished documenting? And in exchange for what? Mere literary immortality . . .

Well, it didn't take that long to decide. There was no way I was going to pass on the spotlight. That was the sad truth of the matter. The arrangements would be a trifle complicated, but it could be done. Instead of boarding the *Sea Shepherd* in time for her Nassau departure, I would rendezvous with the boat a couple of days later, in the Turks and Caicos Islands, and I would attend the awards ceremony in Toronto to help bring attention to the continuing injustices committed against the Native peoples, blah blah blah.

The $10,000 prize would be split, of course, with my co-author. Who had to be located. Which proved to be more difficult than expected. Since I had last seen Bob Royer, he had dropped out of sight somewhere in Western Canada, probably Alberta, but possibly in Saskatchewan. It took a lot of phone calling to track him down, and when I did get hold of him, he wasn't quite as overwhelmed by the significance of a Governor-General's Award as I had hoped. The five thousand bucks sounded all right, though. He could sure use that. Could they just send him the cheque? There was a free plane trip to Toronto and a free posh hotel room for a night in it for him, too, I advised. To say nothing of a chance to make a speech in front of the Governor-General himself, along with Canada's literary elite. A chance to make the case for the Calihoo land claim. But I gathered that wasn't going anywhere in particular. Bob had tried to organize a group of Calihoo descendants, but the group proved preprogrammed to extreme factionalization, and he couldn't get anything political going without it being opposed by one faction or another. He had basically given up, and was on to other things. Vague things. Still pissed at the system. Pissed at his fellow band members in exile too. "I should remember, eh? 'Don't hang out with cliques, pricks, and politics,' " he said, quoting the philosophy of the old rounders who had guided him as a young street hustler.

Bob Royer's whereabouts in the last couple of weeks before the G-G ceremony was the subject of much anxiety on the part of the publicists at McClelland & Stewart, our publishers, who were trying to line him up for interviews with a clamouring horde of media. It was an author's dream. But he never called from the same phone. Left different numbers and was gone before anyone could call back. He was the stealth author from hell. It dawned on me that he had settled back into an underground existence. I explained to his distraught publicists, fine young women all of them, that he was in the habit of covering his trail, that was all. So much so that his movements were impossible to follow, let alone predict. Thus, he entered Toronto quietly, with no one at the airport to meet him, appeared in the flesh only long enough to claim his hotel room, then vanished into the streets. Despite messages left everywhere for him, I found myself being ushered, along with the other winners, backstage at the Winter Gardens Theatre at ten in the morning, as scheduled, to meet Governor-General Ray Hnatyshyn. Not a sign of Royer. By that time, I was seething and hissing at him in my mind. Please don't fuck up, was my simple request. We are, after all, entering the Canuck Pantheon. But no. He was going to be a no-show, and I was righteously pissed. Still, you can't let your big moment be spoiled just because your co-author has buggered up the rather simple assignment of arriving on time. And why was I having to worry about this anyway? Was I supposed to be my Brother's keeper?

I was feeling so stressed, even though it was early in the event, that when my chance came to hobnob with the head neo-colonial oppressor, I asked if he could give the word to somebody to open the well-stocked backstage bar just a little tiny bit early. He sighed heavily and nodded toward the half-dozen security guys with the earpieces scattered among us. "They don't let me drink until eleven o'clock," quoth His Eminence. And I realized the poor devil was a prisoner, too. My anger against the imperialist Canadian state abated slightly in the face of the Queen's Representative's apple-red cheeks and nose and the help-I'm-trapped-in-a-cookie-factory look on his face.

It wasn't until ten minutes into the ceremony, when we were all back in our seats in front of the stage, the house was full of buzzing literary types, the Gov-Gen was seated above us on something looking suspiciously like a throne, and the full primitiveness of this ritual was impressing itself upon me, that I spotted Royer seated by himself off to the side. He had just materialized in the seat. The good news was that he was wearing a suit jacket. The bad news was that it looked like he might have slept in it, not, in this case, a figure of speech. I slipped over to sit beside him. He was a lot more stressed than I was. Whether it was from a lack of sleep, let's say, or sheer stage fright, I couldn't tell. His hands were shaking. Trying not to appear petty and annoyed, I slipped him a feather I'd brought from a collection at home, hoping it would help me to focus when the moment came to deliver a brief acceptance speech. Royer needed it more than I did. And it did seem to steady him. He nodded. For an instant, we were Brothers again. Then we were climbing up on the stage to applause, the Queen's boyo was shaking hands, and we took turns at the microphone.

I had hoped to muster the guts to cry out "Vive l'Oka Libre," but common sense prevailed. Instead, I made a nice little speech about trying to rectify injustices, setting a good example of brevity, and turned the mike, with some trepidation, over to Royer. He held the feather in his hand and quoted from Chief Poundmaker, who had warned his people that the worst ordeal would not be defeat in battle, but the mocking and being spat upon that would come afterwards. Not bad. Short. Lots of applause. We were both off the stage and back in our seats, and the worst, most vulnerable moment had passed, and Bob had behaved. We had both behaved. We were good little prize winners, and we were both clutching our five-thousand-dollar cheques, savouring the applause. As revolutionary radicals, we had totally blown it. Our big moment. Cameras rolling. And

neither one of us said jack shit about smashing the state. I was relieved that Bob hadn't called for the death of the Queen, or something, but couldn't help being disappointed with myself for wimping
out. Roberta, who was sitting next to me, proudly holding my hand,
said: "Nice restraint, tiger."

Afterwards, a glitzy reception. Media superstars everywhere. Living literary and journalistic legends galore. Much subtle sniping. But
it was nice, being fêted. When the bar opened Bob and Ray and I
were right there. In the middle of the witticisms and brilliant repar-
tee, Royer got surprised people from his publishers' office to cash his
cheque for him. He didn't have a bank. In the early afternoon, he
did a fade back out to the streets.

We didn't encounter him again until evening, just as we were
waiting for the elevator to take us to the top floor of a mighty downtown bank. He was ripped. But then who was I to throw stones, as it
were? I was just slightly on the ripped side myself. Sixty storeys up
we emerged from the elevator into an enormous dining area, with a
string quartet playing, looking out over the lights of the biggest concentration of wealth and power in Canada. Surrounded by the nation's economic, political, and literary elite, we were guided to a
round table where we joined our publisher, the urbane, erudite, and
merry Doug Gibson, as well as, among others, one of the vice-
presidents of the bank itself (presumably a human monster beneath
the veneer of charm and breeding), and his delightful and attractive
running-dog trophy bride. It was hard, for an old leftist like me, not
to feel slightly squirmy in the company of the corporate plutocracy.
Supping with the devil, any way you looked at it, really. Who, after
all, has looked upon the bank towers of Toronto, where the mort-
gages are stored, and not felt a twinge of hatred in his heart? Yet they
were our hosts, the VP and his wife, and Doug was our publisher, and
we didn't want to embarrass anybody, did we? We were quickly out-
Canadianing each other with politeness. I think it's called being co-
opted. It was appalling how quickly I went for it, along with the
excellent wine.

We were actually making it through. I was beginning to have
hope. And then the subject of Free Trade came up. The VP was
100 per cent in favour, of course. He had all the numbers about why

it was such a marvellous, brilliant thing. He just had to assume that we common folk understood the benefits too. Wasn't it all so obvious, really? The imperative was irrefutable. At which point, alas, my co-author decided he had had enough of being co-opted. Maybe all those years he'd spent behind bars dreaming of getting even with the bigwigs were kicking in. Here was his chance, for sure. He wasn't likely to be invited back here for din-dins anyway. The banker, being the worldly fellow that he was, tried his best to be gracious, to employ his persuasive skills, underlining his points deftly, trying to keep it light, wry, and clever. But my angry co-author, deploying all the debating techniques learned at Stony Mountain, would have none of it. Basically, his point came down to: *You banking bastards are pushing Free Trade so you can suck more blood from the People, and you should all be hung by the balls with piano wire. On top of that, you're lackeys of the American military-industrial complex, every last fucking one of you.*

Despite the urgency of maintaining decorum, voices began to rise at our table. The banker lost some of his colour. He was now leaning across the table, hissing at Royer, who was snarling back at him. My wife finally couldn't take it any longer and yelled at Royer: "Will you just shut up!" That created quite a stir at surrounding tables. It also slowed my co-author down a minute or two. But he was soon back on the attack. *Banking bastards living off the backs of the poor . . . Free Trade Mulroney goons . . .* It was beginning to look like my now thoroughly aroused warrior-brother was close to leaping across the table and grabbing the poor banker by the throat, although it was a moot point whether the well-fed banker, quite a tall fellow, wasn't about to do some throttling of his own. He looked in a lot better shape than my co-author, although he didn't have the pent-up fury. My money would be on Royer if he got the initiative.

There was a ten-second pause at the end of which the banker's wife—a nice, north-Toronto, respectable lady, who hadn't expected this as part of the "for richer for poorer" deal—finally cracked, letting out a small scream. We all sat there, interested. Gibson, unable to resist a joke, said, "Well, I guess you had to be there." Which was met with chuckles or glares.

Canada's former ambassador to the United States was about to speak, and I had visions of the entire gathering of the high and mighty being disrupted by a fistfight between my co-author and one of the bank's VPs. Resignedly, Roberta got up and signalled for me to do the same. She was right. Better to get it over with before somebody had to call security. Roberta (who has Viking blood in her and had a grandfather who once single-handedly lifted a tipped-over tractor off somebody who was crushed underneath it) grabbed Royer by one arm. I got him by the other. We both hissed at the top of our lungs at him and hoisted him to his feet. I made up the insanely lame excuse to the table at large that I had just remembered our babysitter had to be home early, and we wanted to take our friend here, who's from out of town, *grunt*, home to visit the kids, whom he hasn't, *grunt*, seen in ages. Thus, we grappled with the snarling co-winner of the 1991 Governor-General's Award for Non-Fiction, and now an anti-Free Trade crusader of some note in influential circles. I was poignantly aware that the other hundred diners, including the ex-ambassador, were all staring with expressions of shock and horror as the three of us, struggling and snarling, weaved our crab-like way across the floor to the elevator. I knew they would not understand what was going on. They would just see three crazies fighting among themselves. They would be embarrassed on our behalf, of course, and amused, and I would undoubtedly be remembered, when it all came down to dust, as the famous award-winning writer who, along with his wife and his co-author, made such a spectacular exit from the '91 G-G dinner.

So much for my Great Once-in-a-Lifetime Moment of entering the Pantheon of CanLit.

One thing I had to admit: Royer had *not* wimped out.

9

Flying South with Grizzly Bear Tracks

A nd now, God help me, the very next day the voyage has physically begun.

Urine-coloured morning light pierces the shroud of ground-level ozone above the 401 as Roberta wrestles her station wagon along the edge of the corridor, skirting early Toronto expressway gridlock, grimly trying to get me to my Pan-American Airlines flight to Miami, the first hop in the direction of the Turks and Caicos.

I am hurting. A genuine whimper escapes my lips. It is not just me. Roberta is suffering hideously too as she drives in stoic sunglass silence, no conversation, just the traffic report and the roar of the tractor-trailers and the overloaded flatbeds, with me slumped red-eyed in the passenger seat, numbly clutching my knapsack, sleeping bag, and video-camera case, teeth grinding on a plastic cigarette. Two months, three weeks, four days, three-and-a-half hours off nicotine. Stress stalks the edges of my semi-consciousness, flickering like wonky backlighting around my frontal lobes.

Roberta's silence may very well have something to do with more than just her hangover. She may, it dimly occurs to me, be driving with such hunting-dog intensity to get me to the airport on time because she is still plenty pissed about last night, and probably not unhappy to see me and my crusades and buddies out of her life for a while.

Thoughts of all the things that can go wrong with the days ahead rise up to torment me, I can feel my feeble sense of purpose flickering and fading. My basic assumptions are in disarray. I am not feeling particularly onside with Red Power this morning. I am not particularly sure why I am going out to fuck with Spain. The practical side of things is weighing me down . . .

First of all, there's the fate of Dinah Elissat-Winlaw, my cameraperson, to worry about. Dinah is already on board the *Sea Shepherd*, which departed from Nassau two days ago, and is supposed to be dropping anchor offshore from the Turks and Caicos, where I will rendezvous within hours of my arrival this afternoon on a Pan-American flight from Miami to the island of Providenciales.

The reason Dinah is along as my camera is because she was owed a major out-of-town assignment, and she wanted something that would test her muscle a little, take her out into the world. We're a local station. Don't get as much travel as we'd like. Is Dinah tough enough? Well, normally she wears a black leather motorcycle jacket, jeans, and biker boots. Her shoulders are rolled forward slightly, like somebody bracing for a fistfight. At first glance you are taken by the pixie quality of her face, in contrast to the leather. Bright red slash of lipstick. Grey-green eyes. Short-cropped blonde-white hair. On the model-thin side and a smoker, so you worry right away for her. But when she peels off a leather glove to light a smoke dangling from the corner of her mouth, closing her lighter with a heavy metal clunk, you'd have to be blind not to see that she is projecting a shield of masculinity around the sensitive female within, to which she'd say: "Fuckin' brilliant! Keep the cigar, Freud."

In the normal course of a shift, she pilots a four-wheel-drive Nissan Pathfinder through Metro Toronto streets in pursuit of Stories On Tape, while chauffeuring one egomaniacal on-air person after another, often me. Dinah routinely hoists a hardwired Sony Betacam onto her shoulder that weighs so much I personally refuse to lift it except in emergencies, what with my back problem.

If Dinah ever heard me referring to her as a "cameraperson," she'd have my nuts. "I'm a cameraman," she'd snap. "Okay, bonehead? Let's get that outa the way. What're we shootin'?" How is Dinah doing on board a ship filled with every kind of radical Indian and eco-terrorist imaginable? If anything was to happen to her, I would be stomped to death by the guys back at our TV station, of course. The other question is, how are the rest of the crew doing? Has Dinah drop-kicked anyone in the balls yet?

And it's not just Dinah or any poor male who tried to bother her I have to fret about, or the thought of the engine conking out at sea, which it has been known to do on previous missions, or, for that matter, jumpy Spanish navy boys on the two warships escorting the flotilla who might well open fire on us if we got too close to the *Niña*, *Pinta*, or *Santa María*. Although, as long as we got that on tape, it would be the best of all media worlds, providing they missed. The worst-case scenario, short of somebody actually getting killed, is the one in which, after a long search at sea, we fail to find any of the replicas at all, which would mean that our TV station would have paid hard cash for Dinah and me to be hanging out in the Caribbean Sea for a couple of weeks until fuel and food run out, and our coming home with nothing to show for it except fantastic tans.

The airport has just come into ghostly view through the smog when the news breaks over the radio: Pan-American Airlines has just gone broke. It has been shut down. Locked up. Closed.

What?

Surely, this is a psychotic episode. But no, Roberta has heard it too. From the way her shoulders slump, I can tell she really does want to get rid of me.

After last night, this? I should turn around and go straight home. I mean: A company that had been around for sixty-four years, bankrupted! What are the odds? One of the world's major airlines, its mighty fleet entirely grounded. The *only* airline, by the way, that goes into the Turks and Caicos! Today! This day! Just hours ago. Of all days in the last sixty-four years. How many days is that? If only they could have held on for another half a dozen hours!

Oh no. If this is how the trip is starting . . . Yet I can't bail, God help me. Dinah is already out there. And it is not just the risk of Dinah being ticked off with me. Captain Watson himself might not be too thrilled if I fail to show, what with him having already gone to considerable trouble and expense, to say nothing of having wasted a full day of steaming directly eastward in search of the Spaniards, six hundred gallons of fuel being gulped every twenty-four hours, in order to drop anchor long enough to pick me up from the beach at Providenciales.

And then there's Roberta, her cold blue eyes fixed on me, saying nothing but making it seem like she's asking: "This isn't going to stop you. Is it, sweetheart?"

Of course, Watson wasn't stopping at the Turks and Caicos just to pick up little old award-winning co-author me. The plan was for him to pull in to also pick up a gentleman named Ron George. Ron was the political heavyweight, the highest-level Native leader Watson could find to come along. Like me, Ron had been too busy to leave on time, although his excuse was less self-serving. He'd been speaking at a Parliamentary Committee meeting debating nothing less than the Canadian Constitution. He was a live player in the Constitutional process, and to meet him was like meeting one of the stars of a TV series out on the street after work. Ron was president of the 660,000-member Native Council of Canada. As the elected leader of Canada's presumably militant non-status, mixed-blood, urban Indians, the ones scattered from Skid Road to shining sea, he was up to his neck in the awesomely arcane backroom manoeuvrings behind the drafting of the Charlottetown Accord, a bizarre attempt to restitch Canada, the unravelling vertical mosaic, back together again. This was real Gucci-shoed power-game stuff and Ron was part of it.

I was supposed to meet Ron in Miami as we boarded the now-extinct Pan-Am jet to Providenciales. As it is, arriving in Miami after an unhappy flight from Toronto, feeling like a man who is jumping off into space, I realize I will be damned lucky to find him in the chaos of people madly trying to rebook Pan-Am flights in the Florida humidity.

And what, indeed, do you do if the only carrier into an entire country has vanished over some financial Bermuda Triangle? In Miami, you slog in nightmarish slow motion through the crowds to the Pan-Am counter, which is of course closed, and you demand help of any uniformed person in sight, none of whom knows anything, until, beginning to suspect that you have been beamed into an Asimovian Caves of Steel virtual-reality program, you finally hear a voice blaring something over the PA system about the Turks and Caicos. I want to weep, I am so happy—a variation on Stockholm Syndrome, presumably. Airport soul exchange.

I spot Ron George easily enough. He looks very West Coast Native: shorts, sandals, and a tee-shirt with a totemesque serpent, a soft muscularity to him, high wide cheekbones, raven-black hair already streaked with white even though he can only be in his mid-forties, a thin, also mostly white chevron of moustache, wary Alaska black-diamond eyes, a kind of fake, big-animal slowness that disguises a state of complete alertness. He stands out in the sweaty, crumpled-shirt airport crowd by virtue of the fact that he is mysteriously aglow. Not quite a nimbus around his head, but there is an aura that suggests to me he must just have come down from a mountain, which turns out to be pretty close to the truth. He is talking casually into his cellphone, apparently oblivious to the long-distance charges he must be burning through. The phrase "constitutional rights" comes up a lot. He has a great deep baritone. When he finally lowers the cell from his ear, I introduce myself to him and suggest we head for the bar to ponder our next move.

"Do you know where there's a fax machine around here?"

"I'm sure they'll know at the bar," I promise.

"One of my assistants has a portable fax, but it's no good unless I can find some place to send it from," he explains.

"I hate technology myself," I assure him. It only takes a slight pat on his elbow to get him moving in the right direction. Good sign.

His response to Pan-Am collapsing, stranding us in Miami?

"Oh well."

I sense a certain perspective in Ron that I myself am sadly lacking. As we fold ourselves around a couple of tall cold ones, he admits however that he is beginning to wonder what the hell he's gotten himself into. Having just been elected president of the Native Council, he should by rights be working full-time on the Constitution file—this being the biggest moment, constitutionally at least, in Canadian history since the country was invented—not heading off to sea to chase three recycled make-believe sailboats trying to do a little PR for the Spanish tourism ministry and maybe get their names mentioned in the papers. Speaking of which, at the very least, since he's here, he should be getting out a press release about his journey to protest the Columbus ships. A telegram to the Indian Affairs minister maybe? A demand that Ottawa do something? What good is it being president of anything if you can't make wheels turn? But the waiter doesn't know where a fax machine is, after all, so we tough it out with another drink.

"How long do you think this crazy trip will take, anyway?"

I have to shake my head.

Ron George's traditional name is Tsaskiy, meaning "Grizzly Bear Tracks." He has come directly from a potlatch near Burns Lake, British Columbia, where he assumed his hereditary title as a chief of the Wet'suwet'en Wolf Clan. The Wet'suwet'en hereditary chiefs claim to be the true spokesmen for a lineage going back nearly ten thousand years, legitimate heirs to the oldest surviving royal family and system of government in the world.

Ah, *that* mountain.

My new friend, Grizzly Bear Tracks, has been anointed from very high, indeed, plugged into an oligarchical hierarchy older than the Catholic Church, for God's sake. Not only that, but the almost unbearably ancient (and therefore presumably wise) Wet'suwet'en civilization was a matriarchy—still is—rendering it politically correct to an extent nearly beyond imagination.

"I know what that's like," I agree. "I was raised by my mother too. The good news is, I don't have any trouble with female authority figures."

"That's interesting," Tsaskiy muses. "Most white guys do."

The solution to our dilemma becomes clear after a couple of beers. Tsaskiy calls his Ottawa office and puts one of his flunkies to work finding us an airline. It takes until late afternoon, by which time the pretzels and tacos and beer have turned to lactate in my gut, but we finally get long-distance instructions from Tsaskiy's main aide-de-camp: Caribana Airlines has taken over Pan-Am's Turks and Caicos route. Can't get out, unfortunately, until tomorrow. Rooms are being booked. For Mr. Hunter too? Yessir. Be at such and such a counter back at the airport at 7:30 a.m., at the latest.

I groan—why does everything have to start so damned early?—but quickly find myself assuming the role of the Native Council

President's secretary, digging out a reporter's notebook to mark down our hotel and the departure time. Trying to overlook the horror of being trapped in Miami overnight.

Thus, minimizing our suffering, Ron George/Tsaskiy/Grizzly Bear Tracks and I spent what turned out to be an excellent, manly evening in Miami, shedding as much as we could of our previous senses of identity so we could each embrace a new one, each trip, as I see it, being an opportunity to acquire a new variant of selfhood, as . . . what? This time, it seems to be as a political pirate, seizing somebody else's media treasure on the Spanish Main. Tsaskiy and I relate to each other right off the bat as politically hip shit-disturbing older dudes on the same side, vague as our definition of what that side might be. We become New Age brothers within mere hours. I forget almost everything we talked about, except that by the time we staggered off to our rooms we were exchanging Revolutionary Handshakes, something the other people in the lobby hadn't seen since the Sixties. What kind of time warp were we in? I also can't say I remember where, exactly, we stayed, other than that it was a generic American hotel, or whether my new bro eventually found that fax machine he was looking for, but we did eat and drink and bond, swapping bits of our searing life sagas.

Somewhere in there, I told him the strange tale of my connection to the Hurons. And how I hadn't known about it until *after* I wrote the book. And about the Governor-General's Award. And how I suspected I was on some karmic mission. That is, there were other forces at work here. And I was just a servant of them, whatever they were. So we became Brothers.

Somehow, in the morning, we found Caribana Airlines. I was hurting again. But a few Tylenols fixed that. Some Pepto-Bismol for my gut. A mouthful of Vitamin C for immortality. Tsaskiy had come down a little bit from the mountain. He was much more into his Ron George persona than when I last clinked glasses with him, but he was still moving with the slightly ponderous gait of Wet'suwet'en royalty.

I let him lead the way, parting the crowds. The worst forms of tourist life seemed to be heading to the Turks and Caicos, along with us higher beings with a purpose. The frantic, newly hired Caribana

Airlines staff pushed us aboard, tourists and higher beings alike, as fast as they could, as though they had some important work to do elsewhere and just wanted us out of the way. They did pour drinks to calm us down, always a sign that somebody has been to marketing school.

The 727 must have worked, despite its interior decor. It's not a flight that stands out much in my mind; another interior of a giant toothpaste tube, the only thrill being the pulse of power in those engines. We glimpsed the Dominican Republic off to the left through scudding tropical clouds. We were trundling down the airstrip between low seawind-whipped sand dunes on the island of Providenciales before the head stewardess realized that the customs forms were all still back at the counter in Miami. We applauded the landing, anyway. An unbelievable amount of yelling and screaming went on between the airline officers and the small army of customs inspectors waiting for us. I caught a glimpse into the abyss of the Turks and Caicos regulatory mindset when the last uniformed airport official dinged me five bucks on my duty-free from Miami. I snarled at him, but it didn't do any good.

"It may have been duty-free in Miami," he snarled back, "but you're here now." This was unanswerable. In all the confusion, we found ourselves climbing into a cab without having signed or received any customs forms. "Fuck 'em," I growled, bowing to my bad-boy reflexes. Tsaskiy laughed. "Right on," he said. We had now committed a crime together—illegal entry. We were buds for life.

Nothing on Providenciales grew much higher than waist level except for the palm trees planted around the restaurants and hotels. This was, in fact, one of those places where pirates used to get marooned for being bad, and that was exactly what I was beginning to feel like. I was not impressed so far with the country. Not even a country, really, according to our cabbie. "Just a colony," he sighed. "Sometimes you get a princess coming for a visit."

This would explain the left-hand roads. The taxi itself, a dented and pockmarked Seventies-era Cadillac, had some kind of engine problem and kept conking out on the little sand dune hills as we wound along a half-paved road from the airport to what seemed like downtown Providenciales. Directions were another problem. We were looking for a ship, I told the driver, a black ship. That's right. A ship painted black. You could see the scenarios playing through his mind: black ship? What the hell? Dope? Guns? A Haitian refugee scam? A mass escape from Cuba? He peeked at us warily in the cracked rear-view mirror.

"Ain't seen no black ship, mon."

"Where can I find a fax machine?" Ron George wanted to know. He was getting desperate.

"Dunno 'bout no fax, neither."

I got him to try to gun the Caddie up the highest sand dune around. We made it almost to the top, maybe eight feet above sea level, before the engine grindingly died. Ron and I climbed out into the wind, listening to it *whish* through the bony scrub-brush and the cactus, as we peered at distant horizons, hoping to be able to make out a black ship on the foam-flecked water beyond the endless white beaches. Nothing.

Tsaskiy's cellular rang. It was Ottawa. While I paced, waiting for the cabbie to get his rusting behemoth working again, Tsaskiy unconsciously turned to face north while he fought the constitutional wars far beyond the curve of the Earth. I could tell the battle wasn't going well. The chief started throwing stones that hit the ground in puffs of powder. "There's got to be a fax on this goddamn island," I heard him mutter. How can you fight wars in Ottawa from the Turks and Caicos without a fax? That would be like going into a media skirmish without a copier. Well, at least he had a satellite working for him—and, for a moment, I forgot my frustrations, and watched in awe as a Rainbow Brother, wielding a cellphone instead of a light sword, duelled long-distance with icebound foes trying to hide behind their voice mails. If he'd had a fax as well, I thought, he'd be invincible.

With no *Sea Shepherd* in sight, we got back in the old busted Caddie, rolled down the dune, and limped from one end of the island to the other in search of a dock where a boat as big as a former North Sea trawler could put in. Checking in at the guard post at the one and only such dock, I quickly roused suspicions by asking if anybody had seen a black ship. Ears perked up. What might its purpose be? It would have to come through customs. As soon as they started grilling me, I changed the description to "a big black private yacht. Haven't seen it? Wait a minute, what date is this? Oh hell, I'm a week early. Shoulda put it in my planner, eh? Silly me. Bye. Thanks anyway."

Back in the cab, I anxiously coaxed Chief Tsaskiy off his cell-phone: "Forget the Constitution for a minute." Once he heard my report, he agreed, his wonderful Wet'suwet'en patience starting to flag, that this was indeed a major screw-up, and not even his office would be able to do much about it. With a dozen militant Red Power Indians on board, most of whom must have done time after being arrested at road blockades and logging protests over the years, plus the usual hardcore *Sea Shepherd* crew of animal rights saboteurs and eco-guerrillas, Captain Watson was not going to be thrilled at having to clear a major red-tape hurdle, showing passports and papers, to say nothing of what the docking fees might be (and never mind the duty-free charges), just to come in and get Tsaskiy and me, the well-known rule of travel generally being: the smaller the country the bigger the bureaucracy—Canada, admittedly, being an exception. And then there was the minor glitch of us not having any customs documents proving that we had even arrived in the Turks and Caicos, let alone that we should be allowed to leave.

Just as the light was starting to fade in Tsaskiy's eyes, the taxi driver said: "Why don' you jus' call yo friends on de radio, mon?"

"Radio? What radio?"

"Maybe they'll have a fax machine," Tsaskiy whispered prayerfully.

Minutes later, we were clanking, not daring to quite believe our luck, down a cratered road to an outdoor bar on the beach that happened to have a VHF sideband radio where, should be no problem, mon, I could try to raise the ship and have a pint at the same time. Well! Did my mood improve?

Stacking our knapsacks and sleeping bags in a corner on the Spanish tile floor, Tsaskiy and I pulled up bamboo stools at the bar overlooking glinting razor-white sand and surf, and there, like a birthday cake on the counter, was an actual sideband radio: the blower, as we old sea dogs call it. Used by the tourists all the time, apparently, to keep in touch with how the fishing is going, and which sunburned parties will be coming in next. Faster than you could say karmic transition-point, I was on the marine band, Channel 16, a Pauli Girl beer in one hand, calling the ship. And even more astonishing, after just a couple of stabs at saying "*Sea Shepherd, Sea Shepherd*, do you copy? Over," a voice came back, telling me to switch to Channel 10, and, all hail the electronic goddess, I was in contact.

Half an hour later, a big black ship hove into view on the horizon, taking up a position about a mile offshore. A woman's voice reported crisply over the sideband that a Zodiac would be dispatched to come and pick us up from the beach any moment.

"Hey, you cannot do dat, mon," the bartender complained in Turks and Caicosese. "You gotta go tru' de customs."

"Is that right, eh?" I replied in Canadian, exchanging a look with Tsaskiy, who smiled quietly.

The other guests in the bar, mainly white-haired Americans bored after a week of walking up and down the beaches of Eden, had their binoculars out, examining the *Sea Shepherd*, trying to figure out what the hell it was. One retired navy type could tell from the profile that it was some kind of an old fish boat.

"Ain't that that environmental terrorist ship I seen on TV?" he asked, looking us coldly up and down.

"Not us," I assured him. "Just gonna take some pictures of dolphins. Documenting their behaviour for a university up in Canada."

About the only thing wrong with this scene—our plan to escape quickly from the island to carry on with our supposedly secret high-seas confrontation—was that everyone in this section of the Caribbean could hear my conversations with the ship, and we had a whole bar full of people, including a bartender who must have relatives working for the government, listening in and watching as we prepared to make a run across the beach into the water in broad daylight. It was not quite like escaping under klieg lights from East Berlin, but was probably enough of an affront to legitimate island authority to get us thrown into jail if we got stopped. Therefore the sooner we were out of here, the better. I was even experiencing a trace of paranoia. The bartender laughed slyly: "What's the hurry? Happy Hour comin'." I wondered if he'd already sent someone to rat on us to the cops. Maybe I should speed things up at the *Sea*

Shepherd's end by just blurting over the sideband: "They're on to us! We're running for the beach! Get that Zodiac over quick!" But if there was potential for disaster here, that would surely trigger it. Better to chew furiously on my plastic cigarette, order another Pauli Girl, appear cool, and try not to pester the President of the Native Council of Canada with my petty concerns. The whole time we were in the bar—getting on for more than an hour now—he was on the cellphone to Ottawa. The American tourists, probably Republicans used to paying their own phone bills, were openly in awe of us, more, I think, because of Tsaskiy's obviously Zen-like indifference to communications costs than the mere fact that there was a mysterious black-hulled ship sitting on the horizon ready to pull us illegally out of the country. Coming over to whisper in my ear, an older Yank inquired incredulously: "Is that fella really makin' a long-distance call?" When he got back to his table, I could hear the gasps of admiration.

"This is the *Sea Shepherd* here," the sideband suddenly said. "Someone here wants to talk to Ron George. Over."

Looking just a trifle weary, Tsaskiy took the sideband hand mike, while keeping the cellphone to his ear, and proceeded to carry on two conversations without missing a beat, although I couldn't help but wonder what his assistant in Ottawa made of the boss saying "over" at the end of every second sentence. The message, from one of his militant Red Power colleagues on board the ship was simple: "Hey Ron, we're surrounded by herbivores. Some of the boys are really sick. Bring meat!"

Tsaskiy stared at me, his brain racing: "What are they talking about?"

"Ah yes," I sighed, "I guess no one told you."

I could just see what we were getting into: militant Natives meet militant Veggies. Oh boy.

Tsaskiy was deeply shocked. "No meat? For God's sake." Promising to do something, he passed the sideband mike back to me and abruptly terminated his cellular negotiations over the Constitution. Shaking his head, he reminisced for a few minutes about how it had been on various road blockades he'd taken part in over the years, from Mount Currie to the Queen Charlotte Islands. Food was vital, he recalled. Whenever the troops got worn down in the rain and the cold, a good moose-meat stew would do wonders to stiffen resolve. Or some fresh-killed venison.

Before I could stop him, Tsaskiy took off determinedly to find a taxi to take him to a grocery store. This caused me a certain amount of anxiety because I was sure the Zodiac would show up any minute. And of course so could the Turks and Caicos customs police. While I eased my stress with another Pauli Girl, the retired navy guy, having decided by now that we were too weird to be dangerous, started to give me advice, pointing to a change of colour in the water about halfway between the beach and the *Sea Shepherd:* "See how it stretches from horizon to horizon? That's the great Turks and Caicos killer reef. If your friends try to come through in a Zodiac, they'll be slashed to death. Not an eyeball will get through in one piece. Notice how high the waves are today?"

I took a deep unhappy breath and got back on the VHF: "Hello *Sea Shepherd,* hello *Sea Shepherd.* I have some bad news. Do you copy? Over."

Fizzle. Crackle. "We have some bad news too." It turned out the two pieces of news cancelled each other out. While they were trying to hoist the Zodiac over the side of the boat in rather choppy seas, something had gone wrong. The Zodiac had been pounded against the *Sea Shepherd's* steel hull until it popped. Only a shredded grey balloon remained.

Just then, Tsaskiy returned to the bar, staggering under the burden of probably one hundred pounds of frozen steaks, hamburgers, wieners, chicken, pork chops, and sausages. Judging from the bags the cabbie was lifting out of the trunk, the chief had also bought at least another hundred pounds of canned ham, Spam, shrimp, and sardines. A true British Columbian, he lamented: "Wish I'd brought some smoked salmon, eh?"

I explained quickly about the Zodiac accident. Tsaskiy sat down, ordered a Pauli Girl, and we alternated staring at the stack of frozen meat on the tiled floor and at the distant and suddenly inaccessible *Sea Shepherd* rolling on the swells a mile away. At exactly the same instant, our eyes turned to the bartender, both of us suddenly smiling like old friends of his. Being a saint of a human being (and with us starting to look like paying customers for the rest of the day and night at least), he agreed to let us stash the frozen meat in his restaurant kitchen freezer while we figured out what to do next.

Eventually, the voice of Captain Watson himself came over the sideband. In that laconic, John Wayne kind of drawl he has perfected for radiophone conversations and media interviews, he announced to us and the entire Happy Hour crowd listening over the VHF, all of whom were following our broad-daylight customs-evading escape attempt with increased merriment: "We're gonna have to head out for open water for the night. We, ah, can't anchor. We lost the anchor a couple of days ago. So we'll try again to get you in the morning. Over."

The *Sea Shepherd* belched diesel fumes, put her stern to us, and steamed away over the horizon. Maybe it was mere coincidence, but Tsaskiy's cellular battery decided to die just then.

"We're trapped, aren't we?" Grizzly Bear Tracks growled.

10

"Not Traditional Seafarers"

So I take another deep breath as I splash unhappily along the crystalline beach on Providenciales. I grind my plastic cigarette between my teeth. Chief Tsaskiy/Grizzly Bear Tracks/Ron George, I note, has come another step down from the spiritual mountaintop, a little slower and heavier as he walks, but he did recharge his cell battery last night. So as he stalks the beach, paddling in and out of the champagne-coloured water, his phone cupped like an electronic conch shell to his ear, gesturing and grimacing, still facing north under the overlit smogless sky, wearing sunglasses, he gets to stay in touch with "the world," or at least the constitutional world, while I've got no one to talk to except the half-dozen retired ladies from Kentucky and their dentist, real estate, and manufacturing sector husbands, who, bored silly, have decided to hang out with us while we wait to be rescued.

The *Sea Shepherd* has been lollygagging on the horizon since dawn. I spotted her when I stumbled out of my hotel room onto the beach, hoping an early-morning swim would heal me. *Damn,* I thought, *they're going to be here any minute.* The bar wasn't open, so I couldn't get on the blower to find out what was happening. *They must have fixed the Zodiac.* Driven by an unwise spurt of adrenaline, I rushed to wake Tsaskiy, then ran to get the desk clerk to open the kitchen freezer, which was locked. Of course, he didn't know anything about our meat being stashed in there, and refused to open anything until he got orders from the boss. Which meant me lurching rather faintly, spots before my eyes, along the beach to the house where the bartender lived, the door taking the longest time to open, having to explain to his wife what the problem was, her taking a long time to wake him, and him being the very guy I did *not* want to be dealing with as we made ready for our illegal exit. I sensed as he sullenly stomped along the sand ahead of me a certain reserve, probably having to do with the fact that, being Canadians, Tsaskiy and I had not tipped as lavishly as the American and German customers, even though we considered ourselves big spenders. Hurriedly loading our frozen goodies and canned stuff into seven big plastic bags, trying not to let too much steam escape through the open vault door, we hauled all two hundred pounds of dead animal parts in separate trips down to the beach, expecting to hear either the roar of a Zodiac outboard engine or a police siren at any second. I wondered grimly if meat was duty-free. Each trip I cursed raspingly under my breath because hauling heavy loads of any kind is just what my chiropractor told me not to do, due to a bad parachute landing in my youth, which resulted in two fused lower vertebrae. But other guys don't believe my story, and I keep re-injuring myself trying not to look like a wimp.

Finally, panting, grudgingly tipping the bartender five bucks for unlocking the freezer (not enough, I take it from his reaction, but to hell with him, we're out of here), I slumped on the sand among the plastic bags and knapsacks and sleeping bags and my video case, waiting for this agony to be over and me to be lying in a nice bunk on the *Sea Shepherd*.

But after an hour or so, we had to face the fact that something was wrong. *They must be having trouble repairing the Zodiac.* In the meantime, several hundred dollars' worth of frozen non-human flesh was beginning to thaw under the tropical sun.

We flipped a coin to see who would go back and try to talk the desk clerk into putting the meat back into the freezer. It fell to Tsaskiy. Still talking to Ottawa, off he marched. Money probably changed hands. At least the bartender, who had gone back home to sleep, didn't have to be involved this time. In any event, no problem. So the two of us fumbled back across the loose sand, hauling sweaty hocks of pork and thick slabs of steak with the glaze of frost melted away back to the freezer. The desk clerk was getting edgy, though, what with locking and unlocking the thing.

By the time the bar opened and I could get on the sideband radio it was to learn that there had been "technical problems" with the cherry-picker on the *Sea Shepherd*'s deck, so they weren't able to get their main launch into the water. "Stand by. Over." Fifteen minutes later, a voice reported: "It looks like we're go. Over." So we rushed to get the stuff from the freezer, bribing the bartender again when he muttered, "Sho' hope de customs boys don' blame me," humped the cans and bags down to the edge of the beach, and stood there, panting again. And waiting again. Was it my imagination, or was the sea rougher than it had been yesterday? Definitely rougher.

Still nothing happened except the eternal sloshing of sand and sea. Tsaskiy and I were both betraying a slight edge of tension in our voices as we discussed whether to hang in or haul the damned stuff back to the bar. One more call to the boat revealed that the cherry-picker was finally working but some other glitch to do with a generator had come up. "It might be a couple of hours . . . well, at least. Over."

Back down on the beach, an enthralled crowd of retirees had gathered around Tsaskiy, their binoculars fixed on the distant *Sea Shepherd*. Shadowed by the bartender, I informed them that we might as well start to head back to the freezer one more time.

Tsaskiy shook his cellphone, as if to wring some magic out of it. But who could he call about this?

"Oh, dear," said one of the ladies from Kentucky. "That's terrible. But if you-all are so anxious to be gone, why don't you-all just charter that lovely parasailing boat we saw yesterday?"

I looked at the bartender for confirmation of this possibility. He shook his head vigorously. But the old lady dismissed him with a wave of her imperial American arm and winked broadly at us.

"You-all just wait here, honeypie," she said, flouncing off to a pay phone on a telephone pole . . .

. . . and the next thing we knew, a mighty fluorescent speedboat was skipping over the whitecaps toward our section of the beach, its laminated fibreglass hull throwing blinding explosions of reflected light into our eyes, with dragonfly wings of rainbows fluttering transparently on either side of its knife-edge bow. It was at least twenty feet long, shaped like a javelin, with a mounted pad on the stern deck where you took off and, all going well, landed in your parachute. Flat-planed as it was, it still drew too much water to come right into shore in the chop. Tsaskiy and I had to wade through the surf up to our shoulders before the pilot could reach a hand down to pull us aboard.

"Got any stuff?" he yelled over the throttled-down rumbling of the inboard.

Tsaskiy pointed to the beach where all our bags and gear were stacked. Or rather, had been stacked. To our astonishment, the retired couples from Kentucky had formed a human chain, and were splashing fearlessly, fully dressed, into the three- and four-foot whitecaps, led by the lady who'd made the phone call. Passing the packages of meat along hand over hand, they soon had everything, including our knapsacks and sleeping bags, scooped from the beach and piled up around our feet as we clung to the heaving deck, the pilot shaking his head. I caught a glimpse of the bartender, halfway up the beach, shaking his head too.

"Where we goin', mon?" the pilot wanted to know.

"That black ship," I yelled, pointing.

The pilot recoiled. "There's a reef there, mon! Tide's down. Lotta chop. Too dangerous."

"What's it worth to you?" Tsaskiy asked, digging out his soaking wallet.

A ridiculously high figure was mentioned. Tsaskiy glared but nodded and flashed gold plastic. "You take Visa?" The pilot, no further questions, nodded, revved the engine and swung the bow around with a monstrous gurgle. The first escape from being marooned using credit? We waved to the half-dozen guardian angels from Kentucky who were climbing, dripping, wringing out their blouses and shirts, back onto the beach, laughing delightedly. We'd made their day. And, certainly, they'd made ours. Hell, they'd saved us! I wondered briefly, guiltily, whether they would get busted if Customs found out that they had aided and abetted two illegal aliens fleeing the country. Even if they did, which was hard to imagine, it would give them something to talk about for the rest of their lives.

In a triumphant burst of props, out through the killer reef we zigzagged, and for all the danger—the channel through the reef was indeed narrow and crooked and shallow—I doubt we went any slower than twenty knots, despite the big crackling, spitting white waves our rocket-shaped bow was slicing. I tried shooting some tape, but it was too wet. I had to stash my Handycam back in its bag.

The *Sea Shepherd* loomed dead ahead, rolling a bit like an old black bear on its back in the grass. I'd forgotten how big she was. And how ominous. That black paint really did the trick. Black hulls are not uncommon, but the superstructure is usually painted white or grey or orange. Not this ship. The whole thing was black from the smokestack to the water-line, and you couldn't help but think she was up to something sinister. That was the idea, of course.

As I scanned the ship, I glimpsed Watson watching from an open window in the wheelhouse, his plume of curly white hair standing out against the ebon hull. I wanted to wave but didn't dare let go of the railing. From the moment we cleared the reef and got into the swells, the parasailing boat was out of its element. A wave that induced just a sleepy shoulder-roll on the part of the *Sea Shepherd* was enough to flip the bow of the parasailer up until it pointed halfway to the noon sun, and then slam her down with a drop-kick. Meant for high speed on flat water, her lightweight transformer-toy body, having no keel, didn't quite know what to do in big seas, and neither did the pilot. "Maybe if you slowed her down a bit," I suggested as tactfully as I could, afraid the bags of meat and the gear would go flying overboard. Also, I couldn't help noticing, Tsaskiy had gone deathbed-blue, and there was a wild, trapped look in his eyes. We were pancaking so spectacularly by now, there were moments when I couldn't see the big trawler, so far down had we torpedoed and so far away had she rolled. The clouds seemed to skid suddenly across the sky like displaced cutlery, as a swell from way out in the Atlantic glided mutely and hugely toward us.

Somehow we came alongside the looming dark shape, only to find that the ladder hanging from the *Sea Shepherd* danced snakily just above our high-water point, when a swell lifted us. At our apogee, we were nearly within arm's reach of the crew people, mostly Natives, who had gathered on deck to help, or at least watch. But as the swell swept past, we dropped like an elevator alongside the slimy barnacled black hull. Our pilot was yelping, obviously agitated by the possibility of his fibreglass spaceship being grated like cheese, if not cracked or popped in two, but nobody could make out what he was saying. Self-centred bastard that I am, I was bracing for a leap to the ladder when we came up again when I realized Tsaskiy was throwing a plucked chicken aboard with one hand and a leg of lamb with the other. From the railing, several sets of arms sprang out, and the first few volleys of non-human body parts were deftly scooped out of the air like footballs. Figuring everything was under control on the meat delivery front, with the pilot barking at me, I made my leap, heart rate at fast-forward, not looking down, caught the ladder just a few rungs from the top, and scurried up it with ratlike focus. I was getting hauled the last couple of feet onto the deck by somebody whose crazed laughter I immediately recognized as belonging to Peter Brown, a manic California producer (I guess that's redundant), who, unable to resist leaping immediately into the action, promptly let go of me and bounded like some kind of professional stuntman onto the deck of the parasailer, turning and helping Tsaskiy throw up bags of food, sleeping bags, and knapsacks. After this he leapt lithely back on board the *Sea Shepherd,* and *then* stumbled, having to be caught to avoid smashing headfirst into an oil drum.

At a glance, I could see we had landed, as expected, in the middle of a political war zone. It was as though a boarding party had stormed over the side. In the thick of the fray were half a dozen Indians, identifiable by their long hair and headbands and slight copper tinge and oriental eyes, scrambling to intercept the dead chickens flying onto the ship. From the clunking sounds the various corpses made as they landed on the steel deck, I could tell that the meat was still frozen. The roasts and steaks and hocks and chops and bacon strips too. *Clunk. Thud. Bonk.* The cans broke from their plastic bags on impact and scattered like pucks to be scooped up by eager hands.

Standing well back were the non-Aboriginal members of the crew, almost all of whom, judging from the expressions of horror on their faces, were Vegans. One of them, a skinny, extremely pale, and outraged female, started toward a dented can of Spam, and since she was wearing a tee-shirt that said MEAT IS MURDER, we all knew she was going to hurl it into the sea. But indignation is no match for hunger. Before she could take two steps, a Native guy with a red bandana had snagged the Spam and darted through the hatchway. It happened as quickly as that. Within a minute, the Indians had swarmed the deck, vacuuming up every can and bag of butchered sentient being, and were gone, vanished into the hold, leaving only a cluster of traumatized Vegans holding on to each other, witnesses to atrocity. I bet some of the early attacks on settlers' forts were like that. It was as though some highly efficient smuggling operation had just come down. I could hear the cheers below as Tsaskiy, the Bearer of Meat, was welcomed aboard by the Native faction. Meanwhile, I was left on deck in the tropical sun being glared at by the Veggies. They had all seen me trafficking in slaughtered non-human-entity parts.

But no matter, my old buddy Watson, whose prematurely white hair belies the fact that he is ten years younger than me, was grinning wolfishly as I stumbled around getting my footing on the deck. At first glance, you might take Paul to be a bit on the soft side, like a favourite uncle at Christmas. But that would be before he smashed your boat in half.

"Permission to board, Cap'n?" I half-saluted.

"Permission granted, Bob," he growled in his best cruel admiral's voice. "Gotta find the Armada. Talk to ya later." He pounded up the steel ladder to the wheelhouse. Almost immediately, the engine grumbled and black smoke coughed from the stack. The *Sea Shepherd*'s big meat-cleaver chin swung seaward.

Dinah Elissat-Winlaw, who had been taping all this, swooped down on me with her Betacam still on her shoulder, chomping gum, her black leather jacket shed in the Caribbean air, wearing jeans and cowboy boots and a tee-shirt, relieved, to say the least, to have somebody sane to relate to (me? That's how desperate she was!) after four days in the midst of an ideological killing ground, the Meaties on one side, the Bunnyhuggers on the other. She wasn't keeping very much food down herself, but at least she wasn't outright dying like the brothers and sisters.

"Pan-Am folded," I explained about why we were late.

"You call that an excuse, bonehead?"

Dinah looked ghostly, admittedly, but radiant. She too had been to some kind of mountain. I could tell. Suffering does that to some people. It might also just have been the high of being at sea. We didn't talk about it, whatever it was, right away. Instead, she quickly briefed me on the political situation: the vegetarians had complete control of the engine room and the galley, and since they were all volunteers, the only people Watson could get, even the mighty captain was powerless to resist the hard-line no-meat feeding policy. Watson and Peter Brown were rumoured to have stashes of canned meat and seafood locked away in their own bunkrooms, but the poor Indian buggers had arrived unprepared, thinking they would be provided with real food. "You should have seen it the first night out," Dinah recalled, shaking her head. "They couldn't believe it." The issue quickly became academic, she added, because within a few hours of leaving harbour, every last one of the Indians had gone to their bunks to nearly die from seasickness. "I've only seen a couple of them since we left Nassau. They've been down below the whole time, until just before you guys got here. Somebody said the word 'meat,' and it brought them to life."

Strange, I thought. Tsaskiy had gotten seasick awfully fast, too.

"Aren't these coastal Indians? Didn't they build war canoes and hunt whales?"

"Hell no," she replied, appalled by my ignorance. "These guys are Interior Indians. Y'know, inland B.C. Most of them have never even been on a ferry before. 'Not traditional seafarers,' is how one of the chiefs puts it."

" 'One' of them? How many chiefs have we got?"

"They're all chiefs, for God's sake. Didn't you know?"

I I

"Columbus, Make My Day!"

Returning to a boat you voyaged on, no matter how bad the trip might have been, is always a towering emotional moment in any sailor's life. You get lightheaded. For the first few hours aboard, I tend to touch the *Sea Shepherd*'s steel walls gently, and to step over the hatchways delicately, being careful to avoid smashing my head on ceiling pipes or clusters of wires. From long practice, I quickly adjust to dancing with instead of struggling against the ever-cavorting pull of gravity. I love this Ballet of the Heaving Deck. Some sea dogs move like squirrels, some like rabbits, and a few of us do the *oceanus gravitas* waltz, not afraid to pirouette, if need be, around an invisible partner, waiting for the stage to tilt the other way before carrying on. Energy efficiency is essential, otherwise you exhaust yourself. Sometimes you mince swiftly downhill, sometimes you walk like a crab, sometimes you shuffle, occasionally you hop, and once in a while, you charge across an open stretch of deck, hoping not to slip or trip over anything, lest you be flipped into the ocean.

Dinah points out a Native guy named Wii Seeks, who seems to be the leader, or at least the main hereditary chief among them all, moving like a zombie. The chief of the Gitksan makes it to the railing, where he cries defiantly, shaking his fist: "Columbus, make my day!" And then retches over the side.

But the weather is apparently calmer now than it was on the way from Nassau, and other Native guys are starting to emerge, pulling themselves slowly and warily up the stepladder where they join emaciated Vegans who have obviously been barfing their bean sprouts overboard. At least the factions had this much in common:

the experience of vomiting into the Caribbean, or trying to vomit. The sun still made the decks too hot for walking barefoot, but there was enough of a wind to keep us perfectly cool and perfectly comfortable. Exactly the right temperature for a human body. Yes, this would be a great latitude for Paradise, which, of course, is what it was until Columbus (who viewed atrocity as a routine disciplinary measure, when not practised for entertainment) first arrived and began his grisly work. Like us, he and his men must have smelled the distant beaches and plant life even as they groped their way through sand bars and reefs following the route we had now shifted back onto, the precise route that the *Niña*, *Pinta*, *Santa María*, and escort should be following, meaning that they should be somewhere directly ahead. A watch is posted up in the forward mast with binoculars to scan the horizon for the first sign of a square-rigged sail with a cross painted on it, followed by two more, and two warships. Shouldn't be hard to spot, all things considered.

Watson has given me his bunkroom, preferring to retreat to the smaller quarters next door where he has his word processor, printer, books, scrapbooks, Japanese swords, diving gear, spear gun, Sioux headdress, TV set, video cassette player, tapes, and comic books.

I am pleased beyond measure to have the captain's quarters. Big portholes where the air brings the curtains inward and the steel walls sweat with salt. Ah, the smell of rust and grease, the squeaking and clanging of hatches, the slosh of the hull performing its Archimedean miracle. There is even a head, and, my God, a shower that works, a toilet that flushes! The water is reddish, and I know better than to drink it, but this is wildly civilized compared to my previous experiences on the *Sea Shepherd II*. And, luxury of luxuries, a room all to myself! Of course, I am being granted very special privilege, indeed. What it means is I can unpack my own private stash of Spam and Klik and white bread and margarine and sealed packages of baloney and beef sausages and cans of sardines and smoked oysters and Coca-Cola and 7-Up and half a dozen mickeys of rum and rye and a couple of bottles of red wine, and hide it all away with a fair degree of security in the locker under my bunk. I shower to get the salt off, pour myself a stiff one, and pause for a moment to just wallow and wiggle psychospiritually in how sweet a life this is, lying here on my sleeping bag, stark naked, sipping a rum-and-Coke and chewing on a Spam sandwich, sniffing everything, the rust, the salt air, the wet metal, the diesel fumes, letting the steel trembling of the ship massage my soul, the reverse ions of the air over the ocean like an angel playing with my hair, but doing it inside my head. The swells pick us up in the original cradling movement of the Great Sea Mother, the placenta cushion, the inner sea of the womb.

There is, alas, work to do. Dinah has shot three tapes already, twenty minutes each. I get to watch it through the viewfinder in black-and-white with an earpiece by playing it back in her Betacam, a machine which, I must say, reminds me of a cross between a grey goose that keeps laying rectangular plastic eggs, and a laser spacegun that keeps needing fresh clips: the weapon of mass consciousness-change, the Sword of McLuhan! So far, "with no fuckin' help from you, bozo!" as she put it, Dinah has rolled on just about everything . . . which hasn't amounted to much: "Okay viz," she shrugs.

Back when the Zodiac was working, on December 3, a day out from Nassau, a party of seven warriors, tracked closely by Dinah and Peter Brown, had gone ashore at San Salvador, also known as Watling's Island. The sea, the tape makes clear, was substantial. It seems to me, in fact, a bit nuts to attempt a launching under such conditions, but there's Peter, leaping like Tarzan—actually, more like Aquaman—again, and there's the rubber boat, with seven or eight Natives on board, sloughing through waves. Dinah was shooting all this from the safety of the deck of the *Sea Shepherd*.

It was when the Zodiac came back to get her that the trouble started.

In all, four people were in the rubber boat as it set out for the beach again. Alas, in the time it had taken for the Zodiac to make its first run, deposit everyone ashore, and return, the *Sea Shepherd*, without an anchor, had drifted a couple of miles out to sea. There was work being done on the engine, so it was down. The reason the ship didn't have an anchor: a crewman had let it go without a brake and it had plunged to the bottom, hauling down six hundred feet of chain. The *Sea Shepherd*'s rusting old winch couldn't handle bringing all that weight up, so Watson had had to cut it free.

This being her first time at sea, Dinah started the voyage from the *Sea Shepherd* to the shore with a typical cameraman's indifference to danger. After all, she routinely walks along the edges of freeways where the wind from passing tractor-trailers is enough to stagger a horse, especially if you're top heavy from carrying a Betacam and a battery belt, and there are surely few experiences more likely to rattle one's survival reflexes—it's like being a mouse inching along the edge of a bowling alley during a tournament. Fires, mudslides, floods, riots, football games, rock concerts: she'd been in the thick of them all. This? Hey, it was hot, for one thing, even with this sea breeze. The Zodiac rode like a big beach toy, and so what if, between the swells, they couldn't see anything except water and sky? She was impressed with how quickly the *Sea Shepherd* shrank away. What surprised her was that while she could see the palm-tree-ruffled shoreline of San Salvador quite easily on the horizon from up on the deck of the ship, down here just a foot or so above water level, there was no trace of land. But so what? It was simple enough: you just had to aim in the right direction and go straight ahead.

Funny, it hadn't seemed that far away. Why were they taking so long? Peter Brown, who was driving, explained in the patronizing tone of a veteran sea dog, that they could go a lot faster, but they would be smacked around like Ping-Pong balls attached to a paddle. With all her gear, did she really want to be pounded to ratshit? "Forget it," she agreed. It was all right to take a nice, leisurely run.

Fun, too. She was marvelling at how much higher the swells looked from down here, and was just starting to enjoy the sensation of climbing up them, cresting, with the Zodiac actually bending, when Peter muttered something about the damned thing having an air-leak that should have been fixed. A moment later, the engine conked out.

Dinah grimaced, but only out of irritation. This sun was pretty hot. It would be nice to get into some shade. She'd slathered herself with sunscreen, but had left the tube on the ship. Still, apart from worrying about a sunburn, she wasn't alarmed. She was, in fact, feeling quite proud of herself. After a quick sampling of the food on the *Sea Shepherd*, she had had the foresight to rush back ashore in Nassau and buy herself a shopping bag full of peanut butter, melba toast, and cranberry juice (her favourite stuff when she was a kid— interesting instinct, eh?). It had been touch-and-go the first day or so out at sea, and she had glimpsed the abyss into which the seasick tumble (and keep on tumbling), but the peanut butter and melba toast had had a wonderful binding effect on her guts. Even now, experiencing the powerlessness of being adrift in a sagging air-filled rubber dinghy in swells that seemed bigger than before, now that they were merely wobbling about on top of them, her innards were not only steady, she was getting a kick out of the stuck-at-the-top-of-a-ferris-wheel feeling.

Until the crest of the next swell slopped over the wooden board at the back of the Zodiac upon which the dead outboard engine was perched, its weight, now that it was inert, dragging the stern of the little craft downward. Dinah's sandalled feet, which had been dry until now, were suddenly covered in sloshing salt water. When they were moving under power, she had been crouched on the wooden floorplates, hanging on to the rope along the top of the Zodiac. Now she moved up to sit on the fat balloon side, whose surface definitely seemed less hard than when they had set out.

She placed her camera on her knees, battery belt around her neck, with the equipment bag strapped over her shoulder. Another swell crested over the back and the water in the Zodiac rose abruptly halfway to her knees. Oops. And another slosh. Looking around, Dinah could no longer see the *Sea Shepherd*. And there were still no glimpses of the land. The Zodiac had lurched clumsily on the flank of a swell, so she didn't know which way they were facing. The sun was directly overhead. Funny, she observed, how a situation creeps up on you.

Peter yanked the rope fiercely to start the engine, and when that didn't work, snapped the catches for the hood loose, and started tugging and twisting at spark plugs. She couldn't help noticing that, unfortunately, he had no tools. Or radio.

She watched the faces of the two others in the Zodiac, both Indians. Their expressions were much, she supposed, like hers: rather blank, as though the muscles were still in denial about just how real this was. There was, of course, absolutely no chance she could save her camera gear if they went completely under. If she didn't let it go, she'd sink like a stone. As for paddling around out here . . .

Lighting a smoke, she asked casually: "Any sharks in these waters?"

The laconic answer from Peter, bent over the engine, was exactly what she didn't want to hear:

"Oh, yeah."

Dinah spent quite a while, she admits, looking around at the sky and sea, envying the birds their wings, cursing me: "That Hunter. That fuckin' asshole. I'm gonna die, and it's his fault! Where does he get off letting me go to my doom without warning me I'm in the hands of a bunch of turkeys who don't know their ass from a hole in the ground? If I get out of this alive, I'll rip his lungs out!" (Thoughts to that effect.)

It took nearly half an hour before Peter got the engine going. He consulted his wrist compass, and then they wobbled sluggishly up and down the swells until palm treetops appeared ahead. The landing was something else, with Peter basically crashing them onto the beach, like a dying cetacean. She had the breath knocked out of her and nearly lost her white-knuckle grip on the camera. Gritting her teeth, staggering ashore in the wash of waist-deep rollers with sand sucking at her feet and the water trying to drag her back, the gear bag on top of one shoulder, the camera on the other, battery belt around her neck, she had an intimation of what it must have been like to land at some place like Dieppe.

Going back to the tape now: I watch the whole group march past a sign saying WELCOME TO THE FIRST LANDFALL OF COLUMBUS, LONG BAY. This is raw tape, keep in mind, so everything seems disjointed. The Native guys, in shorts and tee-shirts (a highly unthreatening-looking lot, by the way), find an array of flags representing all the countries of the New World (that is, the colonial countries), including Canada's. Nice pan of flags. Close-up of impressive bronze plaque, indicating this was the official landing site. Now a medium shot as the Canadian flag is being pulled down, and another flag, mainly white, with a black-and-yellow raven-theme tribal emblem, is hoisted. The Canadian flag goes back up, but underneath—and upside down.

"Let's just insult one nation at a time," a voice says. Interviews follow with several of the men, and Dinah raps out their names for me as they appear. The first is a slumped, balding fellow with a wispy moustache, our old Gitksan friend Wii Seeks. He deadpans: "We're discovering the land the same way Columbus did in 1492, except we're not going to injure the local inhabitants." As if.

Okay. A second fellow, looking more like a logger than a Native radical, and who turns out to be named Stanley Stump, adds, somewhat obliquely: "It's too late for us to turn back the pages now but we can look ahead and we can ask that people who have come here five hundred years ago at least in the next five hundred years start giving the people who were here first a better deal than we're receiving so far."

Hmm. A third interviewee, gaunt, high-cheekboned, wearing a headband and a necklace made of carnivore teeth, could pass for an Indian of centuries ago. He is identified as Art Loring, Wing-Chief of the Eagle Clan, a guy who's been on a lot of blockades. He declares, as the other warriors line up in front of the flagpost and the plaque for a group picture: "This way that we intend to hold up our history will be a way that the world will recognize us as Gitksan and Wet'suwet'en people, and other nations within Canada that are Native people that have their own cultures and histories and they will always hold them if we help to work on it." Uh huh.

Now a group of locals has arrived. Dinah is shooting from hip level, which allows you to get in closer in a crowd. She explains: "When this black guy, a bus driver, showed up, wondering what the fuck was going on, somebody told him he was now the King of San Salvador. He thought that was just great." The locals, with their new king, march happily away.

One more interview on the beach. ("Is this guy a hereditary chief too?" "Damn right.") Name of Eric Gilbert, he looks quite bohemian, but in a dignified, older-artist way. His point: "We're undiscovering the Americas and symbolically giving the land back to the local Natives." Ah. So it all does make sense, I guess. Dinah couldn't help noticing as they headed back to the Zodiac that the bronze plaque announcing Columbus's landing had mysteriously vanished, and Peter Brown, eyes twinkling with criminality, was having to put a bit more effort into hoisting his camera bag.

Good home video. So far we do not have great television.

"The good news is I've still got a fuckin' camera, eh?" Dinah observes. "And I'm not at the bottom of the fuckin' shark-infested ocean." I get an elbow in the ribs, and feel lucky to have got off so lightly.

Our hopes for great TV lie ahead. I have, of course, seen pictures of the little caravels that Columbus and his ghastly crew sailed across the ocean blue. They could be smashed like matchsticks by the *Sea Shepherd,* although it is impossible to imagine two Spanish warships standing by, allowing this to happen.

In any event, there is no point pestering Watson with such details as where we are heading and what will happen when we get there, so Dinah and I begin our mission to immortalize this historic voyage by tracking down the First Mate, an Irish lass named Angela Moore who'd gotten involved with the *Sea Shepherd* Society by working in the Dublin office, transferring over to L.A., where Watson's headquarters were, and was now at sea for the first time, already promoted to First Mate. Turnover in *Sea Shepherd* crews is legendary, although, even by those standards, Angela's rise to power has been spectacular. Apart from the usual chauvinist thoughts that I am forced, as a poor male caught up in bodily chemical reactions, to go through in the experience of producing thought, which, of course, as a father, son, husband, and respecter of women, I swiftly dismiss, I can see why Watson promoted Angela so quickly. Her pale green eyes are almost translucent. She notices everything, instantly grasps where your line of thought is going, and has the answers assembled and laid out before you can get to the end of your question. Apart from being eye candy, she gives good clip, as we say in the trade. And good clip in television, combined with good looks, is to die for.

Angela points out our position on the nautical charts. We are about to leave the Caribbean Sea and venture into the deep blue of the Atlantic. The problem is, either our radio equipment isn't strong enough to pick up the Spaniards, indicating they are still far away, or they are broadcasting on military channels that we can't hear. It would make sense that they would use the navy wavelengths for communications. Let the taxpayers back home pick up the tab. In which case, we have to count on radar or the offhand chance of an actual sighting. The radar is only good for a range of about forty kilometres. Out here, it would be easy for us and the little flotilla to pass in the night—or the daylight, for that matter—without us picking up a trace of our prey. What's more, their military radar equipment should easily be able to track us long before we can track them. All we have going for us is the fact that the Spaniards can't keep altering course every time a blip shows up on a radar screen. Until we get into view, they can't distinguish us from an ordinary working boat. Presumably, if we got that close, we could charge, and take our chances on being blown out of the water. It would be a great ending, fab television, but I assume—trust—Paul's not that stupid.

Even as we are doing the interview with Angela, I hear the engine being throttled down. We head up to the wheelhouse where the helmsperson explains she's been ordered to go into a holding pattern, rather than commit to a deep-sea lunge. If we go out too far and the Spaniards get around us, they can make for the safety of any number of islands and we wouldn't be able to catch up to them in time. I see. That would not be good. Very bad television, indeed. See nothing happen. See reporter return to station with nothing to show for the expense slips. Not that I would be fired, or anything. It would just be that the next time I suggested a far-out-of-town assignment, I'd get that death-stare, and there would go my main link to sanity: the freedom to get out of town often enough to make life worth living. I love my family, etc. But you go crazy in one spot. We're nomadic animals. We should be free to roam. It's genetic. Insanity in the world flows from too many people staying on the same chunk of land with the same neighbours for too long.

Or, one might add, from staying on the same chunk of boat with some neighbours for any length of time at all.

It is good, in one sense, to be throttled down, facing into the swell, waiting. We aren't being pounded as heavily as when we were chopping along at eight knots. This is about as soothing as it gets, one minute being lifted as gracefully as a silver tray on the fingertips of a white-gloved waiter, the next lowered in a slow-motion twirl back into the bottom of a basin between the swells. The downside is that the moment you lose your forward momentum in any campaign, the moment you stall, the troops get restless and crazy.

Coalitions are always fragile, and this is about as delicately linked a coalition as you are likely to find. It is quite normal for Watson's crews to be mainly Vegans, who, after all, are militants by definition. On a "normal" expedition, he would be out after ships or men who were in the process of killing wildlife, mainly marine mammals, and his "normal" kind of action would be to ram these guys or chase them away by charging at them through the ice. It's anything but subtle, but enormously effective. Gee, surprise, brute force works. Watson is a pariah in the upper echelons, at least, of most of the big environmental and conservation groups, not just because he is considered an uncontrollable maverick, but more subliminally, because he fundamentally calls into question the effectiveness of the whole strategy of traditional peaceful protest with its techniques of backroom lobbying, political manoeuvring, and the building of a mass support base. Peaceful protest only gets you so far, Paul contends. When that doesn't work, you clobber the buggers. Simple as that. Forget Gandhian principles. Those only worked against the British. Naturally, Paul is considered something of a fascist. And in his own sweet way, maybe there is a certain element of the despot in him. Certainly, he prefers to give orders than to receive them. But then that's just ordinary captain stuff, too.

The Vegans might be willing to put up with the hierarchy of shipboard command for the sake of the higher goal of the missions themselves, but they had learned, through experience, that once one of them seized control of the galley, he or she was in the third-strongest position of power, after the captain and the chief engineer. It was possible to impose Vegan ideology at the critical choke-point of the galley oven. *Sea Shepherd* veterans like myself came prepared to camp out in our own bunkrooms, making our own meals, appearing in the galley only to forage for coffee, vegetables, baked bread, and dessert. What with there being no meat, poultry, or dairy products, and, as a matter of fact, no honey ("You wouldn't exploit the labour of bees, would you?"), I could scarcely imagine a reason to go into the galley unless it was to hang out with one's fellow crew members—except that the crew was bitterly divided over probably the most fundamental question of all—namely, what is murder? Is it murder only when you kill one of your own species, or is it murder when you kill any member of any species? As we heaved about in the swells, waiting to intercept the Spaniards, one half of our intrepid crew wasn't on speaking terms with the other half. And the division wasn't over Spain. It was over Spam.

Native Trappers v. Saintly Vegans

From previous experience, I know how quickly things can get ugly on a boat. I also know the importance of political positioning. You're not going to be able to satisfy all factions, so you might as well pick a side and stick with it. Pandering to everyone just burns you out.

From the moment I clambered onboard amid a hail of little corpses, I was smeared in the Vegan community with the brush of Nazi Meat Collaborator, and I knew there was no going back. I went through the motions of hiding my protein stash, as I liked to call it, but it was the poorest-kept secret on board. Everyone knew I was holding. I think sometimes they can tell if you've been eating meat just by the cruel smirk on your face, and certainly they claim to be able to tell by the stench emanating from your body, the nausea-inducing rot of rendered flesh leaking through the pores. I had thrown my lot in with the meat-eating savages, and it was with them I would stand.

This is not to say that the Vegans were all cut from the same cloth. Nor were all the non-meat-eaters Vegans. Angela Moore, for instance, was a vegetarian, not a Vegan. She would do fish and dairy products and honey, and found the monomania of her Vegan comrades boring. Jimmy Liebling was a vegetarian aspiring to the higher purity of Veganism but with weak flesh when it came to flesh. Myra Finklestein was invariably attired in grubby, shapeless overalls, her face black with grease, but she had a smile that flashed readily and brilliantly, and a soft, throaty laugh. Fanatic she might be—well, to be going out and ramming things, that's a given—but she had a sweet and gentle way of overlooking your failings and seeing the soul inside, even if you were a marrow-sucking monster. A couple of the others, Randy Lewis and Suniva Bronson, were American trust-fund kids looking for meaning in a world of decadent capitalist luxury they had gotten bored with. Suniva started an intense, passionate relationship during the trip with Ian Bamfield, who was the hardest-core member of the Vegan pack, which prompted Captain Watson to pound out a bit of doggerel on his electric typewriter, titled "Vegans in Love." The opening verse ran

> Suniva the slim and Ian the lean,
> Hand in hand, cheek to cheek,
> Sharing soymilk and veggies clean,
> Being strong and never weak.

There were many subsequent verses.

The Natives were a Vegan's worst nightmare. If they were back home right now in northwestern British Columbia, most of them would be out hunting, fishing, or trapping. Yes, trapping! A method of killing that makes the stake so beloved of Vlad the Impaler look like mercy killing. Nobody among the Gitksan, Wet'suwet'en, Chilcotin, or Shuswap onboard ever ate chicken, it turned out, but that was because they didn't wander into supermarkets looking for frozen food. They caught rabbits instead in their own traps. Among the Vegans were people who had sabotaged medical research facilities, liberated monkeys, smashed computers, kidnapped dolphins, saved seals, and sprayed indelible dye on expensive fur coats. What on earth were they doing together on the same boat with a bunch of mad trappers and gun-owners, guys who, when they saw Bambi, saw food on the hoof? For their part, the Natives couldn't believe that anybody could survive on sesame balls, slimy beans, and burnt pumpkin. Something was bound to give. The Vegans weren't the types to lay back with a live-and-let-kill attitude, nor were the Natives any longer used to letting anyone tell them what to do and not do, let alone skinny white guys living on vitamin pills and avocadoes. And wasn't there something *déjà vu* here? Skinny white guys telling them what to do . . . Hmm? Green Robes, I call the Vegans. Eco-Jesuits. Veggie fundamentalists.

Rather than tiptoe around the delicate subject of the mass murder of zillions of non-human sentient beings on this dark charnelhouse of a planet, and my personal complicity in it, I unerringly take the low ground. I'm also a bit of the Vegans' worst nightmare: a lapsed Catholic who is also a failed vegetarian, and a frustrated stand-up comedian, at that. My general line to the Vegans, presented as a joke, of course, goes like this: "Look, if something goes really wrong and we get sunk, and we're lost at sea in a lifeboat or a Zodiac, and we're starving to death, here's the deal. We're gonna need food, and the only source of food will be our fellow human beings. Now the Vegans, bless them, and may Krishna pee in their beer, are too highly principled to stoop to eating me, for instance, or anybody else, 'cause we're meat, and in my case highly toxic from accumulated chemical residues.

"I, however, a Darwinian carnivore," I rage, "am into survival at any cost, and will quite happily eat human flesh if I have to, all the better if it's grain-fed veggie flesh. And, frankly, I expect female flesh is tenderer and easier to bite through in case we're unable to do any cooking and have to eat the body raw. More fatty tissue. So, obviously, the thing for you Veggies to do, if we end up lost at sea, is to draw straws to see which one of you gets killed and eaten first."

This was all cruel and unnecessary, no doubt. But, like I say, I couldn't help it. Somebody had to say something, because the Natives appeared to be far too polite and well brought up to mention the obvious, which was that this was supposed to be a voyage about objecting to the values imposed on the continent just behind us by European imperialists. It was supposed to be a protest against the destruction of ecologically hip cultures that had been around for thousands of years. Yet here were a bunch of white people—calling themselves "Vegans," a name which couldn't be any more meaningless and weird than aliens calling themselves "Spaniards" five hundred years ago on the beaches of the Caribbean—once again preaching a superior way of life, a greater, more compelling moral system; once against trying to force the Native to do things

the White Man's way. No wonder so many of the Natives had been
throwing up over the sides of the ship. Maybe it wasn't seasickness,
after all. It was recognition of an ancient adversary: the skinny, pale-
skinned fanatic whose way is the only way.

I had missed the moment when the two cultures on board the *Sea
Shepherd* had first clashed, but Dinah had been there to witness Ron
Austin climbing aboard in Nassau and asking Vegan honcho Ian
"Where's the nearest McDonald's?" And before Ian could recover
from that shock, Ron said: "Boy, I just barely got my traplines set out
before I had to rush to Vancouver to catch the plane."

Normally, it would be the militant vegetarians occupying the top
of the moral food chain. They were the animal rights movement's
hard core. Their styles in tee-shirts tended toward the didactic:
DEATH TO THE MEAT INDUSTRY, LIFE TO PLANET EARTH. ANIMALS
ARE FOR LOVING. MEAT IS MURDER. There was a certain unavoidable
tone of repugnance for us slavering redneck Australopithecine lower
forms of human life, the ones still using their fangs. The posture of
spiritual superiority was impossible to disguise. Yet for all this, from
their confused body language I could tell the Vegans were ill at ease,
not at all their usual arrogant, more highly evolved selves.

The problem was they weren't just dealing with meat-eaters this
time. They were dealing with Aboriginals. First of all, as eco-
activists, the Vegans had to respect the Natives' front-line role in
the defence of wild nature. As products of the New Age paradigm
shift, they would be completely imprinted with the idea of the
Native Way as the superior ecological path, and their shoulders
would be stooped under the weight of the Industrialized Person's
burden of guilt. Shouldn't good post-industrial mutants be into
going Native themselves? The "Indians" are supposed to be Elder
Brothers and Sisters, custodians of an incredibly ancient harmonic
wisdom. How shocking that up close they turn out to be . . . barbar-
ians? How psychologically upsetting, too. The Vegans were used
to guilting-out white animal-lovers about eating meat, but they
didn't have a system perfected for guilting-out Indians. How could
any white Industrialized Person guilt-out an Indigenous Person, for
heaven's sake? For a Vegan, one presumes the very starting point of
his or her personal philosophical transcendence would be a super-

sensitivity to matters such as race. After all, until you have seen through racism, you can't begin to grasp so refined a concept as speciesism. Ultra-liberals at heart, the Vegans could scarcely allow themselves to "look down" on living, breathing Native people. And certainly the Natives, after centuries of being pissed upon, were hypersensitive to the slightest hint of any white asshole thinking he was superior in any way, shape, or form. Alas, the truth was, the Vegans did look down upon the Natives, and the Natives couldn't help but notice. For them, the experience of being treated like inferior schmucks was hardly anything new, especially coming from white people. Finally, there was an element of awkwardness on both sides which stemmed from the fact that the Vegans were usually the most radical group in any given situation, a position the Natives were accustomed to enjoying, at least among whites. Most-radical status was up in the air—to be claimed as the battle unfolded.

Yet for all the templates of subtext, I suspected that the main problem could be put down to the fact that the food, no matter what it was made of, was shit. And that always makes for trouble on a boat.

How can I put it delicately? The goop our Vegan cook and his hapless assistant served up was either burned, undercooked, steamed into Pablum, fried to a crisp, boiled to transparency, or melted into mush. I had been on trips with bad food before. Once, I had even been down to surviving on diesel-soaked dregs of emergency supplies. But somehow there was always something you could munch or suck on. Not this stuff. The cook, whose nickname was Rainbow Lolly, had been taking so much flak from everyone—even the Vegans—that, by the time I arrived, he was already sullen and vindictive. He was easily the most loathed person on board. That's a position normally reserved for the captain. If the real struggle on board was for the hearts and minds of the carnies, you'd think the Vegans would field their very best chef, somebody at the cordon bleu level of excellence whose poultry- and dairy-product-free culinary masterpieces would delight our tastebuds, leading us gently along the path to vegetarian moral superiority. But no, we got Rainbow Lolly instead.

By the time we reached the edge of the Atlantic, his cooking had become politically embarrassing to the vegetarian movement as a whole. One night certain angry Vegans sneaked up on him while he was sleeping and shaved away his left eyebrow. It took poor Rainbow Lolly the longest time in the morning to figure out what was wrong. As he helplessly pawed at his missing brow, a perplexed look on his face, his crewmates gargled and spluttered with uncontrollable laughter. When he finally looked into a mirror and worked out what had been done to him, the rest of them fell off their benches onto the deck, howling like fiends. Rainbow Lolly was so shattered I thought for sure he was going to cry. It wasn't fair, of course. A sensitive guy like that, a lover of other sentient beings, having an eyebrow shaved in his sleep. I had to admit, these Vegans had a few good tricks in them, and they weren't above punishing their own. But then, that goes with fundamentalism, doesn't it? Rainbow Lolly stamped off to his cabin, lower lip trembling, locked the door, and refused to come out to make supper.

Power abhors a vacuum. It didn't take long for word to spread that no one was in charge of the galley. The oven itself, plus the sacred cooking stove with its four rings—unguarded and up for grabs. The Wing-Chief of the Eagle Clan, Art Loring, whom I had already guessed was a man of action, a natural leader, quickly decided that it was time for a chicken stew, his totemic relationship to his feathered brothers and sisters notwithstanding. Or maybe because of it. Art wasn't quite a full hereditary chief yet, rather a chief-in-waiting, while at the same time being the elected chief of his band. He was both a traditionalist, acquiring rights by inheritance, and a modern politician, elected according to the white man's rules.

For the first time since Tsaskiy and I had climbed aboard at the Turks and Caicos, the full Native crew assembled, about a dozen of them in all, including, to my surprise, a young lady I hadn't seen yet who had been so seasick she hadn't left her bunkroom until now. We were in six-foot waves, which meant that steel pots were clattering together, dishes and utensils were trying to fly away, rubber-footed chairs hopped and squeaked agonizingly, and there were squeals of pain from volunteer assistants as hot water splashed from the sinks. But no one retreated from the galley to their bunks or out to the deck. A giddy sense of festival possessed them. Everybody got into the action, chopping, peeling, slicing, dicing, scraping, mashing. Soon there was a drum beating and the smell of sweetgrass and some chanting. This was more like it. Guards were posted at the door to make sure no Vegans tried to get in, but the rest of us were welcome. Dinah, Peter Brown, and I were right in there, followed somewhat furtively by the agonized young Jimmy Liebling, our would-be saint of an American who was totally New Age, who believed in everything: astrology, *I Ching*, crystals, pyramids, organic everything. He had been trying his best to be pure and true to vegetarian principles. The spirit was willing but he had that same terrible weakness as the rest of us for the flesh. The odours calling from Art Loring's steaming pots of chicken stew proved irresistible, even though we all knew Jim faced ostracization by his Vegan buddies, and, more painfully, rejection by the young Vegan ladies who had made it very clear that their lips would never touch lips that had eaten flesh.

Lord, that chicken stew tasted good, even though the vengeful Vegans had hidden the salt. There was absolutely no salt to be found anywhere. We grumbled about the pettiness of defeated vegetarians, but lack of salt wasn't going to stop the carnage. The Natives and the gringo meat-eating faction bonded for life over those steaming bowls of stew. We laughed merrily. We sang songs.

Dinah, particularly, relished the feast, since it was the first food she had eaten other than peanut butter and melba toast. It was also the first chance to party with the Indians: her buddies. If only the nervous managers back at our TV station could see her now, hanging so naturally with the "radicals." Of course, Dinah's whole gig was to be an outsider in terms of the mainstream scene, and here was a whole gaggle of outsiders.

But there was more to it than just that. From the very first hours onboard, she had noticed something rather odd. Whenever she talked to an Indian, he listened. No—didn't appear to be listening. Wasn't just waiting for her to shut up so he could get back to talking. Wasn't off thinking about something. None of that stuff which normally happened when she was talking to a man. Oh sure, men would hear. But they weren't really listening. Not quite the way they listened to another man. On her own, but like billions of other women, Dinah had concluded that men only take women seriously in some areas, and tune them out in others. And if anything a man did pissed her off, it was this!

But not these Indians. And it wasn't an act. They listened. They respected what she had to say—fully. She had never actually been treated quite this way. She found that if there were a bunch of them hanging around on the deck—usually waiting for their stomach muscles to build up enough strength for another attempt at turning themselves inside out—she could get involved in a conversation with them in which they displayed in their body language and deferential tone of voice an attitude which was very definitely not mainstream: they were treating her not just as an equal, but as someone slightly superior, because she was a woman!

What was going on here? Men honestly asking her opinion? Men waiting for her to completely finish her thought before saying anything themselves? Men letting her lead the conversation? Men deferring to her? Shutting up when she began to speak? Too weird. What was with these guys?

It wasn't until Watson mentioned that the Gitksan and Wet'suwet'en were matriarchal societies that it sunk in: she was among men who had been raised in a world where women were dominant. God, they might as well have been from another planet! Sure, she knew plenty of liberated males. She worked, after all, at a hip news station where overt sexism was totally uncool. Whether the covert stuff had truly been banished, no matter what ripples of political correctness were awash on the surface, was, however, an extremely moot point. There were rare shining exceptions like me, of course, but, on the whole, the Canadian guy thing, viewed anthropologically, was still a European cultural artifact. To put it kindly. The truth is, we're mostly still pigs, boys. But you know that.

I fretted that when we got back to Toronto Dinah might experience culture shock, having been spoiled by the experience of finding herself on a pillar. Not that she had ever taken any shit from men. Let's just say she would be expecting more from her non-aboriginal male colleagues in the future. Having tasted worship, she'd be alert in new ways to any nuance of male chauvinism. *No wonder Native culture had to be crushed*, I think. *It is dangerously revolutionary.* If white women in general ever caught on to the great, ancient North American secret—namely, women running the show—they'd go Indian en masse.

13

Behind Enemy Lines in San Juan

The moment came and went at which Paul had calculated the Spanish flotilla should have showed up on the horizon dead ahead. This meant that they were either moving more slowly than expected, perhaps in a deliberate effort to avoid us, or they had already slipped by. Never one to linger uselessly in one spot, the captain soon gave the order to come about.

The first I knew of this, Dinah and I were trying to shoot a stirring introduction to one of the sections of our planned five-part news serial. The shot opens wide on the *Sea Shepherd II*'s great spade-shaped bow, seen from the roof of the wheelhouse, as the whole forward section of the boat clambers heavily against the pull of gravity toward the sky, rusty steel slicing through the clouds, then falls like an axe as heavy as several freight cars upon the stippled back of the sea, mighty wings of spray lifting in slow-motion silence on either side. That sort of thing. The shot tightens, slowly zooming in on me as I start talking at the bow, lurch across the foredeck, and climb down the ladder, all the time giving my monologue, which happened to be about what a scum Columbus was.

I could understand why Captain Watson had become impatient and turned the boat around without waiting for me to finish—I had done so many takes already.

We were going through endless takes of this—either I'd stumble or we'd have technical glitches—when suddenly the horizon started to swing around as we changed course while I was crossing the heaving deck and groping my way down a slippery ladder, all the time trying to look directly into the iris of the faraway camera.

"We're going into San Juan," Paul shrugged. "Do a little reconnaissance."

Just as it was for pirates in ye olden days, so it is for protesters today. To enter port is to risk captivity. The captain knew this perfectly well, of course. But what was he to do? A deep-sea thrust would most likely have resulted in our overshooting the Spaniards in the vastness of the Atlantic. Unlike the whalers or drift-netters Watson was usually hunting, these guys were moving as fast as they could. If we missed them, they'd be behind us and home free before we could possibly catch up. Besides, it wasn't as if we were out here protesting anything American, which would get us in trouble with Puerto Rican authorities . . . this was an anti-Spanish thing.

At least, that was the thinking as we headed toward Puerto Rico. Just to cover his ass, Watson got on the blower and radioed ahead, explaining that the British motor yacht *Sea Shepherd II,* which had cleared Nassau for Key West, Florida, a week ago, had unfortunately lost an anchor and chain off San Salvador, and we needed to put in to San Juan to replace the chain for our spare anchor. As a cover story, it had the beauty of also being true, an element much sought-after in good cover-story-telling.

Good as the story was, however, it didn't help much when we arrived at the mouth of San Juan harbour on the morning of December 8, a Sunday. The radiophone operator explained that the Port Control office was closed. Could it wait until tomorrow?

"We don't have an anchor chain," Watson replied truthfully. "And we're low on fuel," he added, lying.

In that case, we'd need an agent. The difficulty with getting an agent was that we had picked absolutely the worst possible day to get anything done in Puerto Rico. Sunday was bad enough in itself. On top of that, anything that might have been open was shut down because of the voting in the national referendum being held on the issue of independence.

"Far out!" chortled Dinah. "We're landing in the middle of a revolution. Maybe we'll get a story out of this sucker after all."

A consummate politician, Tsaskiy—who had recovered nicely from his seasickness, no doubt thanks to the chicken stew—sensed a possible Canadian Constitutional tie-in. Maybe there was some kind of press release his office could put out, supporting Puerto Rican sovereignty. The trouble was, that wouldn't play well back in Ottawa, people being so sensitive about Quebec there. And, for that matter, who knew how it was liable to play in San Juan? Nah, better to stay away from that can of worms. A low profile was in order.

That applied to Dinah and me too. We were marked down in the crew list as deckhands. While there was nothing overtly anti-Yanquis about this particular protest, we were meddling with something that could be good for business, and, at the very least, was sanctioned by a NATO-member country. Diplomatically, the Americans would be responsible for the Columbus ships' security. Because we were troublemakers, just on principle the Yanks would be happy to trip us up if they could. And the fact was, there weren't very many people onboard—maybe only Dinah—who didn't have some kind of a record, or were at least entered into some national security agency's file, and thanks to the wonders of computers, probably into all of them. Then there was the small matter of Tsaskiy and me having left the Turks and Caicos without getting our passports stamped. Nevertheless, it was deemed worth trying to sneak through as a pleasure yacht and its happy crew. In that case, there would be no need for *reporteros* on board, would there? Media? What media?

After three hours of circling outside the harbour, Paul finally got connected by an operator to the Club Nautica, a posh yacht club in the very centre of San Juan's historic old harbour. After all, we were a British motor yacht, were we not? How much dock space would we need? Told that our "yacht" was about two hundred feet, the person at the other end paused. You could hear the wheels grinding. How many cousins in how many trades should he phone? Must be royalty, or something, to have a yacht that big. Permission was granted, in a respectful tone, to tie up at the end of the club's dock. It must be fun, I mused, to routinely inspire such obsequiousness.

The next step involved calling a pilot. After much phoning around, one was finally located, despite the national referendum, and came aboard without incident. So far so good.

We had just rounded the old stone fortress that was supposed to guard the harbour when a Zodiac with three Coast Guardsmen on board came whistling by at full throttle. It was impossible to tell whether they got distracted by the sight of a black ship, or if they simply weren't paying attention, but, before our wondering eyes, the Zodiac ploughed straight into a buoy and the Coast Guard guys went flipping head over heels into the water. No one was hurt—but those of us who were watching from the *Sea Shepherd*'s deck made the tactical mistake of laughing our guts out.

The landing was classic. Like a big, shaggy black bear, the *Sea Shepherd II* ambled down a narrow waterway toward what looked like a rookery of beautiful white birds: hundreds of the most expensive sailing and marlin-catching boats in all of Puerto Rico. The docks themselves were like a perfect row of teeth, each ivory hull snugly fitted into its slip, not a single gap. Maybe it was the referendum, but you'd think on a day like this, with a fresh offshore breeze, at least a few of these teak-decked chrome and brass top-of-the-line sports jobs would be out testing their owners' mettle. But no. Instead, there were a lot of bikini-clad yachtspersons, and quite a few executive types in their whites, lounging on the decks with drinks—looking up, at first with curiosity, then with twitches of alarm as the tar-coloured former trawler nosed like a towering predator toward them, its bow-wave, even at dead slow, sending ahead a surge that set the tiny pleasure boats to tugging skittishly against their lines, clacking and squeaking.

As is so often the case, the pilot—who is required by law to take control of the boat in inner harbours—didn't know precisely what he was doing. Accustomed to the experience of his big ship being handled clumsily by a village idiot who got the job through an uncle, Captain Watson stood on the bridge with his arms folded resignedly across his chest as we kalumphed the last hundred feet under the pilot's direction, the engine going too fast, the rudder in the wrong position, stern swinging around ponderously, panic-stricken yacht owners shouting and trying to wave us away as the *Sea Shepherd*'s shadow fell across them—until our starboard side finally collided with the pier with a deck-warping shudder. Watson shook his head wearily, and asked the agent: "Am I liable for this?" With a shriek, a metal lamp post on the dock bent surrealistically as the hull leaned against it, and the glass popped and rained shrapnel. A half-dozen men, including security guys, who had been running toward us, yelling and gesticulating, stopped cold, jumping back out of range. A screaming match in Spanish now began between the agent Watson had hired and the men on the dock, with an exasperated Watson arguing, "Look, I'm just doing what I was told. I was told to come here. I'd rather go to one of these other docks but nobody seems to want to help me out."

Unable to physically stop the *Sea Shepherd*, and more worried about what would happen if she started to move again, the men, who were all officials from the yacht club, backed off when Watson's crew jumped ashore, securing the lines. Paul marched off with his agent and the yacht club honcho to a telephone, to straighten this mess out, while the rest of the Puerto Ricans stayed on the dock, eyeballing the *Sea Shepherd*'s crew with great unease. Maybe they had expected Royal Canadian Yacht Club or Royal Vancouver Yacht Club types in blue blazers, possibly even white ducks, and we did not quite fit the picture.

After ten years of moving ships about in U.S. waters, Paul was used to dealing with Customs and Immigration as one bureaucracy. Here, thanks to some jurisdictional quirk (maybe a pathetic stab at independence), the Customs Department had nothing to do with the Immigration Department. It was necessary to call both, but a purely academic exercise, as it turned out, since there was no answer at either. Only then did the yacht club boss think to suggest Paul call a number at the airport, where he could talk to someone representing both Customs and Immigration. After several lost connections, the captain found himself speaking to a Customs agent named Ellen.

In the affidavit he signed later, Watson described the conversation:

"I asked her what I had to do to clear and allow my crew to go ashore. She told me that all she needed for Customs was the official number and some particulars on the ship. She said for the crew to go ashore she would need the names, addresses, nationality, and birthdates of the crew. I supplied her with these details. She asked if they all had proper identification. I said that they did. She then gave me a Customs control number which is 9212110157. She told me to report to Carrier Control the next day to file the papers and an official crew list. I then asked her if it was all right to let the crew go ashore. She said yes."

The moment the word *sí* sounded over the radiophone, there was a convulsive movement toward the gangplank. The Flesh-Eaters were in the vanguard, which only made sense. Why would the Vegans need to go ashore at all? They had plenty of black beans and lentils left. And of course, not being smokers, they weren't running out of tobacco, like most of their Native and media comrades. In fact, nearly all of them professed not to be interested in booze, and of course the drug word was never used, Captain Watson being notorious for throwing pot-smokers overboard, for one thing. For another, I got the impression that among the Vegans, blowing off a joint amounted to exploiting the labour of kidnapped female marijuana plants. Maybe I'm just being unfair to them again.

The point was, we soon discovered that we were tied up at a crumbling wharf in a neighbourhood that was about as rough as any you were likely to find on earth. A lot of drugs, we were warned. Prostitution. Gang warfare. What San Juan mainly offered was smokes, meat, booze, dope, sex, and violence. In other words: freedom. Dinah and I were right in there with the Ancient North American Brother and Sisterhood of Dead Meat-Swallowers, scurrying down the plank, and if I could find some weed that would be nice, too, while Dinah was focused on tailor-mades, a T-bone, a laundromat, and a Daiquiri.

The first place where we were likely to find any of the above was at the Sailor's Bar, just half a block up the road from Pier 8 along a sidewalk broken into chunks that were sliding into the oily harbour water. Ornate old streetlamps were rusting, their lightbulbs mostly smashed. The surrounding low-income apartment walls were cratered with what looked like bullet holes. Windows were shattered, doors barricaded. Tropical weeds pushed up through the cracks in the pavement. Sickly palm trees sagged against a torn and rusting hurricane fence. Garbage overflowed from battered dumpsters. The New World looked like a very old, run-down world at the moment.

The Sailor's Bar was closed. The referendum, one presumed.

We walked ten blocks through streets that were almost entirely empty, as though a plague had come. Indeed, here we were, a dozen mostly-Native guys, with a couple of white folk (maybe their slaves), coming ashore like characters in an Aboriginal-produced version of *On the Beach*, checking out a post-nuclear war megapolis, hearing haunting, muffled radio music playing behind the shuttered windows. The only people we saw were cops armed with teargas canisters and snub-nosed machine guns, prowling around wearing flak jackets. They turned their sunglasses in our direction but otherwise ignored us. If there was a curfew, it apparently didn't apply to foreigners. The front door of the police station, which we passed a few blocks from our pier, was riddled with pockmarks and craters, like a moonscape. I hadn't seen anything like that since visiting the Black Panther headquarters in Chicago in 1969 just before Fred Hampton was murdered by the cops.

It turned out that we had arrived in San Juan the day after the five hundredth shooting death of the year in a city of not many more than one million souls. (Five hundred gun fatalities per year, five hundred years since Columbus—must be some kind of a message?) Every place you could buy booze was closed, which meant every single restaurant, as well as the bars, which shattered our dreams of T-bone steaks and French wine. Or McDonald's or Wendy's or Burger King either. Or even just a cold can of beer. This was beginning to be like suffering, I whined to Dinah.

"Just fuckin' hold it together, eh?" she replied with a sweet smile, the steel flashing in her eye. Being on the boat that long was getting to her, I could tell. After all, she'd been onboard longer than me, and she was young, still. I do know she was a lot happier when we finally found a convenience store, its windows and doors caged in steel mesh and bars, and she could load up with a carton of Player's. The same went for the bros. You could see the shelf of cigarette packages being depleted before your eyes.

We headed back, still mainly in a group, except for Lloyd Austin, a Gitksan from around Hazelton, a cheerful, moustached fellow wearing large, loosely tied Adidas and a baseball cap, who'd been lagging about a block behind all the way to the store. Just as we were leaving, clutching plastic shopping bags, he was coming in, not seeing the point in rushing: "Just get there the same sooner or later,"

I think I heard him say. The rest of us were back at Pier 8 before any-body thought to wonder what had happened to Lloyd.

An adventure. That was what. He'd got stuck in a long lineup, and was really wanting a smoke bad, when two local guys galloped into the store, high on something, waving shotguns, and shouted at everybody in Spanish. The other customers quickly lay down on the floor. Being from a matriarchal society, Lloyd automatically lay down beside a pleasant middle-aged woman—with her between him and the guns—figuring he'd be safer there. The gunmen looted the till and took everyone's wallets, with the result that, even though he'd walked twenty blocks back and forth through an urban war zone, risking his life and, in fact, coming within someone's trigger finger of losing it, Lloyd still didn't have any smokes. So could he bum one?

The Natives had one of their meetings and quickly decided to get off the boat and take some hotel rooms. It was okay with Watson. A Customs agent had already come and gone. Paul had given him the control number. The agent had said that everything was fine. So off they went, en masse. But no sooner had they vanished than two visibly upset Puerto Rican Customs officers screeched to a stop in their four-wheel drive on the dock beside the gangplank and charged on board, demanding to see papers and threatening $3,000 fines for each and every person who'd left the boat. Watson tried to explain that an Immigration official had said it was okay to go ashore—had even given us a Customs control number, see? But none of this impressed Inspector Garcia, the armed honcho who was in charge.

He was adamant: "I didn't hear anything about anything. There-fore nothing happened. Got it? You better get everybody who is off this boat back to the boat right away. That's an order. Your entire crew is confined to the ship until further notice."

Inspector Garcia and his flunky tromped back into their four-wheel drive while a couple of Vegans ran to flag down a taxi to go round up the Natives. Then several U.S. Coast Guard boys wan-dered over, looked at the old *Sea Shepherd* with barely concealed hostility, and announced, smarmy with power, that they would be back in the morning for a "full inspection." Impossible to tell if these were buddies of the lads who'd gone flying head over tail into the water when the Zodiac crashed earlier, but it might just be that our laughter at their plight was coming back to haunt us. Whatever the reasons, the bureaucratic machinery was kicking in, one puffed-up, arrogant cog at a time. The next arrival was somebody from the agriculture department, who vowed to return in force the next day.

Within an hour, the unhappy Natives were all back on board, told that they faced $3,000 fines. The paranoia levels were matched only by their outrage at having to eat the vegetarian food again, especially since the voting on the referendum was apparently over: the neon lights of the Sailor's Bar had come on, and all along the street we could hear an outpouring of music.

"Oh fuckin' great," growled Dinah. "Now the party begins! What is it with these people? They're starting to piss me off."

There was serious thought of ignoring Inspector Garcia's edict and sneaking ashore—hell, I was prepared to swim—but shortly after supper we looked out the portholes to see a dozen army types in fatigues climbing out of a camouflage-coloured truck and taking up lounging positions at strategic points in the shadow of the warehouse a few dozen yards away.

We were pinned down behind enemy lines and the situation looked hopeless. When I retreated to my bunkroom it was to discover that my remaining loaf of bread had grown mouldy and the margarine was rancid. I wasn't quite out of rum yet, but the supply was dangerously low, and of course I wanted a cigarette so badly I had to pop a Valium to calm myself down while sucking and chewing vehemently on my placebo, hoping the plastic filter wouldn't break before the ordeal was over. Through my porthole, I could see the neon lights of the Sailor's Bar beckoning on the other side of the torn hurricane fence, dancing in the inky harbour waters. Beyond reach. I was a prisoner, for God's sake!

14

Bring Me the Head of Inspector Garcia

There is, of course, a great deal of tightlipped grumbling. Nobody wants to accuse anybody of screwing up, but, obviously, somebody screwed up, otherwise we wouldn't be in this jam. In reality, we are the victims of ineptitude, idiocy, and Little Caesarism. Not our fault. Why do all countries post the stupidest of their goons on the borders? Is it based on an ancient truth that this way, in the event of an invasion, the initial losses are mainly the brain-dead? Sounds reasonable. Alas, reasonableness isn't a *feeling*. The attack-or-flee response is thwarted. You feel pissed right off, and want to lash out. The usual crew response in a situation like this is to blame the skipper. Who else? In a true pirate world, there would be either a fight to the finish at this point, or a vote to determine a new boss. But of course nobody is up for challenging Watson, quite apart from the fact that he owns the boat: everybody knows that if Paul hadn't made up his mind to come in here, we'd still be going around in circles somewhere out in the Atlantic, running very low on supplies—and not just of meat. Everything. Still, even I, his loyal old war-buddy, have to wonder if maybe he hasn't gotten too caught up in the metaphor of war (we came in here to "do reconnaissance") to keep in touch with the threadbare realities of bureaucracy, and what a risk they pose.

We could be bogged down here for weeks! I try not to be bitter. I just barely manage to grab the wrist of my right hand with my left hand and force it downward to avoid accepting an offered pouch of tobacco and papers. A smoke now? Jesus! I could see how, in prison, it wouldn't take long before I'd fold. What else to do?

The Brothers, I notice, are coping with this awful turn of events much more calmly than I am. Glowering, Dinah has gone off to her bunk to read. Good thinking. I make the mistake of prowling restlessly, which means that sooner or later I bump into just about everybody. This is what one does in an emergency. Prowl the perimeters. Seek information. Look for cracks. An animal thing, for sure.

Except that the Brothers, rather than being on the verge of nervous breakdowns, are just wandering the decks, looking at the lights of San Juan. Trading one-liners. Standing around smoking. A few beers here and there. Stress? What's that? One can see the advantages, in a situation like this, of patience. Maybe it comes from having lived all your life on a reserve, or having been in and out of jail. As far as I can gather, pretty much every one of the Natives has done time. I desperately wish I could imitate their sang-froid, but I can't. It's like yoga and Zen. I tried. I did try. By rights, at this stage in life, I should be some sort of beatific Elder Brother, just by osmosis. I read the right books. Listened to the right gurus. But nothing stuck. So all I can do is pace, fixated on escape; restless, thirsty, itchy, starting to feel flashes of paranormal hostility. I do know some people who think there are telepathic battles going on between human beings all the time, and that what we see and hear is but a fragment of the whole picture. It does sometimes seem that way. Especially under the pressure of being confined on a stinking old tub, everybody needing a bath.

I should note that Tsaskiy is responding a little differently than most of his fellow warrior-brothers. He has, perhaps, spent too much time in Ottawa, learning not just how to massage a Senate committee and run up a cellphone bill, but maybe (voice lowers here) he's picked up too much respect for deadlines? Of course, it might also be that he has to be back somewhere. The Constitutional War rages on in the True North, and poor Tsaskiy, his historic moment of leadership at hand, his very role in Canadian history books at stake, is trapped on an old black boat in Puerto Rico. And he is already running into end-of-winter Canuck backlash on the phone, even an undercurrent of it from his own boys. The truth is, nobody in Ottawa is going to listen for long to anyone calling from the fucking tropics! He is squandering political capital every day. There's a

Native Council of Canada election a year from now, with a lot of competition for the handful of top paying jobs, especially his. What's the membership going to say if it turns out the Constitutional War was lost during his time in office, because instead of manning the barricades in the corridors of power during *Götterdämmerung* he was playing around the Caribbean with a bunch of honky Bunnyhuggers, burning up his plastic? So Tsaskiy squirmed, and spent the most time on the radiophone, directing his aides in icebound Ottawa to place calls to Members of Parliament across Canada, trying to get us the hell out of paradise.

It remains that the decision to turn back and come in here was the captain's. And I, for one, certainly hadn't argued with him. Especially after a couple of meetings where he tried to elicit some marching orders from the assembled chiefs. "This vessel is at your command," he must have said half-a-dozen times. "I repeat, I'll do whatever you want me to, up to and including ramming them." It couldn't have been clearer. This scene, too, seemed archetypal. How many generals throughout history must have sat thusly, sword across the knees, in front of their political masters, trying to get a clear directive. No wonder there were so many coups. Near the end—when he finally made the decision himself to make for San Juan—I noticed Watson's face reddening with frustration as the chiefs dithered.

Well . . . "dithered"? A White Man's word, if there ever was one. Granted all that, dithering is exactly what it amounted to. Listening to a dozen hereditary chiefs try to make a collective decision, all of them acculturated to an ornate oratory style, reminded me of the universal truth that there can only be one captain to a ship, and *that* was why it was Columbus who reached these shores rather than Hiawatha running a big canoe up onto the beaches of Normandy. Exploration by ship demanded a clearly defined hierarchy. Just in terms of the organizational requirements to build and launch it, a ship was a perfect instrument for patriarchy, monarchy, monotheism, and militarism. One man ruled. And one man alone. Everyone else was a finger-snap away from being thrown over the side by the captain's lackeys. At least in the good old days.

Paul was bending over backwards in an effort to let the Natives run the show—but they were operating on consensus, as usual, and as old sea dogs the captain and I both knew that no boat can function in such a fashion. Too many quick decisions have to be made, and it only takes one ditherer to render everyone powerless, so you wind up going on the rocks.

Time for a generalization: Among Natives I have fraternized with over the years, I have noticed that the unwillingness to say no to anything expresses itself in the habit of not deciding. Even when they meant "no," the brothers would usually say something that sounded like "sure," or "okay," or "gotcha"—not because they agreed, but just so nobody's feelings would be hurt. It made life easy and painless, but in difficult either/or choice situations, such as when you have to decide whether to plunge out into the middle of the sea or turn and head for shore before the Spam runs out, it made for a lot of nodding of heads at meetings on the wheelhouse and in the galley, enlivened by eloquent, slightly tangential speeches about pride and dignity and not being afraid, but resulting in no specific instructions that a captain (or anyone) could follow.

Paralysis was what I felt. The San Juan situation was unravelling around us, or, should I say, we were in its clutches—and, somehow, horribly, as in a nightmare, we couldn't pick up our cameras and roll, which was surely not the way things should be for a couple of Canuck newshounds with a five-part series to shoot and time running out before the Columbus ships totally eluded us.

Normally, in a tight situation like this—cornered like rats—Dinah and I would be out on the dock, never mind any minor official's orders to stay on the ship, while she swivelled her Betacam around, cocking the trigger, clicking into her sungun belt, flicking on the boom mike. At her side, clutching the hand-held, with my own Hi-8 rolling, I'd be wielding the hardwired mike like a club. We would—normally, I stress—have been right in Inspector Garcia's face. We'd have been in the Coast Guard boys' faces too. We'd have been all over the agricultural guy. We are a crack media team, after all. Pumped up by years of getting away with rude, aggressive, power-crazed behaviour. And we are from Canada, where, for the most part, the police and army really are under civilian control, and you get used to mouthing off to guys in uniforms, because they can't shoot you. In fact, your company's lawyer can slap them around. And, most important, you've got a camera they can't seize without a whole lot of legal bullshit to deal with. Trapped as we were, we would also, in the normal course of events, be on the blower by now, with me screaming to the station back in Toronto that we were being held illegally, get the Canadian embassy on it!

Our position, when we are armed with our cameras and mikes (and it helps enormously if Dinah is wearing her station iden-tification patches on her shoulders), is quite simple: *We are the media*, servants of the new goddess emergent, the electronic morpho-genetic field growing like an extra layer of collective consciousness around the planet, fusing us together as a species, forcing us to evolve at an exponential rate. This is one of those things you either see or you don't. Let me plug an image into the great whirling Jungian media ball of the world and it will be disseminated every-where instantaneously at some level, and it will linger forever in one form or another. Never has such a communications supertoy been around to play with. Never has such power to transform been available. I am a full-fledged media-revolution nutbar who thinks he's wading about in the very estuary of human evolution, stirring up mud.

Such is my delusional state. Objectively, you can see it serves a useful purpose in terms of survival. It makes me feel like I can take on almost anyone. With a camera—better yet an entire camera-person at my side—I am at an outrageous advantage in almost any situation, even if outnumbered. That is, until they reach for their guns or knives or just decide to start stomping us.

In this particular situation, however, by agreeing to pretend that we were just regular deckhands, we had wound up with our camera gear stashed away, suddenly powerless, and Dinah and I were both starting to think this wasn't such a damned good idea. Our media shield was down. It was like being unarmed. Just ordinary citizens. You reach for that trusty hand-held mike and it's not there! In a crunch we still had our business cards, identifying us as employees of a TV station, but it wasn't much, compared to being able to hoist a Betacam and unpluck the lens cap, or blow into the mike and say,

"Testing . . ." It was amazing how quickly we started missing the tools of our trade, now that we were just proletarian sea dogs whose fate was in the hands of bureaucratic goons with guns.

An emergency tactical meeting was in order, everyone agreed. We gathered in the galley, Vegans, Natives, skipper, and media agents, suddenly united. It wasn't a life or death thing, and nearly everyone had been arrested before. But the mission could easily be defeated now. They had us in their clutches and while they probably couldn't hold us for long, they could hold the boat virtually indefinitely. What to do? I must admit my defeatist tendencies were taking over. This would be the easiest way out of this mess, wouldn't it? Surrender. Go have a drink, maybe a cigar, head for the airport. The trouble with cutting-edge protest is that at first it always seems faintly ridiculous. Here we were, trying to do PR battle with a long-dead white man. Remind me, why are we doing this again? Oh yes, continued injustice and oppression . . .

It was Gordon Sebastian, the Gitksan Frog Clan lawyer, who came up with the observation that each and every one of the individuals who was now facing $3,000 fines was a Native person. "Of course it was just coincidence that we'd all headed off looking for a hotel," Gordon said carefully. "We all know that. But to the outside world, it must surely look awfully suspicious that not a single white person on this crew was charged, only the Natives. All we have to do is get that message out."

Brilliant! The only question was, how? Tsaskiy was hot on having his office put out a press release, but the concern was, what with it being Sunday, the sleepy wire service operators in Ottawa might not copy the release fast enough for it to be picked up by Associated Press and relayed down to Puerto Rico, where it would have to wind its way through the various government labyrinths before it could come down on the head of Inspector Garcia in time for tomorrow morning's meeting, and before the other goons started tying us up in serious red tape. The solution: Peter Brown, who could speak fluent American, would call the Associated Press office here in San Juan and tell them about the seizure of the anti-Columbus ship and the arrest of all the Indians onboard. Blatant racism being practised against North American Aboriginals on the eve of the arrival of the *Niña, Pinta,* and *Santa María.* How ironic. How sad. A terrible message being sent out.

The story didn't get picked up anywhere outside of Puerto Rico that I was able to trace later, but the instant it went out over the Associated Press wire that night it appeared in every newsroom in San Juan, and that was what counted.

Imagine Inspector Garcia's surprise when he drove up with his flunkies to the *Sea Shepherd* at 0900 hours to discover half a dozen television, radio, newspaper, and wire service reporters crawling all over the ship, interviewing everyone in sight. He'd said we couldn't go ashore. He didn't say anything about journalists and cameramen coming aboard. Unaccustomed to hard thinking, Inspector Garcia apparently made no mental leap to the realization this was bad news. Instead, he puffed up with confident authority the instant the cameras went near him. I couldn't tell what the reporters were asking in Spanish, but, whatever it was, he had no trouble coming up with a self-important little speech that ended with him wagging his finger sternly.

The media were sent packing while we simple deckhands were ordered to muster in the galley. It was plain from his ongoing arrogance that the good inspector hadn't quite realized that the *Sea Shepherd* had anything at all to do with a protest against the Columbus ships, nor had he figured out that the crewpeople who had gone ashore were all Natives, nor that the reporters waiting out on the dock were asking about anything more than a routine immigration bust. It wasn't until Watson, more in sorrow than anger, handed him the Status Indian cards which the Natives used instead of passports that Inspector Garcia finally realized what he had stumbled into. The cards matched the list of people he had threatened to fine. Everyone else had passports. Everyone else was white. He knew what he would be accused of. His face reddened until it was almost purple. He started to yell at his flunky, but realized that he would just look more idiotic. The galley was packed with thirty-three *Sea Shepherd* crew members. We all managed to keep a straight face, only the occasional lip twitching with pleasure at his discomfiture.

The inspector glared at Watson: "Captain, why didn't you tell me about this delicate situation sooner?"

Replied Watson laconically: "Well, Inspector, you had more important business to attend to, as I recall."

As his face worked we could see the real meaning of the media waiting out on the dock registering in the poor man's frontal lobes. Puerto Rico was not quite the Third World, after all. Freedom of the press existed, thanks to the benign imperialism of the Americans. This was a legitimately good story on a smoggy Monday morning in San Juan: a boatload of Indians busted for trying to stop the Columbus ships from landing. Look, real North American Indian chiefs! An Indian logo on the smokestack. A big black ship famous for ramming things. The referendum story was yesterday's news, and, as it turned out, the voters had turned down the independence proposal by a wide margin. No revolution after all. Today was the perfect soft news day for something like this. Novel, distracting, visual, resonating with historical imagery, even mythological archetypes, and easy to shoot. With a ready-made villain right on their doorstep.

It wasn't until Inspector Garcia had retreated from the boat to make a phone call to his superiors that Dinah and I—what the hell—rushed to dig out our gear and join the local media on the dock as they wrapped the story, awaiting only the sweating immigration inspector's final report on his consultation with the authorities. If Inspector Garcia recognized us in the small crowd of newshounds as former deckhands, prisoners of his, he gave no indication. He was busy covering his own ass. And it was amazing how quickly that was accomplished. By this time, from talking to a local radio reporter who spoke excellent English, I'd found out that the city of San Juan hoped to reap a serious tourism bonanza from the arrival of the Columbus ships. The last thing the tourism department people wanted was any negative publicity.

Without knowing the workings of the San Juan media ecosystem, I can't say exactly how the message flashed on in the collective mind of the oligarchy that rules Puerto Rico. All countries are, of course, run by a small percentage of the population. The truth of the matter is that you only have to aim your publicity blast at the elite. In a small, stable American protectorate—probably not all that much more violent, really, than pockets of the U.S. mainland itself—where vested interests were in a few experienced hands, the alarm bells rang quickly. Nowhere was such a message actually typed out, so far as I know, but the gist of it did get passed down verbally to Inspector Garcia: *Do not cause public relations nightmare just before the arrival of the Columbus ships. Release Canuck Indians immediately.* Suddenly, the high and mighty neo-fascist with the big fat .45 in his holster looked like nothing more than the nervous cipher of a clerk he was. Swallowing hard, he quickly announced that it had all been a misunderstanding, there were no charges against anyone. The ship was free to go.

Satisfied, the media mini-horde turned its attention to Wii Seeks, our ultimate chieftain. His nearly bald head sweating in the unfamiliar tropic temperatures, Wii Seeks got straight into his role as a geopolitical leader: "Spain has two choices," he announced, looking from camera to camera. He might have made a Gandhi-like figure in his shorts and sandals, but the effect was ruined by the bright red tee-shirt he wore, saying: b.u.m. This was too bad because he really tore into Columbus: "Columbus himself was a despicable slaver and mass murderer who deserves no more admiration than Pol Pot, Adolf Hitler, or Saddam Hussein. He may have been a great navigator but he was an even greater monster of prey."

Thoroughly pumped, Wii Seeks ended up proclaiming: "Spain can apologize and begin a new era of cooperation with Native peoples, or Spain can continue to be arrogant and to perpetuate conflict between the two cultures. What we're hoping to do is create a new beginning, a new start so that some of these injustices or all of these injustices can be corrected."

Alas, while that might have been a good warm-up, the ending wasn't quite what the media wanted. Correct injustices? The last Indian living in Puerto Rico was probably killed 450 years ago. Spain hasn't been a player over here for centuries. The reporters were looking confused. What was the angle?

Tsaskiy made a stab at explaining about the Indian Act in Canada. "Until the Indian Act is dismantled, Canada has no right to call itself a democracy. Until the Indian Act is dismantled, the Native people will remain prisoners in their own land."

Nada. The press corps is still shaking its communal head. What's Canada got to do with this?

That's when they decided Art Loring must be good for a clip, mainly because he was recognizably Indian, wearing his bear-tooth necklace and the headband and a red button-blanket waist jacket, no shirt. He too immediately took to the high ground, speaking one-on-one to the entire nation of Spain. I love this moment when someone goes from anonymity to megafame. The transition is made in a flash, like a crystal forming. One moment they were ordinary, and talked like ordinary folk you knew. The next they were elder statespersons, speaking of "our people," accustomed to addressing a global audience. When it happens, it happens so smoothly you don't even notice the change. It is only afterwards, when you listen to the tapes, that you think, my God! And it's not just vanity and vexation of spirit. There was, after all, a pretty good chance that this stuff would be beamed back with Spanish subtitles to Madrid and relayed from there across the whole Iberian peninsula. By tonight, depending on the time zones, the image of Art Loring, Wing-Chief of the Eagle Clan of the Wet'suwet'en and Gitksan nations, would in all likelihood be radiating out from millions of television screens, maybe not only across Spain but throughout Europe, and quite possibly the States and Canada, Australia, Asia, you name it. Sensing his moment of destiny at hand, Art decided to dispense with the diplomatic bullshit.

"We are willing to seek peace with Spain," he let them know, "but they should not underestimate our anger. One hundred million of our people have died, our culture has been raped, our people continue to be victims of a racist system. We will not be ignored or dismissed. An apology or else their voyage will be ended. It is as simple as that."

Ah, this was better! And finally, inevitably, the cameras swung to Watson, the man in charge, who declared: "For myself as captain, I have placed myself under the orders of the hereditary chiefs. If they want the ships stopped then I fully intend to stop them. The Natives onboard my ship plan to board the *Santa María* to demand an apology. If Spain doesn't apologize then the ships will not be allowed to proceed to Puerto Rico."

Not be allowed to proceed? What did that mean? How? Wait a minute! But before he could be pinned down, the wily captain was off to the bridge to ready his ship for immediate departure. The media people started streaming away, facing editing and transmitting sessions before going to air. The megastars of the hour coped with their moments of fame by smoking like crazy and making radiophone calls to media back home, maintaining the momentum.

Several of us lower-deck types seized the moment to check out the Sailor's Bar. This included Art Loring, cousins Lloyd, Ron, and Jason Austin, me, and young Jimmy Liebling, who was in trouble with the Vegans again over being caught gnawing on some cheese. I don't know what drew these fellows here, apart from avoiding a ten-block hike to the next boozery, but I was drawn as though by a force like magnetism. There was nothing I could do about it, and it wasn't quite as simple as the lust for a cold beer from the tap with honest head on it and condensation on the glass so that your fingers squeak when they touch it. I sometimes suspect that in dozens, if not hundreds, of previous lives, I must have hung out in a lot of cheap seaside drinking establishments. This one was classically seedy. The plaster was flaking away, revealing old brickwork. Cracked tiles. Tiny lizards skittering across the walls. Slow, noisy fan. Smell of limes, something dead nearby (what is manhood without the smell of death?), diesel fumes from the street, strong cigarettes and cigars. Ah, sí! Mucha cerveza, por favor, señor!

Judging from the reactions of the locals, it really had been a long time since anyone had seen a gang of North American Indians around here. Lloyd and Ron and Art and Jason and Ralph were used to running into rednecks in northern British Columbia, and having to fight their way out of bars in little towns. But this was different, they assured me. We tried to figure it out. First of all, San Juan was a big city. Second of all, these guys around us were the direct descendants of the Mediterranean invaders of the Americas, led by Columbus himself. These were not the usual northern European types they ran into back home. Spanish blood, sí? Probably carrying guns and knives.

When hearing or trying to use Spanish, my experience has mostly
been in Mexico. But in Mexico, there was a lot of intermingling
with the Natives, forced or otherwise. Here, in this part of the Caribbean, they were just wiped out, so the population today is almost entirely Mediterranean. My guess was that these boys around us had
probably never seen an Indian except on TV or at the movies, and
guess what? The Indians had been jumping around waving toma-
hawks and scalping people. This was like being part of a biker gang:
our image radiated outward, creating a little standing wave of con-
sternation, or at least cognitive dissonance.

Whether we could fight our way out of here alive, I didn't know.
In the event that somebody decided to avenge the massacre of poor
Custer, or for that matter, come to the defence of Columbus, by at-
tacking us, I was pretty sure we'd be in deep trouble fast. The boys
might be great street fighters, but I hadn't seen them do their kung-
fu thing yet, and we were outnumbered and surrounded, as usual.
Eugene Pierre, the official police officer for the Wet'suwet'en, was
trained in all sorts of martial arts, and could probably be trusted to
take on most anybody in the bar, but once he got wound up we
might have trouble stopping him, or else somebody would pull a
weapon. It wasn't that anybody around us projected hostility. They
just gawked in our direction a lot. And laughed quite a bit. What
you do in a situation like this is laugh and wave and yell something
like "To the Queen!" If that doesn't work, wave a beer around and
yell: "*Bueno, bueno!*" Something to let them know you are even stu-
pider than them, and therefore not a threat. Above all, be very respectful to the bartender. Treat him like a higher being. Do not flash
peace signs. Don't look nervous. Drinking in seedy, dangerous bars
where people can get killed is a sport, or ought to be considered as
such. Some people like to ski. Some hang-glide. Others have affairs.
I like to drink in a place where the air is alive with a sense of potential out-of-the-blue craziness, what with the mix of booze, drug
deals undoubtedly going down, narcs probably everywhere, money
changing hands in washrooms. More awful stuff can happen to you
in a portside bar than is likely to happen to you at sea, that's for sure.

Because it was crowded, we sat down in a different section of the
bar and I looked up to see a faded old print in an ornate smoke-

stained frame over the cash register: a depiction of Custer's Last Stand, with the painted Indians riding in circles around a barricade of dead horses and overturned wagons, aiming bows and arrows as they closed in on the white soldiers, whose guns were blazing under the torn Star Spangled Banner. And there was the old Indian-hater himself, mad George Custer, sword in one hand, revolver in the other, surrounded by the bodies of his men: one of America's greatest heroes. Via mythology, this version had become The Truth.

Certainly it was the truth in the minds of everybody sitting around us. The Brothers, and by inclusion me, might as well have been mere projections from the mindset that painted that picture in the first place. As Indians, we had to be packing scalping knives, just *had* to be. That print of the Last Stand had loomed over the Sailor's Bar since it opened generations ago. It wasn't a painting, any longer, so much as a window on the past. It was true history, exactly as it happened. That's how it was seen. And in true history, the great hero Custer fell bravely, trying to save us and our descendants from the human-wave tactics of the godless atrocity-addicted Injun hordes bent on mass rape and mutilation.

Staring up at that Last Stand print as we chugalugged our first few beers was one of those moments when the inherent strangeness of life in this particular dimension leaps out and hits you square in the neocortex.

"He shoulda took treaty," Art Loring deadpanned, meaning Custer. And we all laughed.

The truth was, the Oglala Sioux, under Sitting Bull, had used guerrilla tactics against the Americans, and defeated them just the way the Viet Cong would defeat them again a century and a half later. Riding around in circles, trying to aim while bouncing on horseback, was not something your average Native guerrilla fighter did during the War To Save The Buffalo, which was what the fight with Custer at Little Big Horn had been all about. The Oglala Sioux had gone to war to defend an endangered species and a threatened ecosystem from the European hordes, and in the end, outnumbered and outgunned, they lost. A foreshadowing of the rise of militant conservationism and the eventual defeat of the environmental movement?

A warrior-brother moment falls upon me, unbidden. You *do* have to challenge myths, I realized. And there *is* a place where myths collide. That's where you shape the great mindscapes of the future. You topple statues made of false collective memories. You deconstruct the historic lies of the conquerors. You disconnect the cultural programs of the teachers, priests, politicians, artists, publishers, and, in our time, advertisers.

Yes! And I was actually hanging out with actual Indians, and I *was* one of the boys. If this was a clubhouse, I was in it. If I wasn't quite a member of the gang, I was riding with them in this battle to dent the great myth of Columbus, and by denting Columbus, dent Custer, dent John Wayne, dent whoever runs the Multinational Capitalist-Industrial Military Conspiracy. Change the planetary mindset, change the planet, I say! Attack!

I certainly *should* be considered a Brother by now. I had helped come to their rescue with meat, sided with them immediately on the vital philosophical question of the human right to kill and eat, joined in the takeover of the galley, shared chicken stew and wine with them, and now we were drinking beer together in a cracked-tile bar deep in traditional enemy territory. You could hardly bond much more than that, eh?

We drank to Inspector Garcia's health. We drank to Associated Press. We drank to the *Sea Shepherd*. We drank to the captain. We would have kept on drinking, of course, except that First Mate Angela appeared at the side of our table, reminding us sweetly that the boat was about to leave. I started to argue in my grumbling old rebel mode, but the other guys got up as one without hesitation, abandoning half-full glasses of beer, and I was dragged along by sheer peer pressure. It was astonishing, such acquiescence. No wonder they lost the continent, I thought cruelly. In a matriarchy, of course, you would learn to listen to women. To do what they say.

Oh well. I had been there, God knows. In fact, I had to wonder, following my Gitksan and Wet'suwet'en buddies as they obediently tramped along behind the First Mate back toward the boat, if I had *not* been raised by my mother, would I have folded at the table just now like that, almost as easily as the Native guys did? Of course, we're liberated. I know that. I am happy about it. Really.

As the *Sea Shepherd* swings out past the old stone fortress guard-
ing the mouth of San Juan harbour, Wii Seeks climbs to the bow,
and for the exclusive benefit of our own onboard video cameras,
utters the battle cry: "Columbus, make my day!"

And this time, he does not throw up over the side. We are ready.

15

Playing Chicken with a Frigate

M y first rush of hope that this might actually work came when
I climbed to the wheelhouse after sunset to find a tense, jubilant scene. People had that look of ecstasy and dread which means that the long stalking of something bigger than yourself is ending and you must face the next moment. Half the crew had gathered inside or around the radio room, where Spanish voices had been picked up on Channel 16. Just a few minutes before, the words "*Santa María*, read you loud and clear" had been heard. A cheer, from Natives and Vegans alike, had gone up. And about half an hour before that, somebody had reportedly signed off from the *Niña*. Great stuff. Dinah rolled on a bit of the radio room drama, but not much, because she'd felt the flicker of hope too, and so now she was into making very sure she kept enough tape for the big encounter.

Even though the seas quickly rose to ten feet, enough so that the old *Sea Shepherd* wobbled like a rhino shambling along, not a single person seemed to be seasick. Either the break in San Juan had restored the Interior Natives' interior equilibrium or the thrill of the chase was producing enough adrenaline to neutralize the urge to barf. We weren't quite in hot pursuit of our prey but we were on the edge of it. Everybody felt it. The decks, which had been uninhabited during the leg of the journey from the Turks and Caicos to Puerto Rico, were downright crowded now, especially the forward deck, despite the occasional shower of salt spray and enough upwelling motion so that you felt like a mouse on the shoulders of a slow-motion gambolling elephant. *Sea Shepherd* had begun her charge. The only problem was, she couldn't see anything yet, so there was an inevitable tentativeness no matter whose hand was on the wheel. During the day, there was almost always someone up in the mast with binoculars, as well as somebody else staring intently into the radar screen.

I climbed the mast a couple of times myself, partly for the physical thrill, partly to show how easily I could do it, old fart that I might be, gasping but stupidly pushing myself, as if anybody gave a shit how fast I climbed, mainly as a sop to the kid inside who wanted to be the hero by being the first to spot the enemy. This wanting-to-be-a-hero syndrome goes way back into the mists of boyhood. I keep waiting to outgrow it, but it seems to be almost as intractable as lust itself. And then you are forty, maybe fifty feet above the deck, and the ship looks incredibly small from up here, as though you were balanced at the top of a broom handle, with just a broom down there, and why doesn't the whole works fall over due to your enormous size and weight? There is a whiplash effect up here too, so you must hang on with both hands, never mind the goddamn binoculars, can't focus on anything anyway, whanging back and forth like this, wind stinging your knuckles, scanning squint-eyed, tears half-blinding you, for a glimpse of a sail with a cross on it.

Nice scenes, I recall, in the wheelhouse at night: the glow of the compass light pushing shadows upward on the helmsperson's face, everything else pitch dark except where the panel of front windows and the open doors let in the stars. In the radio room, fresh night sea air flaps the porthole curtains and the charts rustle on the table. The sizzle of the phosphorescent ghosts around the hull, whirling away into darkness in our wake. And if there was ever an excellent time to pray, this would be it. Swooping down into sloshing darkness of the deep, emerging as though from death's grip (especially if the bow goes deep and ploughs right up to the lip of the deck into the infinitude of black liquid mass), rising into the wind, the Milky Way going from being above you to being around you. And now the moon comes up over an island on our starboard side and throws its spotlight upon the deck, hurtling my own shadow back as far as the wheelhouse wall where it dances even though I'm hanging on perfectly still, braced and gripping with my toes. Moonlight creating a blinding silver path across the water which we seem to be unerringly following . . .

I love this stage of a campaign. Impossible not to have a sense about omens. At 1530 hours December 12 a pod of dolphins is spotted off the bow. What can that possibly mean? Which way are they going? Oops, not the way we're going. The trouble with signs is that they may not be good signs or maybe they are signs that have nothing to do with you. There was a time, of course, when I took all signs seriously, and lived a blessed but stressed existence which others took to be merely impetuous, and if, along the way, I dislodged a little pebble of destiny or two, it was strictly accidental, you understand. We must all be humble, brothers and sisters. Nowadays I try to take everything with a grain of salt. Miracles happen, sure! All the time. But what isn't a miracle? Sail on, dolphins! We won't place the whole burden of our success or failure on you.

Our best bet, it had been deemed, was to head east by northeast, skimming along above the Virgin Islands out to a position just north of Anegada Island at the tip of the chain. If the Spaniards were indeed making straight for San Juan, and if they haven't been blown far off course to the south—which would see them approaching along the other side of the islands—we should quickly be in the best possible location for an ambush as they parade past. Of course it is not really possible to hide yourself on the open water from the radar eyes of a warship escort, but we were not far off a major shipping lane, and there were lights bobbing everywhere in the night. We could be any old fishing boat.

Well, not quite. Captain Watson has been on the radio fencing with U.S. Coast Guard aircraft 1712, whose radio operator had expressed amiable good-buddy concern about our situation. Were we experiencing any "distress"? Assured that such was not the case, he politely asked for our position, "just in case." Paul gave it to them. What else could he do?

"They're not going to have any trouble finding us," he mused. "If worst comes to worst they'll get us by satellite. Might as well appear to be cooperating. See if we can get anything out of them."

Clicking on the mike, he asked bold-facedly: "Hello Coast Guard, this is the *Sea Shepherd*. Do you, ah, have any information on when the *Niña*, *Pinta*, and *Santa María* are expected in? Over." The look of innocence on his face, a method-acting approach to getting the voice right, was so convincing most of the radio room folded up laughing, and had to be shushed so we could listen for an answer.

After a surprised pause, the radio operator's voice came back: "Negative. We'll get back to you on that. Over and out." He did come back a couple of hours later to tell us to call on another working channel, but when somebody tried it, there was no response.

We had high seas all day on the 13th. I was three-quarters sure we'd catch them that day for no good reason other than that 13 is my lucky number, and on my last *Sea Shepherd* venture we had caught up with a Japanese drift-netter fleet in the North Pacific on a 13th. Accordingly, I chewed hard on my plastic smoke, paced the decks, prowled the wheelhouse, haunted the radio room, and rode the bow. Bigger seas meant a better ride, being lifted up higher and descending further, with the *Sea Shepherd* kind of throwing her head around, shuddering, as the whole weight of the bow came pounding down, and it was like I was riding a shield being thrown into the sea.

I still had no idea what exactly was going to happen when we found them.

We changed course several times, swinging toward anything that showed on the radar. A plume of smoke over the horizon was enough to trigger a course change. But it was all just thrashing about. We listened to a Spanish ship, the *Sevoilia*, broadcasting on the VHF sideband, sounding very military and very much like a vessel giving instructions to other vessels within visual range of each other, somewhere tantalizingly near, but the signals were too brief for anybody to get a fix on the radio directional finder. You could almost smell them out there, three small sailboats like nuns being hustled along by a couple of burly security guys past the bad old protesters.

At 1345, a U.S. Navy submarine surfaced a mile ahead off our starboard. It sluiced effortlessly across our bow, heading north. It was probably nuclear: huge, grey, square-dorsalled, so heavy that the waves splashed against it as if it was mounted in cement. It didn't so much sail or steam as ride like a train on a monorail.

"That's it," snapped Paul. "They've been watching us all the time. If they're showing themselves now, it means they figure the job's done." He immediately ordered the helm to come about.

"They're behind us. Passed us on the other side of the Virgins last night," he growled to the surprised helmsperson as we began a U-turn in the Atlantic. "They're lamming it for San Juan. Gonna be close."

When Peter Brown got through to the U.S. Coast Guard radio operator in San Juan later in the afternoon, he was advised that there was no information available on the position of the Spanish flotilla, after all, and, furthermore, none would be forthcoming. The operator ended his frosty little speech by saying: "The United States government cannot be responsible for marrying you with the vessels in question."

In retrospect, it seems clear that while the sub tracked us up the north side of the Virgins, the Spanish boats, tipped off, quietly slipped by through Anegada Passage to the south. Presumably, if we had taken the Passage, they would have gone around on the open Atlantic side. The impeccability of the timing of their move suggested that the Navy and Coast Guard and probably a satellite or two had been monitoring us from the moment we left San Juan, with the information being relayed to some Spanish ambassador in Washington. The little fleet, hoping to dodge negative publicity, had undoubtedly held back just long enough to lure us out to the edge of the Atlantic, where they could duck around a chain of islands and get behind us and make a run for it. So weird has the world become, here were guys from a major industrial country with 50 mm cannons on their front decks sneaking around in the dark to avoid a handful of Indians armed only with television cameras—well, admittedly, also a 210-foot steel battering ram of a ship with a Captain Nemo-style madman at the wheel. Whether it was just fear of a PR nightmare or genuine security concern that the *Sea Shepherd* might actually try to ram one of the caravels, the Spanish were doing the prudent, civilized thing—bringing their people in through the back door to avoid trouble.

Now it was a race. Moving all night at full throttle, the *Sea Shepherd* closed the gap swiftly. Spanish voices could be heard over the VHF, the signals getting stronger every hour. Soon the radio directional finder was quivering, pointing dead ahead. As dawn broke, we knew by the chatter from other ships, including the Coast Guard cutter *Nantucket*, that the *Niña*, *Pinta*, and *Santa María* were in the home stretch, nearing a place called Puerto Del Ray, which we couldn't find on the charts, which meant it had to be the name of a marina—somewhere between where we were on the open water and San Juan. Ahead lay the northeastern coast of Puerto Rico.

"Got 'em!" someone finally yelled, straining to see through binoculars.

Maddeningly, I caught a glimpse of sails flapping wildly as a wooden ship disappeared behind a seawall—dammit, the last of the three caravels tucking into the refuge of harbour. They were too far away and it was over too quickly for Dinah to get anything on tape.

"Twenty minutes sooner and we'da had 'em," Peter Brown muttered bitterly.

My first reaction was disbelief. *You mean we actually blew it? We came all this way, nearly two weeks at sea, and missed by twenty lousy minutes? What kind of a lesson in karma is that?* But before I could plunge into complete existential despair at the futility of life, Dinah poked me on the shoulder.

"Take a look, buckaroo. I think we've got somebody pissed right off."

Indeed. No sooner had the last caravel disappeared into the mouth of the harbour than the big grey Spanish navy frigate which had been herding it along had turned ponderously, belching smoke. It was now steaming straight out toward us, throwing up a bow-wave—rather like an angry man rolling up his sleeves. In the wake of the onrushing frigate, an equally stout-shouldered seagoing Spanish navy tug came crashing along. It was impossible not to think of the music from Ravel's *Bolero*. Showdown music.

Watson's eyes gleamed. Until now, he had been prowling in and out of the wheelhouse, his eyes taking everything in. We were still going at full throttle, for all intents and purposes still hot on the heels of the caravels. The seas were around ten feet, choppy, with a morning wind behind us, keeping our own wings of spray hovering in the air as we lunged forward, but taking the bow-waves from the

Spanish boats and lashing them back across their own decks. I was amazed at how black the smoke from their stacks was. And, of course, I noticed that their deckguns were pointed directly toward us as they punched out through the waves, a couple of big guys looking for a fight.

Personally, my heart sank. Somebody could get hurt here. I've always had a certain fear of huge manmade machines smashing into each other with me anywhere in the vicinity, let alone hanging on to one of them. Dinah, still ahead of me, had already decided the foredeck wasn't the place to be in the next few minutes. Nimbly, she danced backwards, heading for the ladder to the wheelhouse, looking for high ground. I lingered for just a minute. And what a lovely minute! With the wind behind us, whiffs of our own diesel blew across the deck. For me diesel has always been an intoxicant, sometimes an aphrodisiac. The *Sea Shepherd* made a noise like a train coming into a subway station. The decks were wet with spray so there were reflections of the sky to be seen at your feet, as though you were standing on a broken mirror. From my position on the deck just in front of the wheelhouse, the bow kept rising and falling, obliterating the view of anything but the sky, then dropping down to reveal a new flash-frame of the Spanish frigate: slightly bigger, slightly closer, its bow and our bow aimed directly at each other, and the tugboat hard on the frigate's tail.

Out of the corner of my eye, I saw Jimmy Liebling yelling and pointing, and there, just surfacing off our port, maybe a mile away, was the big grey American nuclear submarine. It was a leisurely emergence that suggested the Navy boys were just coming up to watch, not to interfere.

"They're bored," shrugged Peter Brown. "It's like a cockfight. They've gotta have bets going on the outcome of this."

"What kind of odds, you figure?"

"They've looked us over," Peter laughed. "They know how old this heap is. It'd be like a horse and buggy hitting a truck. Ten to one on the Spanish, easy."

Paul was standing in the doorway to the wheelhouse, the wind in his hair, binoculars in hand, to all appearances as calm and blasé as a tour guide, talking to his helmsperson:

"Steady. Straight ahead. Steady as she goes."

"This is a collision course, isn't it?" came a faint voice.

"Only if they don't move over."

By now the foredeck had been completely vacated. Everybody had found something to hang on to.

We were actually now playing chicken with a frigate, I realized, almost sadly. Surely this wasn't the most mature thing to be doing. But then that line would probably make a good caption underneath any picture of any battle in history. Maturity—what's that got to do with anything, son? We're talking pride, nationalism, race, machismo. The Spaniards seemed to be overreacting, was my thought. But then Paul wasn't helping any, was he? If I were at the wheel, we'd be seriously slowing down right now. But then that was why Paul was the captain, and I was just along for the ride.

As I recall maritime procedure, when two ships are head-on-head, you are to maintain course until a collision is imminent, then move to the starboard and the other ship is to do the same. *Sea Shepherd* just kept going, no course change at all. A serene, detached feeling, that, just before the machinery connects. I imagine this is the same serenity that possessed every warrior throughout time at the moment just before the spear impaled him or the bullet bit: an utterly false sense of security. (Some lingering genetic illusion or memory of immortality?) Maybe there is no such thing as courage, anyway, only ignorance and some kind of chemical broth that clouds the brain, or, rather, wipes it almost clean so that you seem to be seeing and smelling and hearing everything perfectly, even better than normal, precisely because there is no interfering smog of abstract thought between you and the experience of the moment. Here and now. This is how people get to be action junkies. And now, I must admit, I am enjoying himself. Hey, other people are in little offices bending to their little clerical tasks, or commuting, heads bowed, to and from work, or even watching television, for God's sake! I've got the wind and a pounding deck and a seagoing train collision staring me in the face. Sure, my throat's a little on the dry side, heart's *bumpity-bump-bumping* a bit, and I would really like a smoke. But other than that, I'm feeling a glow all over, a warm buzz inside, a little squirt of exultancy. I realize I've got a sort of acid grin on my face. Nobody's actually said "Charge!" But that's what we're doing. Immature? Hell, insane! But there's no fear any more. Reached that seemingly clear madness zone where it's all just amazing and bizarre. Life on Planet Earth, eh? I really do believe in Watson's combination of instinct, luck, shithouse karma, and chutzpah. Maybe I'm not standing close enough to him. I should climb up and stand right next to him. I do.

We might turn to pulp if the two bows ever slammed into each other, but it doesn't feel that way. And it certainly can't look that way. By now the captain of the Spanish frigate must surely have realized that he is up against somebody his own size, and he's not back at home on his own turf. Still, I would say we were down to half a small city block before the frigate's bow inched over to starboard.

Game to us. They blinked.

I had been pretty sure it would end this way. If nothing else, Paul was driving his own old wreck. The captain of the frigate was in command of government property. He was the guy who faced the paperwork if anything got dented. Paul could just write it off. Believe it, that's how a bureaucratic mind thinks, and the captain ahead was primarily a bureaucrat.

The captain, I should say, who was now off to our port.

If there is anything to media war, we had them outgunned. Surveying our decks, I counted half a dozen Hi-8s in the hands of various Native guys wearing headbands and baseball caps as well as Dinah's Betacam aimed at the Spaniards. Rather than firing back at us, the sailors assembling on the foredeck of the frigate as it chopped past us about thirty feet abeam stood stiffly, almost at attention, staring in our direction but, dear me, no one waving or smiling. I guessed this was the eye-to-eye part of the *mano a mano* exercise. I noticed our own crew froze where they were on the decks, little cameras rolling, staring sternly back, no one smiling or waving either. The Natives had all adopted their absolutely-most-solemn expressions. Dinah was happy because she was finally getting some decent shots.

Watson let the frigate make a half-circle, with the tugboat tagging along, so that they had rounded our stern and were starting to overtake, before he gave the order:

"Hard over to port."

The *Sea Shepherd*, still at full throttle, came about quickly.

Good Christ, I thought, *what is he going to do now?*

My throat got a lot drier. But he was having so much fun I didn't want to spoil the mood with questions. Instead I soaked up the scene, savouring it. One thing about this guy, it occurred to me, was that he didn't care about odds. Just beyond the two Spanish ships, the nuclear submarine was idling closer. Over in the mouth of the harbour a U.S. Coast Guard cutter was belching smoke, swinging toward us. I spotted a chopper coming along the coast. Too early to say if it had anything to do with this. But the setting was suddenly busy. And just what did Watson think he could get away with, surrounded, as we were, on all sides by armed naval vessels, including one of the greatest weapons of mass destruction ever invented? *I keep giving him the benefit of the doubt,* I fretted, *but maybe this time he really is going to do something profoundly dumb, like ram a frigate in front of everybody's eyes and guns.*

But no, he was just playing a little game. As we churned across the frigate's bow, a good one hundred feet ahead of the bigger ship, Paul grinned with kidlike glee. "That's called 'Crossing the T,'" he explained. "Back in the days of sail and broadside cannon, you'd be able to fire on the enemy without them being able to fire back." The Spanish captain—and his officers and men—would know perfectly well that, with this textbook manoeuvre, Watson had just thumbed his nose at them. They could hardly overlook the fact that he was flying a British flag, either. Ancient enmity. You could feel it radiating out from the frigate's wheelhouse.

And they weren't quite through. As Paul straightened out so our bow was once more pointing toward the harbour mouth, the frigate and the tug rather deftly swung out, one to port, one to starboard, and booted up their engines so that they began to overtake us at flank speed in a pincers movement.

"Interesting," Paul grunted. "Looks like they have a game plan."

Whatever it was, they didn't get to exercise it.

By now the Coast Guard cutter out of Puerto Del Rey was kicking up a bow-wave of its own, coming straight in our direction, and her captain was on the blower to Watson and the Spaniards, snapping out orders in a distinctly no-nonsense tone of voice. Watson was to pull back a mile immediately, and the Spanish navy ships were to hold their positions to accept a pilot to take them into a nearby military base. The Spanish warships rumbled off, fuming.

Immediately, a Zodiac was launched from the *Sea Shepherd*. Half a dozen Natives jumped in, as the intrepid, wetsuit-clad Peter Brown took the helm. As skipper, Paul had to stay with the ship. There was barely room to squeeze Dinah and her camera in. The idea, I gathered, was to head over to the marina and at least get some footage of the caravels. I could have got myself onboard the Zodiac, but my heart wasn't in it any longer. I really didn't give a shit what the *Niña*, *Pinta*, and *Santa María* looked like. The harsh reality was that we had missed them. Shots of a few military boats splashing around in the water were fine, but they didn't add up to a confrontation. So Watson and the Spaniards manoeuvred around each other— exciting if you happened to be there, but so what? We did not have a five-part television news serial. We had a lot of media foreplay, but that was it. As for the Natives, I had no idea what they were thinking, but if they had hoped they were going to do something that would at least get into the footnotes of history, they might as well get a new fantasy. This protest wasn't going to get to be a footnote to the daily goddamn news.

I wanted to bang my forehead on a wall. I wanted to smoke myself to death overnight. I wanted to drink copiously. Fortunately, Dinah came back from rolling on the famous caravels as the Zodiac circled around in the harbour beside where they were moored, and assured me that we had pretty good stuff and we could maybe patch something together, a sort of a travelogue of San Juan, if nothing else. Or a cultural thing: Natives and seagoing art.

"Don't freak out, buckaroo. We'll figure something out." Despite everything, she had become the nurturing female while I broke down into childish helplessness.

A flop! I couldn't believe it. So damned close! As Watson set a course back to San Juan, I made my plans to go straight to the Sailor's Bar and cry in my *cerveza*.

I was not the only despairing crew member to seek solace in the Sailor's Bar. The cast around the three or four beer tables we had pushed together against the back wall kept changing through an increasingly blurry evening. The one sensible thing I did was stay away from tequila. Otherwise, I ate the food (meat) and drank the *cerveza* and didn't worry about Puerto Rico's equivalent of Montezuma's Revenge. What did it matter? I was outa here. The campaign was toast. We had lost by twenty minutes. Might as well get seriously wasted. It's a farewell, eh?

I noticed that, except for me, the older guys were taking our defeat more calmly than the younger ones. Wii Seeks had announced before we got into San Juan harbour that he would be leading a delegation of hereditary chiefs to the Spanish Consulate's office tomorrow, seeking "redress." Tsaskiy was into this, along with Gordon Sebastian. Dinah rolled her eyes. I just looked away. Watson and Brown drifted quietly away. The Vegans went off looking for wholesome food. Soon, we were down to a hard core of young Turks, plus me, an Old Young Turk. Somehow, I ended up with a cigar in my mouth as we griped and plotted, chugalugging *cerveza*. Lloyd Austin, Art Loring, Ron Austin, Stanley Stump, me, and Jimmy Liebling in the hot San Juan night looking up at the picture of Custer's Last Stand, and maybe we are symbolically the other mirror image: Wii Seeks's Last Stand. I give in to that mouth of mine that just won't shut up and start ranting about how nobody should kid themselves, we blew it bad. Wouldn't it have been nice to win something for once? I can't say I remember very well, but I suspect that I slipped into my "Native" mode, which was still then very new to me. Every since discovering about my Huron great-grandmother, I had been suffering bouts of Indianness. Add to that the fact that the experience of researching and writing my history of the occupation of Canada was still fresh in my mind, and it is highly probable that, late in the evening, I slipped into my Huron act.

Which, of course, might not have been an act. If, indeed, the oral tradition was true, there would be Huron genes inside me, and maybe, every once in a while, after the Scottish and French genes had gotten sick of upstaging each other, lo, the Huron genes got a chance to speak. I made some kind of a speech in this Three-Faces-of-Eve transformed state, revealing a hitherto hidden "third" ethnic personality. An insensitive observer might merely perceive me as three-quarters pissed, zonked on macho tobacco leaf, maybe with some residual Valium or Gravol or Spam in me, and not much else besides nachos and hot sauce. I got . . . Indian. I spoke to the Brothers as a Brother. I was one with them. If I was Bradbury's Martian, I would have shapeshifted into Blood. I became proud. I was indignant. I was aggrieved on behalf of my people. Fortunately, at another level, as they say, I was fully aware that I was also probably crazy from decades of substance abuse, and was just slightly out of control. Harmless, of course.

There comes a point in a booze binge when you either notice that the people sitting around you are giving you strange looks, and you become paranoid and get up and flee, or you don't, and you go over the hill. I was just at the top of the hill, holding onto my glass like the stick shift of a bar-sized streetcar about to start the descent. I was also—note—just at that moment when you transcend to a presumably higher state, or you fall short and splash into the mush. I could see the mush coming up fast. I got out of there.

I staggered along the torn hurricane fence, finding my way down to the pier but getting lost in the shadows of the crates, spending what seemed like hours wandering through canyons of produce boxes, until finally I spotted a couple of Vegans who guided me in a very saintly fashion, considering how cruel I'd been to them, to the gangplank, and only quit hovering at my elbows when I growled at them. I paused for one blurry look at the lights of San Juan, my stomach not feeling very good, trying to remember where I packed the Maalox. I vaguely remember groaning aloud, then laughing at myself and shuffling into my cabin and crashing into my bunk without taking off even my sandals. A wave of relief and happiness passed over me. It was over. I could sleep in. Catch a late-afternoon jet. Get down to Customs early. Check out the bar. Be home in my sweet baby's arms by midnight tomorrow, with luck. I won't get fired over this, I assure myself. Not my fault, et cetera. It'll be a long time before they let me go out on a road trip, though. Damn . . .

No sooner had I plunged into the sacred oblivion of sleep than my cabin door clanked open. It was The Boys, led by Art Loring. They were shaking me, pulling me out of the sanctuary of my bunk. It was worse than a nightmare. It was like they were tearing me up out of the ground. Oh, I did *not* want to re-emerge in the world just yet, thank you.

"Listen, you can't just walk out on us like that, brother," Art Loring told me fiercely, squeezing my arm. "We came all this way. Come on. Get up. Come talk with us. Just a few of us. We need to figure this out."

Well, I had been summoned, hadn't I? That's all I'd been waiting for: to be asked. Or was it that I couldn't say no? Uncertainty, doubt, failure of will, weakness, fear, cynicism, disbelief, pessimism: this was my mindset as the Brothers hustled me out of my cabin, marched me off the boat again and down the pier.

We did some more power-drinking. Can't say where. Art did most of the talking. He and the boys had decided the older chiefs were crapping out, settling for a bullshit meeting instead of action. It was time for the warriors to step in and do something. I recall half a dozen of us ending up sitting on the upper seats of a huge stone staircase outside a smog-rotted cathedral, leaning against cracked and pitted Corinthian columns, as though squatting under the moonlight on the edge of the ruins of a devastated civilization: looking down on pocked, dug-up roads, half the streetlights blacked out, boarded-up windows, piles of garbage. Yet in the midst of the gutted warehouses and vacant lots, the streets were impressively, vibrantly alive. There were drums, mandolins, accordions, and electric guitars blasting echoingly through loudspeakers. People were dancing in the middle of the road. Along the edges, vendors had set up stalls and parked their taco wagons. Plumes of blue kerosene smoke mingled with the fumes from charcoal. Crowds of Puerto Ricans, clad mainly in white, many with sombreros, rolled peacefully along in family groups, swaying, whooping, laughing, singing. Firecrackers, horns, dogs, distant sirens. And there we were, ghosts huddled in defeat in the shadows.

Somewhere in there, inspiration hit. It was me, witnesses insist (and, yes, I do vaguely remember), who came up with the harebrained idea of going down to the marina where the ships were moored and seizing the *Santa María*. Seizing it. That was the idea. Walking onboard dressed in warpaint and feathers and claiming it. Right under their noses. *Fuck you. This boat is ours. You owe*

us, baby. In their face. This mad, drunken proposal was greeted
with late-night cries of "Right on!" It was followed by a brotherly if
somewhat stumble-footed round of Revolutionary Handshakes. And
then the group shambled unsteadily back through the crowds to our
pier. The battle plan got fleshed out as we went. A predawn departure under cover of darkness to Puerto del Rey. A lightning guerrilla
strike. Breach security at the marina. Seize command of the *Santa
María*. Demand that the Spanish Ambassador come down to the
dock and apologize for . . . whatever. Worry about that later.

I managed to keep my act together enough to go to Dinah's cabin
to alert her. She didn't even blink. Seize a ship? Under cover of darkness? "Sure. Fine. Wake me." As I half-crawled back to my bunk, I
began to suspect that I might have said something insane, and now
people were going to act on it, and probably get shot. I told myself
not to panic. Maybe the rebels would forget. Or they'd sleep in. Or
they'd have second thoughts. Chicken out. Yeah. Don't panic.

16

Warbonnet Time

First, the noises: gulls yokking, a rubber Zodiac squeaking against the hull, an engine turning over somewhere, a hiss of air, a metal door grating on its hinges. And far away—could that be a jackhammer? The smells: tar, diesel, fresh paint, salt air, dead things out in the harbour, a sleeping bag under me that badly needs washing. Feeling: have to piss like a horse, and there is a gentle warmth on my feet. Wait. Warmth? Jackhammers? An alarm explodes in my head. My eyes blink wide open, although my drinker's instincts make sure I don't move my head a millimetre yet. Sure enough, the morning sun beams a spotlight through the porthole onto my bare feet. And it *is* a jackhammer. I hear trucks rumbling now, too. The work day has already begun in San Juan.

So much for the cover of darkness.

I close my eyes in angry defeat. Our predawn attack window would seem to be gone. And what the hell's the point of even getting up then? We blew it. We slept in. What an ignoble way for it to end. The full weight of existential angst settles upon my still utterly motionless form. Does it matter? Who cares? Why bother? Abort the mission and head home. Maybe take a leak and catch a few hours' more sleep first. Maybe forget the leak . . .

I am just easing back into the blissful void when Art Loring materializes in my cabin, gets his hand behind the back of my head and lifts it up as you might a corpse's in order to speak to the dead.

"We're running late," he confirms flatly.

It is my voice that answers him, not my brain. Listening to the conversation between us, I wonder who the hell is it talking anyway? Not me. I'm back here in the basin of my skull, hiding.

"Everybody up?"

"Sort of."

"Taxis?"

"Not yet."

This bare-bones exchange gives no hint of the electric exchange between us, which involves his spirit's energy coming to the rescue of mine. There is not a shred of suspicion in him that I might be thinking of copping out. I am just wounded by booze, he knows. That's why I'm having so much trouble making my body move. He has apparently shaken off the firewater madness of last night. His eyes gleam. He is high and clear and strong. I feel his strength pulsing through his fingers into the back of my skull. My last hope of getting out of this vanishes. He fully expects me to rise literally to the occasion. He trusts me. Without a media bodyguard he and the boys might as well go straight to the slammer with no Warhol moment of glory in between.

The way I figure it, Fate manifests itself through the medium of other people who come to you at certain moments in your life and steer you in one direction or another. In this harbour on this boat on this day, Fate's name for me is Arthur Loring, Wing-Chief of the Eagle Clan, a Gitksan warrior ready to avenge the Columbian Holocaust. And I, who have been playing Indian since I can remember, am being invited to join the battle on the Indians' side. A moment of destiny, surely. At least, if nothing else, a great working-out of a boyhood fantasy. Do the genes remember? Is it the Huron blood I feel stirring? Something subliminal, in any event, is getting the adrenaline going, and before I quite know it I am moving purposefully if somewhat gropingly about the cabin, scooping up gear, cameras, wallet, tape recorder, pulling on my yachting whites; numb as I may be, some instinct says: *Look like you can afford a good lawyer.* I wash down a couple of Tylenols with the remains of the bottle of Maalox. I blame the shaking of my hands on last night's substance abuse, but it is also fear, is it not? And there's not much I can do about that except let it work its way through my system. Within minutes, gulping back the fear and the desire to puke, I am shambling along behind Art like a good Boy Scout, hiding my angst.

There is a certain ritual quality to our movements which cannot be accounted for solely by the hangovers, although when we meet in the galley, Ron and Lloyd Austin look like men whose souls have been nailed to something during their sleep. I have already looked at my face in a mirror and seen an aged, wrinkled map of journeys. We barely grunt at one another. Jimmy Liebling flashes me a clenched fist and I give him a croak of "Right on." His jaw is clenched with determination, which must mean he's coming along.

"What tribe are *you* from, Jimmy?" I have to ask.

Before he can answer, Art lays the doctrine on the line: "Any warrior who goes into battle on the side of the Gitksan people is eligible to be adopted into the clan as a brother."

My heart sinks. This is our boarding party. Three Native guys, none of them much more than five-foot-seven, two of them so hungover they can hardly walk, and one white kid with a college haircut. With Dinah and me riding media shotgun.

Dinah, who is tapping her fingers on her camera bag, watches the rest of us with an expression that certainly doesn't suggest awe or hero-worship. I can't read her mind, but from the way she keeps shaking her head, I get the feeling she's not quite sure she should accept this as reality. She notices my hands.

"DTS, eh?"

Captain Watson himself has gotten up to bid us farewell. I don't particularly remember telling him about the results of our late-night scheming, but obviously he knows everything and approves. In fact, it suddenly strikes me that this is probably why he went to all that trouble to bring me aboard, calculating that if all else failed, I could probably be counted on to revert to form and stir up some kind of trouble, especially if I got drinking.

Art had stayed up all night, it turns out, preparing himself, putting together a make-up kit from his artist's supplies, digging drums and feather headdresses out of various cabins and stuffing them into a suitcase. But there are going to be four people going onboard the *Santa María,* and he can only find headdresses enough for three. This is seriously holding us up.

I start to lose it. I hate that when it happens. Aspirants for saint-hood aren't supposed to yell at people. You're supposed to be gentle and peaceful and lead by an example of all-seeing calmness. Instead, here I am, starting to rant and rave: the firewater still speaking, no doubt. The Bad Bob is coming to the surface. I am immediately ashamed of myself for berating my brothers, but at the same time I want to whap them over the head.

"We've got to get it together . . ." I rave. "This is global street the-atre . . . you gotta look the part . . . we're dealing with archetypal images here . . . dramatic counterpoint is what we're after . . . it has to register at a non-verbal level . . . the protagonist and antagonist have to come together . . ." I throw buzzwords from film school around in a desperate effort to browbeat everyone into listening to me because I so obviously have a higher intellectual grasp of it all. But nobody's hopping to do my bidding, which is to round up one more set of feathers. With Art having loaned a headdress to Jimmy, Lloyd is the one left wearing his usual baseball cap on backwards. This is not quite the regal touch we want.

The good captain steps in: "Hold everything for a minute, boys. I've got just what you need."

He marches off to his cabin and returns with his authentic Oglala Sioux eagle headdress. It's almost like a living thing, the feathers shimmering with a faint hue of rainbow. Paul carries it as you would a flag, draped in his arms. Again: very ceremonial. He hands it to Lloyd. Major moment, I think.

But instead of being thrilled, Lloyd backs away.

"I can't wear that," he says. "I can only wear my own clan's stuff, eh?" He looks at Ron.

Ron weighs in slowly but implacably on Lloyd's side. "It would dishonour their ancestors, whoever owned that."

"Are we talking primitive taboo here?" I groan, starting to panic because I'm still caught up in the fantasy that we were going to get started before dawn, and now it's broad daylight, and with every minute that passes we are going to find the Puerto Del Rey marina busier. There will be more people to deal with, more security, less of a chance to break through to the *Santa María*'s side.

"This is a warbonnet," Watson explains solemnly. "As a warrior-brother of the Sioux, I was told by an Oglala medicine man I could pass it on to another warrior when he went into battle, as long as his cause served Mother Earth."

"Nobody ever told me anything like that could be done," Lloyd replies warily, not buying it at all.

"Me neither," confirms Ron.

"Just wear the fucking thing, Lloyd," I growl, turning nasty under pressure. "You gotta look like an Indian. Any Indian! It doesn't matter, for Christ's sake. We gotta get going."

Indifferent to my White Man bullying, Lloyd and Ron turn to Art for guidance on this delicate ethnological matter. The young Wing-Chief hesitates. Destiny flaps her wings impatiently while he ponders. Then, with the authority of age-old traditional wisdom, he judges:

"It's okay. No offence will be taken by the Eagle Clan."

Into the suitcase the Sioux warbonnet goes, along with the make-up and instruments.

I am beginning to feel like the producer of a small-scale travelling medicine show. It is a good idea to keep my primary job description in mind, so I'll know what role to play when the time comes. As it is, my identity has fragmented. I am reporter/activist, insider/outsider, director/narrator, manipulator/observer, participant/witness, exercising what you might call multiple "either-or" functions. But mainly just gulping down several cans of tomato juice from the fridge to ease my dehydration.

I ask Paul if he's interested in coming. "Nah," he says. He doesn't need to explain himself any more than that. He did his part of the job, which was to try to engage the ships at sea. A veteran like Paul knows when he's finished with a campaign, and I can already sense his attention shifting to whatever he's going to do next. A pro. That's what he has become.

This is a new one for us. A role-reversal. We've gone into action together, and then, when I quit leaping into the fray myself, I kept seeing him off on planes or trains or boats to fight the good fight. This is the first time I have marched off to the squeal of bagpipes with him staying behind, waving goodbye. There is one problem with this, of course. When the shit hits the fan this time I won't be able to wander over and stand beside him or behind him, will I?

It is hopeless to try to get a taxi to find its way down to the *Sea Shepherd*'s location, so we clamber down the gangplank and wind our silent way single-file through the maze of crates around to the front of the storage depot, with Lloyd trailing, as usual, and up to the foot of Pier 8, where we wait for him to catch up. Can't lose him now. Not with a crew as pitifully small as this. The 7:00 a.m. weekday rush-hour traffic plugging the street leading past the Sailor's Bar has already congealed into the San Juan version of gridlock. The air is so thick with diesel molecules that the crawling trucks and cars look as though they are moving along in the ghostly slipstream of some interdimensional warp zone. Christ, we'll never get taxis here! Despair washes over me again. I even try jumping on a bus, after we have been waiting for ten minutes, but when I ask "Where is Puerto Del Rey?" the driver gives such a complicated answer in Spanish that I give up and step back out through the door. Ron and Lloyd are sitting on the sidewalk, backs to a wall, leaning on each other.

When deliverance does come in the form of two taxis, one on the heels of another, Dinah, Art, Jimmy, and Peter Brown pile with the camera gear and the suitcase into the first one, agreeing that we will all meet outside the gate at the marina, leaving Ron, Lloyd, and me to climb into the second, me telling the driver to take us to Puerto Del Rey. He speaks English. Knows where the place is. Good.

"How long to get there?"

"An hour." I try not to wince, thinking about the cost. After all, in my yachting whites, I'm supposed to look like a rich gringo.

I count on my stress levels to keep my eyes open in order to enjoy the scenery as we inch our way out of the smog-shrouded harbour district and onto a coastal highway, with San Juan dropping behind us, but I keep falling asleep, being wakened rudely when we hit bumps or come squealing around sharp bends. Ron and Lloyd have both passed out in the back seat, and are snoring like big hibernating animals, their heads rolling from one shoulder to the other in unison as we weave along the coast. Thank God we have air-conditioning, because it is already a humid jungle out there. In the short bursts while I am conscious, I feel almost choked by the sense of being inside a survival pod of some kind, with a menacing alien biosphere all around.

The pod ejects us outside the marina. I wake the warriors. Dinah and the others have just finished settling, somehow, with their driver. I fumble for money in my pockets. Ron and Lloyd are quickly robbed of whatever coins they have on them so we can pay the bill. My pockets are empty now. I'm down to plastic. Oh Lord, don't make me go into the Visa again! It looks like we've all peeled away our cash, so I hope there's no fee at the gate.

There is only one place to enter, the rest of the marina being obscured by a high brick wall topped with cemented shards of glass. A yellow-and-black metal guard-arm dangles across the asphalt road leading in, revealing a profusion of docks with bare-poled sailboats lined up saddle to saddle at least a quarter of a mile out, or so it seems. Huge! Where the hell would the Spanish be in all that? We could easily get lost just stumbling around looking for them, running up one long, long dock after another. On the left side of the gate is the open-windowed, open-doored guardhouse, where a cop in a grey-and-blue uniform and mirror sunglasses waits, his revolver hanging like a folded leather wing from his hip. We all cringe, spotting him at the same time.

With a furtive glance around, I can count three other armed, uniformed men in clear view, within probably thirty steps of each other—not soldiers but a little too clean-looking to be private goons. Maybe some municipal or maritime unit—not the sort of presence you'd normally expect at a marina unless there were VIPs around, or—and this is chilling—unless this is just how it is in Puerto Rico, anyway. How many deaths by shooting in San Juan? One guard has a shotgun, I notice. Another a machinegun-looking thing. The third guy has a carbine. Freedom of choice in weaponry suggests a non-governmental corporate structure behind the defence perimeter, but maybe with a government contract. We'll never get through that without ID, is my first thought.

We're all huddled together, on a wide, newly cobbled sidewalk. It would look odd to just loiter, since there's nothing else around here except the marina. So this is my moment. I'm the guy in the yachting whites who looks like he can afford a lawyer, and therefore maybe even a yacht. And since we all just climbed out of cabs from San Juan, obviously I must have money. My crew might look a bit motley, but that's not unusual.

We just have to keep our momentum. Fortunately, I've hung around a fair number of yachting clubs, and can easily get into thinking of myself as a yachtsman. There's a certain way you treat the workers, including the guards. Casual *mano a mano* friendliness, but not too friendly. You are the customer, after all, and in this cruel, scratch-for-it world of starving people and collapsing mutual funds you have managed to acquire and hold onto something so monumentally useless as a sailboat. It says something about your self-indulgence as well as your wallet.

"You guys carry the stuff," I whisper to the boys. "You're the crew, right?"

Dinah instinctively hesitates to let go of her camera, but for purposes of deception, sees the point right away. After all, we are anything *but* media right now. We may, for expediency's sake, have played at being humble deckhands back in San Juan, but at this moment I am a rich American-type sonofabitch and she is some kind of weird probably European jet-setter. Art, Lloyd, Ron, Peter, and Jimmy work for us.

"Are we ready?" I ask, my voice sounding calm enough. I know how hard my heart is beating. But my hands have stopped shaking. I am actually quite steady, which is a major relief. I hate shaking when I'm trying to bluff my way through something.

"Let's fuckin' do it," says Dinah, flicking a butt away.

"Columbus, make my day," the rest of us say at once, like a mantra. We are finally at the edge of the cliff. Up until now, we have done nothing, barring the Herculean effort of getting out of our bunks. We have breached no local laws, triggered no automatic alarms, galvanized no guard dogs. We all take a deep breath. And start hiking.

It is amazing how long it can take to walk just a couple of dozen steps, moving at what I hope is an easy-does-it, executive-level, arrogant, alpha-male pace straight for the pedestrian gate right by the guardhouse. The gate, steel mesh with razor-wire coils on top, is wide open.

"*Buenos días,*" I grin at the guard, making sure not to slow down or speed up. I apply Method Acting. I *am* a Yanquis yachtsprick. My boat with the teak deck is down there, I'm thinking. I've paid a lot of money for the privilege of tying up here. I don't have much time for little guys. I am so used to power I wield it without thinking. Dinah is right beside me, letting him have her best Hi-big-fella look. He nods impassively at me, gives her the once-over, and ignores the "crew" bringing up the rear with the bags.

Into the marina we march, the other guards not even giving us a second glance.

17
Storming the Santa María

I've had this feeling before: that you are being picked up in an invisible palm and carried along just above the ground. We have taken no more than three steps onto marina property than I hear a *beep beep* to my right. An open-topped electric golf-cart-type dock shuttle, driven by a pretty young female in the marina colours of dark blue, glides silently to a stop right beside me.

"Where to, *señor?*" the driver asks brightly. Luxury marinas, eh?

"Go for it," Dinah nudges me.

I clear my throat. "The Columbus ships, if you please."

The young lady flashes a dazzling smile, waves her arm at the six empty seats in the cart, just exactly right for us and our bags. We clamber aboard, laughing giddily and exchanging meaningful looks among ourselves. Indeed, the gods do seem to be with us. I take the front passenger seat in order to distract her (okay, enjoy her too) while the necessary furtive costume changes take place behind her back. Dinah retrieves her Betacam, climbs in behind me, and starts rolling.

"You are making a movie, *señor?*" the driver asks, impressed by the size of the camera.

"Yes," I admit. "About the *Niña, Pinta,* and *Santa María.*"

"Oh yes, very beautiful!"

A blissed electric car ride! Our magic carpet, on cue. There is enough wind off the sea to slosh the champagne-coloured water against the pilings, so that we splash through puddles as we whirr along the two-lane main floating dock out to the end, where the seawall rises. We hang a tight left and start down a narrower dock, parallelling the shore, bumping softly over metal ramps from one float to another. The bows of massive American yachts loom like overhanging cliffs as we wheel through their shadows. Beneath their keels, schools of little tropical fish are hovering in the shade. We pass sloops worth millions of dollars, cabin cruisers that could only be owned by executives at multinationals. The smallest boat we see is in the forty-foot category, with twin inboard diesels. Hardly anybody is up yet. The few people out on their decks have jobs to do. They pay scarcely any attention to us as we proceed like a Stealth bomber zeroing in on its target, disguised as just another boat crew being shuttled out on the golf cart. Except for the light flopping of the rubber tires on the planking we make almost no sound.

Without the driver noticing, Art gets his suitcase open, unscrews a little jar of paint, and starts to work on his face, swabbing bright white Vs on his cheeks. He hands the jar off to Ron, who repeats the move and passes it along to Lloyd, who slaps some on expertly and passes it to Jimmy, who dabs self-consciously at his face, embarrassed. The others have done this before. He hasn't. At least, not as an adult. In fact, in my eyes, there is something almost foppish about how casually Art, Ron, and Lloyd apply make-up to themselves. Poor Jimmy shares my white male heterosexual uneasiness with facial paint, deeming it, from lifelong conditioning, a girlie thing. (Well?) His jaw muscle is taut as he drags a forefinger of white paint along it. But he does it.

There is something else bothering me. Belatedly, I realize I should have taken a piss before leaving the boat over an hour ago. Oh Christ. There's no place out here, surrounded by posh yachts and anti-pollution regulations. You could try just whizzing off a dock, but somebody'll be able to see you for sure. Politically, it wouldn't be a good move. I try to imagine my bladder as a thing of steel. I guess Art notices me squirming, because he taps me on the shoulder, and hisses:

"You gotta take a leak, too? So've I. What're we gonna do?"

"I dunno, man. Hang on. They'll have a shitter on board. Maybe you can seize the shitter first."

"There they are, *señor*!"

I'm not sure what I had expected. I knew they would be small, especially compared to the fibreglass and ferro-concrete monsters tied up all around us. And I vaguely imagined that they would be crudely built, by the standards of half a thousand years later. As a man of the "future," surely I would end up looking down on them, poor primitive craft that they were. The cheapest one-man sailboat today incorporates sail and hull design changes that long ago revolutionized sea-travel. How could you compare a horse and buggy, say, to a Mercedes-Benz? Different eras, different technologies. Evolution should have passed those little Spanish caravels so far by that one's only appropriate reaction upon sighting them would be to snort derisively, or shake one's head with pity for the sailors who had to go across an entire ocean in them.

Instead, what I see are the three ships silhouetted against the sun like fantastic harps, the planking of the high prows and sterns elegantly folded together, like wings. As we come in view of what amounts to a collection of gorgeously crafted antiques, I am struck by plain old culture shock: the feeling I got the first time I walked down a narrow rainslicked harbourfront alley in Genoa, or stood in whirling snow under the arch of Cologne Cathedral, or pressed against the bar by a fireplace in a little pub by the Thames, or sniffed the late-afternoon August streets of Pamplona: a sense of Europeanness. Then, as now, the little Caucasian countries between Asia, Africa, and the Atlantic were part of the same continental civilization. The wars were all civil wars. Their science produced one technology. A distinct style, those crazy Europeans! One thing I did not expect: I am filled with an ache of appreciation such as when your eye falls upon a great artwork for the first time. Damn, those evil imperialist bastards built beautiful boats! Look at those things! Could this be another of the great secrets of life being revealed: Behold, evil comes riding sometimes upon the back of a noble steed? It seems especially cruel, somehow, that the Black Legend of Spanish atrocities was made possible because European genius-level engineers and artisans and craftsmen were so good at building intricate, exquisite, sensitive, almost musical instruments for the sea wind to play, and in the process unleashed near-demons like Columbus and his various sadistic crews.

When I can tear my eyes away from the perversely graceful lines of the caravels to sneak a look back to check on my own crew, it is to find that the silent transformation into a Native boarding party is almost complete. The war paint is on. The bonnets are on and tied under the chins. Amazing what a bit of paint and some feathers will do. Lloyd, in particular, is unrecognizable. In the place of the hung-over guy with the backward baseball cap sits a young Oglala Sioux chief, his face coloured in stripes of white, red, yellow, and blue, a deerskin drum clutched in his lap. With his warpaint and headdress on, you would never take Jimmy for a white kid in a hundred years, although you might question his choice of a "native" instrument: a tambourine. Ron has acquired a drum, feathers, paint, and a bone necklace. Art has fully assumed his Gitksan alter ego, clad in a cere-monial vest with his bear-tooth necklace, plume of eagle feathers, and warpaint. He has pulled out what I recognize immediately as a Talking Stick, understanding its significance as a ritual communica-tions device from the days before microphones. But, of course, if you didn't know what it was, you could be forgiven for mistaking it for some kind of huge club for pounding people over the head.

With sincere *muchas gracias*, we hop off the shuttle at the begin-ning of the very last dock, which is too narrow for us to be driven any further. The Columbus ships have this last section all to them-selves. Up close, the three caravels aren't as small as I'd imagined, and there is something wrong with the woodwork, as though the hulls had been sprayed with some high-tech fibreglass material. Still, their elegance is undeniable. For a moment, it seems as though they are abandoned, and I'm wondering whether that is good or bad, but no, there are bodies cocooned in string hammocks above the decks, smoke is coming from what must be a galley, and a portable radio is playing low. Clothes are strung on cobwebby lines. I keep expecting an armed security type to challenge us from somewhere, but there's nobody in uniform in sight.

Art and Ron have taken the lead, marching shoulder-to-shoulder, with Jimmy right behind, and Dinah, Peter, and me on his heels, their big cameras and my little camera rolling. Dinah and I have both clipped on our plastic-coated Ontario Legislature press passes, a nice touch. Lloyd is lumbering along after us as per usual, but at least this time he has an excuse: he is carrying the biggest drum, after all.

The ships are secured by spring lines, as well as bow and stern lines. I get a sense of how much heavier than modern sailboats they must be just by listening to the agonized squeaking of the wet rope binding them to the docks. The tide must be running at least at a couple of knots, trying to pull the ponderous wooden shells back out to sea.

The *Santa María* is moored at the very end of the dock, wouldn't you know, which means we have to get past the other two caravels without arousing any alarm. This is the beauty of surprise, and I can certainly see why military folk have always enjoyed making use of it. We are waltzing straight to our positions, already firing, and nobody knows because they have been caught with their guard down and our weapons happen to be silent as well as non-lethal. We hustle past the *Niña* and *Pinta*, their identities made clear by the names posted on their sterns, and although it is the bow of the third vessel which faces the dock and there is no name plaque visible, we can safely assume the remaining boat to be our target. It is slightly larger than the others.

It is also not quite unguarded.

A large hunk of sailor with a black beard and a tattoo on his beefy bare shoulder is lounging on the bulkhead beside the portable gang-way, presumably on watch. He looks down sleepily at us as we come around the *Pinta*'s stern. At the sight of painted savages striding purposefully toward him, the sailor sits bolt upright. His jaw drops. Rather than slowing down as we approach him, Art picks up the pace so that by the time he reaches the gangway, he is almost running. He bounds up the steps, waving his Talking Stick, and leaps onto the deck beside him. The guard—if that's what he is—makes no effort at interception. Instead, he jumps off the boat and scurries away along the edge of the dock, his face registering genuine terror. This is marvellous. The man looks to be at least one hundred pounds heavier than Art, with biceps as thick as Art's thighs, but in the face of an apparent attack by Redskins, no matter how short and skinny, he is ignominiously abandoning his post. The warpaint has done its job, scaring the shit out of the enemy.

A soft lot, these modern Spaniards, I think contemptuously. First we breach their security, then we scare off their watch. If this was the good old days, say five hundred years ago, our side could have fallen at this point upon the sleeping sailors and killed them all. That would have held off the European invasion for a while, wouldn't it? Only a while, but hey! We might have gained time to organize the tribes on the East Coast and wiped out each new explorer's expedition as it arrived, destroying everything, leaving not a trace. Too bad you can't go back in time . . .

Although this has a bit of the feeling that we *have*. Through our cameras' eyes, Dinah, Peter, and I behold a little mini-movie, a historic re-enactment production with admittedly low-budget costumes, but a million dollars' worth of props in the form of ancient ships brought alive. The ships remind me of pirate movies, since that's where I have seen these kind of boats most often, and since the crew, as they appear, are wearing not much more than bathing suits. You could take them for near-naked brigands on the old Spanish Main. Earrings. Tattoos. Long, curly hair. Bandanas over their skulls. And as for the Indians, well, it's too good. We have gone back centuries to bear-tooth necklaces. True to the Hollywood style, we even have a white actor playing the part of one of them. Jimmy's cute. He'd be the honkie love-interest for the mass teenybopper audience. I'm waiting for him to give a war-whoop. Please Jimmy, don't. So far this thing has an amazing amount of dignity. Let's not spoil it. To do this as a feature, I estimate, we'd have already spent way over a million, more like two. But by doing this as a live action segment, a *real* live action segment, news in the making (rather literally), we allow the Spanish government to shoulder the costs of getting this fabulous stage and pricey backdrop together. Thank you, King Juan Carlos! Within range of our lenses (and that's all that counts) we are looking at some pretty high production values. And the key is, so long as we don't turn our cameras on each other, we are invisible. We see only the set and the players: The angry young warrior striding across the small, sloped deck, slowing down now that he knows he is unopposed, climbing toward the stern where he takes a position beside a storage box at the foot of the mast and pounds his Talking Stick on the planks. A Spanish deckhand awakens in his sleeping bag in a hammock a couple of feet away from where the Talking Stick bangs down. At the sight of a painted, befeathered, probably scalp-taking heathen towering over him, the Spaniard, still inside his bag, thrashes his way in a panic out of the hammock, landing with a muffled *thunk* on the deck, and scuttles away in his underwear like a lizard leaving its skin behind.

Hard on his heels, two more crewmen scramble out of their bags to get away from Art the Barbarian, although one of them has the presence of mind to scoop up his camera as he flees the stern deck. The moment he reaches the safety of the wall of the fo'c's'le, as far from Art as he can get, he turns and starts taking pictures. Oops! There's our first sign of resistance. The Spanish are firing back with a Leica.

Art has to yell just to be heard over the loud squeaking of the ship's lines as the *Santa María* heaves her keel around in the tide, straining to pull away from the dock. About a dozen Spaniards have popped out from the interior of the fo'c's'le and below decks, all of them big, burly men, I notice. Art is joined by Ron Austin, who is still putting on his warpaint, and as a producer I wince because this should all have been done already. Oh well. On balance, considering what Dinah and I have in the can already, things are going extremely well.

"My name is Gitwangak," Art announces, jabbing his chest with a thumb. His voice wavers slightly, crackling with emotion. I worry about it carrying, but thanks to the partial canopy of furled sails directly overhead, there is a boom-box effect, and an echo across the water. You couldn't ask for better acoustics.

"I am from the Eagle Clan," Art declares. "I claim the *Santa María* for our people in North, South, and Central America."

By this time—we could not have scripted it better—one of the Spaniards has started translating in a loud voice so the crew, most of whom obviously do not speak English, can understand. Art picks up on this immediately and pauses at the end of each sentence to await the translation.

"I'm seizing this ship and I'm staying on it." Pause. "We will see that corrections are done right by our people." Pause. "We are not gonna get off."

The translator gets lost in the middle part of that, but catches the spirit of the last bit, because a murmur goes through the Spanish ranks, and more cameras click. No one is running away any longer, but no one is moving toward Art and Ron, either. At which point, Lloyd Austin clambers on board in his Sioux warbonnet, pounding his drum, with Jimmy right behind him, rattling his tambourine. And no one moves to head them off, either. It is only when I march up to the side of the boat, brandishing my own camera, with Dinah and Peter behind me and rolling, the three of us plainly looking like media, not protesters, that the Spaniards come to their senses and block us from coming onboard.

"No camera!" one of them barks at us.

"Well, we'll just stand out here on the dock then, bozo, and shoot all the pictures we want," Dinah growls back.

I go through the motions of looking like a frustrated-but-obedient reporter, but in fact I am perfectly happy to remain here on the dock where we have everything in clear view. So far, no one is challenging our right to be here, even though we are on private property, and could be ordered away at any moment if the proper authorities show up.

Up on the deck Ron Austin takes a turn making a speech. He makes it in Gitksan, which leaves the translator, as well as the rest of us, utterly in the dark as to what he might be saying. But he speaks in a righteous, angry tone, and whatever he is saying, he seems to mean it. The fact that he is speaking in neither Spanish nor English but in his own Native North American tongue gives him instant credibility. It is a perfect case of the medium being the message. The Spanish are unlikely to have heard an authentic "Indian" language spoken before. At the end, for everyone's benefit, Ron descends into English and says:

"I also have suffered the indignities."

This great line is enough for the translator to work with, and it brings out another round of murmuring in Spanish. *Sufrir! Indignidades! Ah, sí!*

Ron, Lloyd, Art, and Jimmy are standing shoulder-to-shoulder at the stern now, drumming, tambourining, and chanting. Sailors have come over from the sister ships. There are easily three dozen Spaniards on the dock now, on the *Santa María*'s deck, on the fo'c's'le roof, with several of them up in the rigging and perched on the yardarm, watching the performance. The travelling medicine show would seem to have settled down on stage in front of its audience, and I almost expect the Spaniards to break into applause when Art and the group, as I am starting to think of them, get to the end of their chant. In the meantime, it is spellbinding stuff.

They are still at it when the first cop arrives.

Until now, there has been something wrong with the picture in front of our cameras—something so glaringly wrong that you don't notice it at first because it is as obvious as the nose on your face. Four little guys say they have taken over somebody's big, expensive boat, and are apparently holding three dozen much bigger guys, the crew, at bay. Yet the little guys don't have any weapons, just drums and a tambourine. How is it all four have not been grabbed and tossed into the briny, along with their musical instruments, amid much Spanish laughter? If you want to get technical about it, unauthorized seizure of somebody else's seagoing property is at least attempted theft, if not piracy. What's wrong with these big guys? Are they wimps? Can't be. They have just sailed the Atlantic. They are men's men, after all. It must be that the little guys pose a diplomatic problem which can't be settled by muscle or sheer numbers. The presence of foreign media is a factor in the Spaniards' self-imposed passivism, no doubt, but there's more to it than just that.

The cop seems hip to this. Even though he is packing two pistols, one clipped to the back of his belt just under his flak jacket, and has a truncheon in motorcycle-gloved hand and a Plexiglas-screened crash helmet, he makes no effort to climb aboard or even talk to the miscreants. Not macho enough for his taste. Slightly bored. Dinah and I swarm him busily as he stops on the dock, trying to make ourselves seem like more than a two-person media scrum, documenting him in-close, hoping to make him feel so important he might forget about ordering us to get our asses off the marina's property, pronto. I have a bad feeling this is about it for us, no matter what we do, and I don't have a fallback plan, I'm afraid. The first thing the law anywhere does in these situations is order the media away from the scene. We're used to that. The trouble is, the moment we're gone, those restrained Spanish sailors might forget their manners and decide to thump our boys something awful. But I can't think what miracle is going to keep us around here more than a couple of minutes longer. Maybe I should signal to Art for him and the boys to dive into the ocean and swim for it. I am just puzzling out how I would do that when it dawns on the cop that Dinah, the camera *hombre de televisión*, is a camera *señorita*.

The idea of a woman operating a television camera is a little avant garde for rural Puerto Rico, apparently. We can guess this from his reaction—which is to puff up even more pigeonlike than our previous armed nemesis, Inspector Garcia, and to switch into his hunk-of-hunks Latino Lover mode. Here we are in the middle of a virtual declaration of war between the indigenous peoples of North, South, and Central America, no less, and the nation-state of Spain itself, and when a cop finally shows up, what does he do but start hustling my cameraperson! He completely ignores me, the Spanish sailors milling about, the war-painted "occupiers" of the ship.

"What is this?" he wants to know. "A good-looking woman like you with a big camera like that? Why isn't *he* carrying it? Where are you from? Ah, very cold, *sí*? You are staying in San Juan?"

His whole attention zooms in on her, just as she is zooming in on him. God knows what bondage fantasies are pulsating through his little chauvinist mind. Scary. But Dinah has been dealing with sexist cops for years. She hides the smirk behind her cupped hands as she lets him light a cigarette for her. It looks like we are not going to be told to leave immediately, after all.

The amorous cop is jerked back to his senses by a burst of agitated jabbering from his hand-held radio. His eyes quickly refocus. He stiffens as he takes in the sight of the four Indians with their dozens of "prisoners" on the *Santa María*. His eyes narrow as though pantomiming somebody discovering something unbelievable going on in front of their eyes. Remember, he only sees the images: the warpaint, the warbonnets, the war-drums, the war-club, while facing the Apache Redskins, or whatever they are, as obedient as prisoners of war, a couple of dozen Spanish crewmen are sitting and squatting. Handcuffed? Legcuffed? He can't tell. The drums and chanting echo across the waters of Puerto Del Rey. Is someone being tortured? What the hell has he stumbled into? His expression is so comical it doesn't occur to me to worry about what he is trying to say into his hand-held as he fumbles to give his report. Whatever it is, he has to repeat it, trying to keep his voice low, turning his back on us.

They must have been already well on their way—they couldn't have responded that quickly. It is mere minutes later, it seems, when I notice that other cops are unobtrusively moving into position. There are more sailors and yachts people and marina staff crowding in around the *Santa María* every moment, lured by the drums and the commotion, with the cops mingling and trying to make themselves as invisible as they can, which is tough given their black leather Dark Force stormtrooper gear—the truncheons, pistols, boots, whatnot.

A build-up, that's what's happening around us. A very rapid build-up.

I have, of course, figured out where I'm going to stand when the shit hits the fan. As close as I can to Dinah, right? After all, I tell myself, my job will be to protect her. Besides, if you are going to hang out with guys from a matriarchal society for too long, something of their attitude is bound to rub off on you. There is the recent example of Lloyd, lying down on the floor beside the older woman during the robbery, as a model.

Apart from Dinah, there doesn't seem to be a single other female in the crowd, which is up to probably fifty or sixty visible players and onlookers now, although it is impossible to say how many more might be watching from hiding on the other boats, peeking through portholes, or spying from rooftop positions on the shore. For that matter, how many guys in this crowd are undercover? As the situation settles into a stalemate—with Art stoutly declaring "I am not giving this ship back until the Spanish consulate comes down here and apologizes to our people"—I amble with studied nonchalance down to the end of our dock and surreptitiously check out the shore through my binoculars. My heart does a little flip when the first army truck comes into focus. Yep. That would be military, all those young guys climbing out with the rifles.

So they *are* taking it seriously.

A binocular scan of the rigging of the *Pinta* from this angle reveals a gentleman in camouflage gear, rifle cradled in his arms but still fortunately aimed skyward, perched on the mast above the mainsail, and hidden from the *Santa María's* view behind a fold of canvas. Okay. What else? Maybe it's time we *did* call this off, before someone gets hurt. Forgetting to be covert, I start nervously panning my binocs along the storage sheds, offices, clubhouse, parking lot, and fuelling dock on the shore. Oh God. A sniper on the roof there . . . another guy over there . . . behind that . . . inside that . . . All with scoped weapons, flak jackets, antennaed helmets. Fully alert now, my eyes rake the water. Sure enough, over there behind the *Pinta*, a line of bubbles on the surface: one diver, at least, maybe two. What the hell are they doing—surely not checking for limpet mines?

The boys have still got the drums and the tambourine and the chanting going. I slide back to Dinah and whisper, more unnerved than I want to admit: "Remember the ending to *Butch Cassidy and the Sundance Kid?*"

"Don't worry," she whispers back, having noticed the SWAT-team type in the *Pinta's* rigging. "I just heard, the local cable station's at the front gate. They're not being let in and they're pissed." She nods toward her source, the admiring cop who is busy maintaining a holding position a good ten feet back from the *Santa María*, squelching static from his hand-held as though he's not supposed to be noticed in the crowd but some idiot back at HQ, unaware of the need for deep cover, keeps calling over the radio and our boy Romeo can't turn the damn thing off.

So—we are saved! When no one's looking, Dinah and I give each other the thumbs-up. *The Local Station is coming! Ta rah!* If this was a movie, the theme music would signal the approach of the U.S. Cavalry. It is a known media effect that once the ratio of reporters and cameras to police and military reaches a certain critical mass, you are almost surely safe—assuming you are up against some kind of rationally organized human force that needs to avoid bad publicity. A mass slaughter of unarmed ethnic protesters performing peaceful civil disobedience and making music is surely way too bad PR-wise to be contemplated at any level in a society as relatively advanced as Puerto Rico—I resolutely still believe this. This is my analysis, and I am clinging to it. *Nobody* will shoot *anybody* in front of the eyes of the "international media." In reality, of course, on this particular stretch of dock, that just means Dinah and me. Not much of a media shield, you might argue. But by our presence, we should set a precedent. There is a foot in the door. Since the "international media" is known to be at the scene of the event *already*, the case for keeping out the local media should be rapidly collapsing up at the front gate, where the guards are belatedly trying to block the advance of the Fourth Estate. The news business here is just as cut-throat and competitive as it is back home. Giving anyone an advantage unleashes the repressed fury of the rest of the pack. It isn't just an issue of keeping out the regional cablevision station any longer, either. The national and big-city media from San Juan are on their way—print, radio, video, wire services—with two live-transmission mobiles dispatched, alongside a host of low-rent stringers and paparazzi looking for a surefire freelance photo sale. Associated Press is rumoured to be sending its bureau chief in person. Hey, we have made it! We are a story!

Now all we have to do is get out of this in one piece. And, boy, do I have to go to the can! I look over at Art Loring, who is still chanting and thumping his Talking Stick on the deck, as though casting a spell on the Spaniards. It is a plaintive, wailing sound, that chant of Art's. Ancient Gitksan? A trickle of perspiration streaks the warpaint on his forehead. He is straining mightily, I realize. We make eye contact for just a couple of seconds, which is enough to communicate his desperation: he has to piss like a horse too. How do you do that without breaking the spell?

The spell is indeed fragile.

Some of the Spaniards onboard the ship are remembering their *cojones*. Although I can't understand a word, a couple of the conversations they are having among themselves take on an angry tone. One of them, I just know, has to be saying something like "Why don't we just kick these assholes overboard? Look at them! They're squirts! What are we waiting for?" I am squirming now, and not just from the urge to pee. If even one of these guys begins to wonder why one of the Indians has such pale skin and blue eyes, The Boys could be in serious trouble fast. But obviously the word has come down from the captain level at least, as it naturally would in such a situation: *Wait, compañeros, sit tight. Somebody upstairs will handle this.* And they are, after all, a highly disciplined crew despite their shaggy, piratey look. The cops, too, are disciplined, and presumably the undercover guys as well. The rest, the gawkers from the marina, are like any other crowd: entertained. I resist an urge to rush along the dock like a barker rounding up an audience for the big show. Besides, no need now. In groups of six (having to *pay* for the shuttle ride, I hear) the Puerto Rican media is pouring in.

It is a wondrous thing, the Attack of the Media Spawn. As a reporter, I have had to take part in enough scrums and pressers and news events to be perfectly aware of the herd impulse that takes over among the poor journalists. It is not, after all, much more civilized than blood sport, and media worker bees do occasionally get hurt. Dinah herself once got knocked down in a scrum and trampled. (Just once, mind you.) With television, it's all "live" until it's on tape or transmitted, and then, wham, it's history. The instant, the now, is entirely the thing, which is why the camerapeople move like a flock of birds (or vampire bats) responding as one to stimulus. It has to be a form of telepathy or a morphogenic field that is so densely packed its members experience the human equivalent of a Vulcan Mind-Meld.

Something happens to the players and onlookers, too. It is the reverse of suspending your belief systems. Instead of having to pretend, as in a movie or book, that what is happening is real, you automatically believe that it *must* be real because the media is there to record it (even if somebody is faking it to begin with). Everybody snaps into their roles, becoming *more* themselves than they were a minute before. After all, they are now portraying themselves, and what other roles have they been practising for all their lives?

With the arrival of the media, even the most restless Spaniards realize that their chance to beat the crap out of their unwelcome visitors has passed. The posture of the police improves slightly as they sense that events have taken a quantum leap in importance. The onlookers manage to look harder. The reporters and cameramen jockey for positions alongside the *Santa María* where they can focus on the scene. The caravel has truly become a stage.

Dinah is still a major hit. The media boys haven't seen a *señorita* with a Betacam on her shoulder before, either. Through them, we learn about what went on at the gate, and we also learn that a major event is about to occur: The Indian Chiefs are on their way, being brought by the police to negotiate a settlement. It seems that their meeting at the Spanish Consulate has been called off because of the "emergency." And not only are the mighty Chiefs Wii Seeks, Tsaskiy, and Gordon Sebastian coming, but the Spanish Consul-General, Raphael Marcus, is rumoured to be planning to come down to Puerto Del Rey to defuse the situation.

Now if only I can keep my bladder under control. I notice Art shakes his head sternly when a Spaniard offers him a swig of bottled water. It looks good. No compromise. Stoicism. But the truth is he doesn't want to worsen his delicate condition, especially not with all the cameras having arrived. There is still definitely the risk of the papers coming out tomorrow: NATIVE PROTESTER WETS SELF. His face is red, and it's not just the heat or the genes. The Boys are all sweating under their bonnets and headdresses, and their warpaint is starting to run, which could spell trouble for Jimmy.

When The Great Chiefs do arrive, they are indeed escorted by police. In terms of dramatic effect, this makes up for the fact that every feather on the boat had been commandeered by the boarding party, so there were no headdresses or even drums left, and The Chiefs, at a glance, are not quite as regal as you might hope. Wii Seeks is wearing his red b.u.m. tee-shirt. Gordon Sebastian and Tsaskiy are in shorts and sandals and tee-shirts, looking like tourists. Only Eugene Pierre has really got his military bearing figured out. He's wearing his Gitksan Police badge and a beret, marching sharply just ahead of The Chiefs as their guardian, shoulder-to-shoulder with what must be, judging from his body language, the top cop in all of Puerto Rico. And just ahead of them, backing hurriedly down the dock, camera rolling: Peter Brown. The phrase, "We've got 'em surrounded" comes to mind.

I must say, Wii Seeks, Gordon, and Tsaskiy have wonderfully determined, serious looks on their faces. Having had no contact with any of them since early last evening, long before the plot to seize the boat was hatched, we have no way of knowing just how pissed off they are going to be with us rebel troublemakers. There's nothing they can do to Dinah, Jimmy, or me, of course, but maybe there's some age-old procedure for excommunicating bad Gitksan or Wet'suwet'en boys who break ranks and do unilateral actions, in which case Art, Lloyd, and Ron could be in for some kind of serious ethnic spanking.

Intercepted by the media, The Chiefs give clip according to their ability. Maybe it's the hangover, or the sun, or the piss backing up, but this spectacle gives me a dizzy sensation, a feeling that Time is a revolving door. Or that I am standing at a place in time where the Past, in the form of caravels and Indians, is encountering the Future, in the form of men (and one woman) with strange one-eyed machines on their shoulders, humanoid slaves being ridden by robot masters. Is that possible? Very! If the future is inherent in the present, and therefore automatically also inherent in the past, maybe I'm getting a glimpse of the blueprint, the DNA, as it were, of the Future, revealed here in this real-life restaging, according to new rules, of the day the Indians and the original conquistadors came face-to-face under the Caribbean sun five hundred years ago. If there is such a thing as collective karma, it just might be that some therapy that the human race needs to experience is being attempted within view of the mass mind. A healing? Reconciliation? Could that be what we are really seeking? Trying to close the old wounds of history. In which case this is an optimistic venture, after all. The painting of Custer's Last Stand in the Sailor's Bar back in San Juan superimposes itself in my mind over the sight of a horde of white guys armed with bazooka-like weapons circling in on a little band of Indians, and the Indians, with a phalanx of cops around them, making their own last stand after all those centuries of losing. Having seen the entire continent overrun by hundreds of millions of invaders from every part of the world and some of the planet's biggest cities sink roots subway-deep in ancient tribal lands, the entire land mass tied so tightly by rails and superhighways that it bleeds, the tribes of Turtle Island would seem to have long since made their last stand, and this can surely only be a mirage, an echo of Little Big Horn.

Being videotaped.

A flurry of negotiation takes place at the *Santa María*'s side. Art Loring has come to his feet (with his thighs pressed close together so it looks like he is standing at attention). The drums stop. Art's voice echoes marvellously (although, to me, it is a little high-pitched) as he announces that, as warriors, he and his brothers have done their duty. They now put themselves at the command of their Chiefs, and will do their bidding. "But, make no mistake, we will not hand this ship back to you unless they instruct us to!" No one blinks at the incongruity of such a statement from the spokesman for a handful of unarmed guys cornered on a boat by ten times their numbers, half of them with guns and truncheons. Instead of exploding in hysterical laughter, the Spaniards go into a huddle around the man I assume to be their captain, which would be Santiago Bolívar, the descendant of Columbus.

A handsome, bearded, aristocratic-looking fellow, immaculate in his whites. I can't get a fix on his emotions. He should be angry about his big moment being upstaged by these clowns. But he is trapped. These are, after all, The Indians, the very people who accuse his family of unleashing a holocaust. He knows, if nothing else, he must tread more delicately than his ancestor. It is a measure of the times—and a rather exquisite experience, I must say, watching him squirm. The Spaniards are joined on deck by the head honcho cop and his entourage of officers. When that confab breaks up, the Top Cop climbs ponderously back onto the dock to talk to The Chiefs. But they are one step ahead of him. It would not do, after all, for The Great Chiefs of the First Nations to deal directly with a mere military functionary, no matter how omnipotent. Which is when Eugene Pierre's moment of destiny arrives. As one Top Cop to the other, it is he who gets to speak on behalf of The Chiefs. Mucho *mano a mano* stuff. He looks the Top Cop right in the eye, standing in the at-ease position, nose-to-nose. This is great! One by one, everybody is getting their Moment. As producer, I can stand back and watch. Savour the performances. Smile a little. And pray they hurry up and get it over with. I try Art's trick of standing at attention.

Finally, thank God, the Spanish Consul-General arrives, surrounded by yet more cops.

Raphael Marcus is short, stout, white-haired, and somewhat harassed-looking, very much with the air of a weary dignitary having to attend to important matters of state. He wades through the media and cops to shake hands with the Chiefs, introduced one by one by Eugene, with the Top Cop right by his side. With boom mikes dangling above the close-packed crowd, Tsaskiy and Gordon Sebastian seem to be dominating the intense conversation that ensues, with Tsaskiy playing the heavy, Gordon assuming his lawyer role, and Wii Seeks nodding a lot, which seems to set the Consul-General to nodding a lot himself—his head bent forward respectfully, eyes on the deck, for all the world like a repentant kid, I think, surprised. I had expected an arrogant bureaucrat, not somebody with his head bowed almost sorrowfully. There is something very Catholic going on here, it suddenly occurs to me. The body language. The bright red crosses on the pennants. The genuflecting before the cameras. And, of course, the sailors with the crucifixes on chains around their necks. I almost want to make the sign of the cross.

Ah, something has been decided! The players straighten, the Top Cop and Eugene turn on their heels and start marching toward the boat, followed by The Chiefs and the Consul-General in a little knot, with the media and *policía* surging around them as though they were celebrities. And for this Moment, they are! One by one they are welcomed onboard by Captain Bolívar himself. He is extremely polite and gracious, shakes their hands warmly and bows. The Chiefs nod stiffly, careful not to smile yet. Good, good. They are playing their roles to the hilt, enjoying themselves to the hilt. Look! A large wooden table has been set up on deck in the shade of the fo'c's'le. The captain seats himself at the head of the table, the Consul-General and a couple of guys in sunglasses and suits whom I hadn't noticed before on one side, Gordon, Tsaskiy, and Wii Seeks opposite them, the Top Cop at the other end of the table. Wii Seeks sits in the middle across from Señor Marcus. I catch a glimpse of Tsaskiy pulling a piece of paper out of his pocket, then the crew closes in around them to listen and the *policía* arrange themselves on the dock, keeping the media back. My God, it's working!

Suddenly, I'm emotional. It passes, but for a few seconds there I think I'm going to cry. At the merest hint of tears, alas, my bladder reminds me that it has priority on the passage of bodily fluids. I grit my teeth and pull my quivering scrotum up higher. Got to remember to yoga breathe. Fuck! Why does the banal always have to intrude? I'm starting to get seriously stressed, and want a cigarette baaaaaaaaad. A sincerely unwanted thought flashes into my mind: During all the great Moments of history, how many of the heroes and warriors and kings and popes were beset by the need to pee? How many bad decisions were made because somebody wanted to get the battle over with? For that matter, when did the sacred act of pissing acquire a bad press? A kaleidoscopic vision swirls through my consciousness: of Caesar pissing, Genghis Khan pissing, Churchill pissing, Hitler pissing, Jesus pissing, the Buddha pissing happily. I hear the clanking of a marching Roman Legion stop, replaced after the barest pause by a *whoosh* like a flash-flood. Help! I could sneak away through the crowd, slink down to one of those docks between the other sailboats, and with everybody's attention on the *Santa María* (including the snipers, I trust), take my chances on getting caught having a whizz. But (a) that would betray the empathetic bond I have with poor Art and the sterling example I set by hanging in (he looks over at me from time to time for sympathy and support), and (b) things are happening awfully fast. The story could climax (another unfortunate image) any minute, and while Dinah will get it on tape whether I'm present or not, I'll miss my chance for that live-on-the-scene standup that makes for great gonzo television.

Besides, the most manly thing Art Loring is doing isn't facing-off against this gang of sailors and soldiers, it's not pissing. Holding it, despite the heat, the pressure, the tension. Holding it for the pride of his people. Holding it for history. Holding it because he's going to look awfully goddamn stupid running to the side of the ship, in the midst of all this pageantry, and squirting into the sea. I wonder briefly if the Gitksan have any initiation-by-torture manhood rituals that would give the brave young Wing-Chief extra strength and stamina in his hour on the urinary cross. There's nothing, I'm afraid, in my background to help me. But I admire his fortitude, and don't want to be less of a man than him. So I hang near Dinah, who is très amused by my dilemma, and wait for something to happen.

A miracle! A mere twenty minutes after they sat down, The Chiefs, Consul-General, aides, captain, and Top Cop climb to their feet like men putting their shoulders under a mighty keel and lifting. Bootheels click. The media stirs. Some monumental decision has been reached with far-reaching effects on the future relations between Spain and the indigenous peoples of North, South, and Central America. Flanked by The Chiefs, Señor Marcus steps to the side of the *Santa María* and looks into the multiple eyes of the cameras. He makes a short speech in Spanish, then holds up the piece of paper Tsaskiy had pulled from his pocket, and begins to read it. Microphones strain forward hungrily. At the end, the Consul-General puts the paper down on the wide wooden railing where the cameras can all see it, pulls a ballpoint from his shirt pocket, and signs the document with a heavy, portentous hand, Tsaskiy and Gordon Sebastian peering with burning intensity over his shoulders. A murmur goes up from the onlookers and there is scattered applause which turns into wider applause, and not just from the onlookers but the crew themselves, until everyone, even a few of the reporters, are clapping. An ovation, for God's sake! The Chiefs' faces are radiant as they look around in triumph, accepting the applause. Wii Seeks turns a full circle, waving like a rock star at the end of a long set.

I am looking around desperately, thighs trembling, trying to find out what the fuck is going on while not losing control of my bladder.

Dinah confers with one of her *policía* admirers, then turns to me, her jaw slightly agape from shock.

"What'd he sign? What'd he sign?" I hiss.

"An apology," she says in a tone of awe. "For five hundred years of oppression."

The drums start beating. The warrior-brothers burst into a high, keening chant.

In the hush that immediately follows, Art Loring announces: "Justice has been obtained. I obey the will of my chiefs and thereby release this ship."

There is an after-the-game jubilance in the air. The Chiefs clamber off the *Santa María*, followed by the cops and consular people. A media scrum of impressive proportions engulfs them, interrupted only when the cameras pivot away, their attention hooked by the sound of approaching drums, to capture the spectacle of the Indian warriors climbing over the ship's railing and jumping onto the dock, led by Art, Talking Stick held high in victory, a ragged, dog-crazy grin on his flushed face.

Our eyes meet. No words need be said. While the other heroes linger to pontificate for the benefit of world public opinion, Art slips nimbly and urgently through the crowd. We meet on the other side, where everyone's back is to us. We fall in shoulder-to-shoulder and march double-time down the dock, past the empty *Pinta* and *Niña*, letting instinct take us directly to the first spot in the shadow of a ship we can find where no one can see us, and with trembling hands, we claw at our flies, and let fly. With the first splash in the ocean, we begin to convulse with hysterical laughter, and stand there, one arm around each other's shoulder, Brothers of the Bladder, pissing joyously, ecstatically, historically into the Caribbean, undoubtedly breaking the anti-pollution laws, so lightheaded by the time we have finished it seems we must surely float away into the air.

18

Counting Coup

The media disappear as quickly as ants when the picnic is over, the Spaniards drift back into their routine, buzzed because now they'll have something to talk about—the day the Red Indians attacked. The snipers have long since vanished and the army trucks are gone, leaving no trace. Like a street scene after an accident, the marina goes back to its languorous routine. We are left, Wii Seeks, Gordon, Tsaskiy, Lloyd, Art, Ron, Jimmy, Peter Brown, Dinah and I, out on the street in front of the main entrance, doing high-fives, hugging, giggling, burbling, having just won an apology from Spain for the oppression of tens of millions of indigenous people in North, South, and Central America over the last half-millennium, and there isn't a taxi in sight. (That's another question: What happened after the big historic scenes? The history texts don't tell us, do they? But I guess everybody just limped or wandered away, or, if they were lucky, caught a cab.)

Finally, a lone taxi shows. Tsaskiy moves faster than anyone else, hails it, and orders Dinah, Peter, and me in.

"I'm buying you guys drinks."

I take it from this we are forgiven for our unilateral action.

Oops, but we're not quite out of it. Just as we are climbing into the cab, a big plainclothes cop whom I'd noticed lurking in the background comes over and announces that he wants to express his happiness that things worked out so well. "I am a Christian. I did not want to hurt anybody." He introduces himself as Detective-Superintendent Manuel Ruisanchez from San Juan. He makes a point of shaking hands with each of us, and there can be no doubting his genuine relief that, for a change, the day has not ended with spilled blood. He is almost giddy. I wonder how many guys he has had to shoot.

"Please forgive us for overreacting," he begs. "We did not know if you were peaceful or not. The message that went to all the police stations in Puerto Rico and all the security forces, the Army, Navy, Air Force, Coast Guard, even the fire departments, all of them, do you know what it said? It was not good. It said: 'Terrorists have seized the *Santa María*.' So we came prepared to—" He finishes the sentence by pointing an imaginary pistol at Wii Seeks's head, pulling the trigger, and saying: "Boom."

A chill runs through me. So that's how close we came! A dangerous game we've been playing, shaving it thinner than we'd really figured on. I don't remember, last night, asking prudently: *How will our action be greeted in a gun culture like Puerto Rico's?* It might have been a good thing to at least discuss. But then we'd have probably lost our nerve. How far were Art and The Boys from having bullets put through their heads? From any number of twitchy trigger fingers. And who'd have been responsible? Hello!

Suddenly, I just want to go home and hide and not get into trouble ever again.

"*Señors*, it is a long wait for another taxi to San Juan," the Christian detective says to the Chiefs. "We have room in our cars. Happy to take you back." There is some shuffling of feet, indicative of a collective quiver of paranoia, but the superintendent seems to be enjoying getting in touch with his nurturing side. Why would he bother to fake being nice, since the Puerto Rican media is already gone, and he could have the shit kicked out of us with impunity? Of course, it might just be that it would be in everybody's interest to see us all moved as far away from the Columbus ships as possible. So Peter, Dinah, and I carry on, unimpeded, with Plan A, and pile into the cab with Tsaskiy, while The Chiefs and Jimmy head over with their new buddy to where the squad cars are parked.

There's no Plan B. We just want to whoop and drink. Our cabbie leaves the cop cars far behind. Impatient to celebrate, I don't want to wait the hour it takes to get to San Juan. No one argues. As soon as a bar appears along the side of the highway, we order the driver to head straight for it. Tsaskiy is good to his word, buying us food and drink.

"You gave us our power," he repeats over and over again, as astonished as the rest of us that it worked. We bask in the glow of the noon news, which leads with shots of the *Santa María,* a wide of the marina, a couple of medium views of army trucks and troops. Cut to a shot of the *Sea Shepherd.* Perfect! Then Art and The Boys beating on drums, police and onlookers milling about on the dock, and there, right in the middle, Dinah, Peter, and me! Now we see the sullen-looking Spanish crew—uh oh, the bad guys. Captain Bolívar himself huddling with his men. Suddenly, the Consul-General reading from the document. The word for apology. The Top Cop giving baritone clip. Wii Seeks saying something that we can't hear because it is muted under a Spanish voiceover—but our paramount chief manages to looks magnificently indignant, despite his red b.u.m. tee-shirt, which, after all, doesn't mean anything in Spanish, and we cheer. And there—sequence out of order—a zoom-in on Tsaskiy and the others negotiating around the table on the deck. I understand why the editor placed that shot there. That's the tableau that will stick in the files for eternity. And, finally, The Boys marching off the ship, with a close-up of Art's victory grin, which says everything except how badly he wanted to pee. Television being what it is, although scarcely a couple of hours old, the footage is history already. By tonight the tapes will be mostly blacked-out, with only a few sound bites saved for the archives.

At our table, we are pretty much satiated. Weak from spent media juice. The rush we get out of seeing our production staged on the little coloured screen in an anonymous bar in a strange country is narcotic-like in its intensity. A good media hit satisfies at many levels. Crudely speaking, you know when you have popped the mass mind. By the time the images you have sent out come boomeranging back via satellite into millions of cathode tubes, and you are sitting in front of one of them, you are in fact back to being part of the mass mind yourself, so you can judge your own shot, how good it is. You get to be audience as well as performer, and you get to applaud yourself: a sort of holographic narcissism . . . or something. The al-

cohol and shrimp sauce and limes are kicking in. And we must remember that the sun is barely over the yardarm.

But the bottom line is, we will be able to say on our deathbeds we
were on TV in Puerto Rico. And when they play the old archival
tapes in the year AD 2492 to commemorate the 1,000th anniversary of Columbus's landing, they will not be able to avoid showing
today's footage. It will go on playing through time until the end of
recorded history. The 2,000th anniversary. The 5,000th anniversary.
The 10,000th anniversary. How long can history be expected to
last, anyway? Our morning's piece of guerrilla street theatre will be
there, a little jewel of a scene from the Early Times, carried right
to the end, probably beyond, after humanity has been crushed under
the ice, because we will surely send out spacepods bearing the trea-
sured tapes of our species' story, and this little scene has a chance to
be in the collection.

A *small* chance, but hey! If we didn't make history, we at least
made the footnotes. What more can you ask? Yay, media team! More
high-fives. More drinks. Of course it is also a sweet, sweet detail that
Dinah and I have a complete five-part news serial in the can, with a
beginning, middle, and end.

This is too good. I make a stab at bumming myself out (just to stop
myself from getting too high) by musing aloud about motivation.
What did I really want out of this situation? There are only strategic
interests, isn't that right? Every creature is out to satisfy its own
needs. What selfish goals have I been serving? Apart from saving
my job . . . Ah, and my reputation. Face. Hey, probably I'm just a
reporter in the tradition of Randolph Hearst, who invented a war
right down here in San Juan simply to sell newspapers.

But Tsaskiy will have nothing to do with such self-flagellation
and absorption. His baritone vibrating, he says something to the
effect of: "We, the Wet'suwet'en, don't believe the individual acts in
isolation. We are a collectivity, first and foremost. It's exactly like
this thing we just did: individuals show up to play the roles that
need to be played, captain, chief, warriors, but what we do is always
determined by the actions of others around us. On our own we can't
do sweet bugger-all. There's no such thing as an act that isn't a col-

lective act. We all share the responsibilities. We all share the victories. We do things for *all* of us, not just ourselves. It's impossible to do otherwise. If there's something to be ashamed of, we share that too . . ."

Ah, it is the voice of the hereditary chief of the Wolf Clan that I hear speaking now—clear, knowing, open. I glimpse the gift for oratory which makes him also a political leader. Dinah, I can see, is slightly mesmerized, digging this unseen side of old Grizzly Bear Tracks. Of course, she didn't see him in action back in the Turks and Caicos, rounding up supplies for the troops. He has, after all, been somewhat preoccupied with the distant constitutional wars, and wasn't fully engaged on this voyage until now.

"But what Bonehead's getting at," Dinah says, disrespectfully, "is *why*? Why are we really here, doing this? There's gotta be subconscious forces at work. Maybe even some weird historic shit coming down."

Tsaskiy nods solemnly.

He suggests we gave them a chance to atone, to seek redemption. They're Catholics. They *ought* to go for it, eh? Actually, atonement and redemption are big words in Wet'suwet'en thinking, too, he adds. "You know, what happened today? It was a spiritual thing, which means it helps everybody's evolution. You have to understand that political and spiritual development go together."

You could see it in Art Loring's eyes when he climbed off the *Santa María*, with an almost rubbery post-coital twist to his grin, and it wasn't just the urine backing up in his system. After five hundred years of being hit on, a Red Man had symbolically counterpunched and floored a European cultural projection. Sure, it was *just* a media score, with virtually no usable additional political clout gained, or even any diplomatic leverage that anybody could apply, but it was a mountain that had been climbed, a spiritual mountain maybe, and coming down from it, Art and The Boys looked lit from within. This would go down in Gitksan and Wet'suwet'en legend, for sure.

"You know what the fuck this whole exercise was about?" Dinah demands. "Forgiveness!" She jabs a finger at Tsaskiy. "They've apologized. You guys have to forgive now."

Was that the game? To set up a situation where atonement, redemption, and forgiveness could occur and resonate through the
electronic skin of the world? I think about it. Forgiveness. If the Jews
could forgive the Germans, and the Muslims could forgive the
Hindus and the blacks the Afrikaners and the Chinese the Japanese
and the Macedonians the Turks, and everybody apologized, and
meant it, political miracles of liberation from the vicious circle of
history might actually become a fact of global life . . . Big-picture
stuff. And who sent us? "It"! We laugh a trifle hysterically.

But there are still niggling little practical things to do. Mop-up
stuff. Soon, dutifully, we are back in the traffic grinding and butting
our way into downtown San Juan. Tsaskiy hauls out his cellphone,
like a sheriff drawing his .45, and gets talking to Ottawa. He in-
structs his aides to get the fax machine ready for a major press
release.

"We'll be writing it as soon as we get to the hotel," he announces.

"We," I gather, means me. Well, why not? For this, I'll come out
of retirement. In my PR days, I must have ground out a hundred
releases. One more, a freebee, won't hurt, especially on the occasion
of Spain's apology to the indigenous peoples of North America. For
me, secret PR agent man, it is a final little counting of coup.
Absolutely, my chief! I will be honoured to write the most historic-
sounding release imaginable. I know the cadences. I know how to
make it roll sonorously. It will be a press release with the rhythm of
the wind in the cedars, the pulse of the ocean breaking on barnacled rocks, a drumbeat in the great Prairie Earth, maybe even a
shushing of jack pines clinging to lichen-mottled rocks. The booze I
have had so far, lack of sleep, lack of anything to eat but pizza and
shrimp, and now one cigarette after another, *could* be getting me
slightly wasted, but nevertheless it seems to me, in all seriousness,
that deeper than my pleasure at being here as a television docu-
mentarian, and deeper even than my secret pride in being a radical
flack (rad-flack, I like that!), there lurks a sick desire to write the
Great Canadian Press Release. My innermost private *goal. That's* the
secret selfish thing, the dark truth, the great collectivity be damned!
This is what I was born for: to write the release about Spain apolo-

gizing to all the Indians. Hey, I have written historical non-fiction in my time, but from the usual distance. This, on the other hand, is a matter of cranking out almost primary material.

I do write it. It is a magnificent release, everyone agrees. It is a nice, clean thing, yet it piles up gravitas. The words arrange themselves like the footpads of distant elephants marching. I've got some chicken wings in me now. I am unstoppable. Another package of cigarettes. Somebody brings a rum-and-Coke. It is truly a gestalt. I am using an electric typewriter supplied by the hotel. There are no carbons, there is no memory. I should know better, but what choice is there than to plunge ahead with a single copy? Tsaskiy, Wii Seeks, Gordon Sebastian, and I huddle together in a room overlooking the poor industrial-wasteland waterfront, and they throw triumphant lines for me to quote while I put together the narrative. Datelined San Juan, naturally. Yes. A few nice journalistic riffs, the slant built right into the structure itself, a certain elegance in the way the significance of the action is spun, a subtle shading of values, almost a signature layering of catchy phrases, just a touch of searing rhetoric. We manage to catch the essence of what has transpired here today, and what we want to say about it (and this is the art) from *our* point of view, the Indigenous Peoples of North and South America. However, there is soon so much excited jabbering going on, I am quickly driven insane, until I yell at the others to shut up and let me start writing. The rest of the job is done mostly by telepathy. Minimal verbiage. I concentrate on the page. The words start to flow, squeezed out by some inner, probably collective, subconscious, group mind. They are not just *my* words. They are *our* words, and we are all amazed at how it happens, the electric typewriter almost like a Ouija board taking command. Somehow, I become the instrument of their urges to communicate. A slave, again! At the end of it, as I type 30, my hereditary-chief friends applaud. I rise from the typewriter and take a bow, thinking perhaps this is one of the major moments in my life, somehow.

Alas, it is Wii Seeks himself who decides to take charge of the Sacred single-copy Press Release, and I worry briefly that as the Senior Hereditary Chief, he might get distracted by affairs of state, and lose temporary track of what should be his singular humble mission in life, namely to get this magnificent, historic two-page piece of rad-flack poetry down to the boys at the hotel front desk who are in charge of the fax machine, and who go off shift in half an hour. The full resources of the Native Council of Canada are at our disposal, Tsaskiy's staff in Ottawa standing by with the media lists cocked. But when I dare to wonder aloud if Wii Seeks is the right guy to be heading off with the one and only copy of my (pardon me, *our*) little masterpiece, I am immediately chastised. Wii Seeks is hugely indignant at my impertinence, and insists that he will get the release there on time: "I just have to take the elevator five floors. What can go wrong?" I cringe but then think: *Hey, things have worked out so well so far, we must be on a karmic roll. Trust the Collectivity! Let go of vain individualistic urges to control! Be one with your brothers . . .*

Wii Seeks did reach the front desk, but not before the people who ran the fax machine had long since gone home for the night, locking the office door behind them, and no one else knew how to get in. Apparently, he did drive around in a taxi trying to find a fax machine in the petroleum-haze San Juan night, a noble effort, but everyone else was closed down, too. And somewhere along the way the Great Canadian Press Release got lost and probably wound up drifting in a gutter along with the other litter until the rain turned it to mush and it got washed down into a sewer . . .

Reality as art? If you wrote this kind of stuff into a script, you'd be accused of being heavy-handed in your dark Canuck nihilism. And what are we to learn from this? Something about hubris, I presume.

Ah, no. I remember now. Dinah put her finger on it: Forgiveness. I must forgive Wii Seeks, just as he must forgive Spain . . .

So we get on with the partying, which continues for the next fourteen or so hours.

First there is a major reunion with Art, Ron, Lloyd, and Jimmy at the Sailor's Bar, and we find out what happened to them after we took off in the taxi from Puerto Del Rey. They had climbed into the squad cars, feeling a little on the nervous side, having been arrested so often in the past, and found themselves—not exactly to their liking—dispersed among three vehicles, sitting beside Puerto Rican cops who were friendly enough, sure . . . But then, a few miles down the highway (this is why we lost them), the lead cop car carrying Wii Seeks and Gordon had veered into a police station, and stopped, the other two pulling in behind. "Uh oh," thought Gordon, "this was all an elaborate deception to lure us here, and now they'll bust us. Off we go to the Spanish Inquisition." But no, it was just so Detective-Superintendent Ruisanchez could attend to some quick bit of business, namely dropping off the shotguns and rifles. The other cops all laughed when they saw how stressed their paranoid guests looked sitting parked outside the cop shop . . . From there it was straight into San Juan, up the gangplank of the *Sea Shepherd* to drop off gear, and from there to the Sailor's Bar—where our boys are celebrities! And we, their media entourage, are good buddies too, worthy of free drinks, including tequila. Oh, just *one*!

I am cured for a while, I realize. The disease has run its course. I don't need any more madness. I am overwhelmed, now that we are safely through the pass, with a desire to get home to my family, and never leave. We could have got hurt out here. For a piece of paper that is probably already lost. I have been in the grip of weirdness. Let me go home—and by that, I mean let me find that little cave of sanity, hidden away, where we can huddle and be safe, and not take chances. Ah, but why kid myself? After a few weeks of playing house, I will be restless again. There doesn't seem to be any peace. Maybe there shouldn't be. It is a strange sport, media-eventing, but what a rush! I am feeling alive, *sí*?

I get through to Roberta from an outdoor public phone with diesel buses and trucks going by, a lot of shouting in the background, and a bad connection, but the telepathy must have been working because she started getting a feeling of excitement and jitters about five hours ago. A few minutes ago, driving home along the 401, she barely heard something on the radio above the traffic about an apology and the *Santa María*. "But I couldn't get who was apologizing to whom. Did you guys run into them?" She can tell enough from the satisfied chortle in my voice: "You old shit-disturber, you did *something* you shouldn't have."

"Don't wash," I croak hungrily.

She laughs. I am forgiven. I am loved again.

"So," she concludes, "I take it you're back in touch with the monster within?"

I growl.

My son Will gets on the phone: "Did you kick butt, Dad?"

I make gross devouring sounds.

Lord, how life scares me! How fitting, I think. How perfect in the Zen sense. We set out to do television. It took a bit of pushing, but we got what we needed in the can. And now here, in real life, is a television ending—a family sitcom, no less! In the end, old Dad finds his *cojones*, kicks butt, and gets Mom hot for him again. Lord Shiva, who writes this shit? You can't have hokey stuff like this! Now I go home and get laid, right?

It can't be too soon. We end up that evening, the entire crew, Vegans, Veggies, Meaties, and Trappers, reunited for the big victory blast, in a large hotel room, with cases of beer piled up in the kitchen. Captain Watson himself expresses formal satisfaction with our achievements. He's in a terrific mood, having spent the afternoon at the casino, winning seven hundred dollars, while we fought the Spanish Empire. It is amazing. Even the sullen Vegans seem at least respectful. Suniva Bronson, the skinny Vegan-in-love, was the first to break ranks and come over and start hugging the war party as we filed in, breaking the my-lips-will-never-touch-lips-that-have-touched-flesh rule. Even Ian Bamfield, the hardest core carrot-lover, came around to Revolutionary Handshakes and embraces. Jimmy Liebling is welcomed back into the fold of the untainted ones with more handshakes and hugs. He was, after all, the lone professed believer in the Vegan Code actually in the thick of the fray, so he is politically useful to them again, is how I read it, cynical old dog that I am. The prodigal Veggie son. At some point, Art Loring raises his hand and hushes us to make the announcement that because of his courage in joining the battle as a warrior-brother, Jimmy Liebling is being invited to join the Eagle Clan, as a full blood brother, an honour never before bestowed upon a white man.

While everyone else is cheering, I have to fight back an urge to yell, "For Christ's sake, don't you remember whose idea this was, who insisted on the feathers and paint, who got us into the marina, it was me, me, me, me!" Fortunately, I am able to mask this burst of immature, egocentric petulance, and make myself clap and grin along with the others, so that no one suspects that I could be so childish, so ungenerous, so jealous, so petty, so unbrotherly. Brooding hugely in secrecy, I party bravely on, trying to be satisfied with basking in what slight glory there is to be had in being a behind-the-scenes operative instead of an on-air personality. Unrecognized, unheralded. A faceless backroom guy. An adviser. An aide. A gofer, basically. Still, I am saved from a complete crash into the pit of self-deprecation by virtue of being a bona fide member of a returning media boarding party, having counted serious coup, and there are, among the Veggies, a couple of young ladies who seem interested in what I have to say, or at least who are kindly pretending to be. It is a sweet-enough ego-stroke to keep me from whining aloud about having being deprived of probably my one chance in life to be adopted as a member of an Indian clan. But hey! Not everybody can be a winner.

To our amazement, we are joined by Detective-Superintendent Ruisanchez and half a dozen of his men, all of them in business suits. Much coming and going. Hotel staff keep bringing in more pizzas and Chinese food. I gather we are local celebrities for the night. The party spills out into the hallway, but no one complains. These cops can really knock it back! Somewhere in the evening, we discover that the cops got a very big kick out of us tweaking the Spanish like that. It has not been all that long since the Spaniards were the colonial masters here, and the residual nationalist bitterness has not had time to drain away. We would seem to have tapped into that. Nationalism! I always get nervous around it—such an easy thing to tap into. (Want to get the peasants worked up? Wave a flag!) My view is that, as an intellectual achievement, nationalism ranks with athlete's foot. Naturally, I do not espouse this view on foreign soil. Especially not at the point in the celebrations when I see the Superintendent wearing the Sioux warbonnet and dancing to Fifties rock 'n' roll with a Vegan lady.

Paul and I click glasses several times on the balcony. Good moments are a great thing. It seems to me I see another scene superimposed on this one: *Another lifetime . . . a mountain pass . . . still the two of us . . . I am sure . . . We fought together against a common foe . . . Victory was ours . . . Maybe defeat too . . . We are getting back on our horses . . .* Ah, the hallucinatory power of good Spanish wine! Thank God Spain folded like that, otherwise we'd have had to boycott the stuff, which would be stupid here in San Juan. Long may we boogie unscathed!

A moment comes when Art Loring and I are standing shoulder-to-shoulder, surveying the party, and I get around to telling him the story of my Huron connection, which I hadn't mentioned to him yet, and the tale of the Huron trapper finding me in the forest just in the nick of time, and, finally, I blurt out the story of my mother's death, the Medicine Man coming, the lightning bolt that seared the hair on my brother's arm. My years of doing media for the Kwakiutl. The dance in the Big House at Alert Bay. Writing that book. And now being here, involved in this. It must add up, make sense. But I can't see it. Serendipity isn't an answer. I *know* something must be going on, but what is it?

Art has followed everything I said with grave concentration. When I am finished he nods, as if it is all so obvious it hardly bears repeating—a truth as big as the sky. "The spirit lives on the mother's side," he explains.

Ah! And for a second I *see* it, glimpse behind the veil obscuring the inner world. It triggers a quake of emotion. I blunder onto the balcony, turning my face to the smog-wreathed lights of the city so no one will see the tears pouring down my cheeks. Once again— what a day!—I think I understand: it was somehow my mother's spirit *that made all this happen.* I am content to accept this as the literal truth. A spirit that just touched me and set me in motion to do its bidding. Something. Another "It."

Later: I am still on the balcony, one arm around Paul, another around Lloyd Austin, who has an arm around a plainclothes detective, and we are singing along to "Hey Jude" with the lights of San Juan spilling away into the blackness of the sea, steam coming off the palm fronds in the sulphur light, ground-level ozone draped like a see-through gown over everything. More things undoubtedly happen, but I am losing it. Much to my shame and horror, I am starting to lust after certain youthful female crewpersons.

As she had promised to do should I become unfit to make decisions for myself, Dinah steps in and gets me out of there. "Move, bozo. Time to go nightie-night." Yes, ma'am, whatever you say. A female authority figure, that's what I need to extricate myself from any unintentional entanglements, intriguing as they may be. But I can't say that aloud. Can't shape the words. Tongue too thick. She gets me to the ship. Somebody takes over from there and half-drags me up to my cabin.

Morning. I am sitting, one hand cupped over my eyes to keep the light out, in a booth in a restaurant, trying mechanically to force some eggs and toast and bacon down, not quite sure how I got here. I was walked over to this table by somebody guiding me by my elbow, pushed gently down into the chair, and abandoned. At least they saw fit to arrange for me to be fed. I must be trusting. Someone will come and get me when I am finished. They will not leave me alone to die. My head and body feel like they are made out of concrete and not really joined, just piled one on top of the other. I wish it was all over. I am in pretty bad shape. I find a half-finished package of cigarettes in my shirt pocket. Thank God. I smoke one. Even though I want to throw up, and I start hacking immediately, that feels better. Great. I am back to chain-smoking immediately, of course. So now I will have to go through withdrawal all over again when I get home. Almost as bad, I discovered this morning that the Valiums were all gone. Somebody must have got at my stash. I couldn't have munched them all. *I'll kill the fucker!* I have to unclench my fists, decouple my jaws, and try again to yoga-breathe. Easier said than done. The trouble is, my plastic cigarette is gone too, wouldn't you know? And who took that, for fuck's sake? No Valiums, no plastic. Far, far too early to start drinking. And we are about to plunge into the labyrinth of the San Juan airport, which we have already been warned is one of the worst in the known universe for bureaucratic intransigence. Smoking allowed anywhere? Dream on, junkie-boy. That would be like getting away without being punished for bad behaviour.

As I wait for whoever it is who is going to rescue me, I hear Art

Loring and Jimmy Liebling in the booth behind me. I am still smouldering with jealousy over not being offered Brotherhood, so I eaves-
drop, partly just to make myself feel worse. Apparently I am such a
twisted low-life form that I enjoy rubbing salt into my own wounds.
Suffer some more, Bob, you're not suffering enough!

Art is explaining to Jimmy what his duties and responsibilities
will be as a blood-brother of the Eagle Clan of the Gitksan Nation.
He will have to memorize the names of all the Chiefs, and there
have been a staggering number of them.

"All of them?" I hear Jimmy inquire weakly.

Definitely. And not only all of the Chiefs over the years as far
back as the oral tradition goes, but the names of all the Wing-Chiefs
too.

"Really?"

There are the special days with the special rituals that have to be
performed and the special observances. The Dance of This and the
Harvest of That. He will, of course, have to learn to speak Gitksan.
And there are the potlatches, which he will have to attend every
year, bringing gifts for his new family.

"How many are there?" Jimmy's voice is almost inaudible now.

How many? Art starts rattling off names. He is still rattling them
off when Dinah appears and signals for me to stand and walk. Time
to go. The last thing I hear Art doing is telling Jimmy how potlatch
gifts that only cost a few dollars are okay for most of his new relatives, but for the Wing-Chiefs and Chiefs, you should by rights
be shelling out at least twenty-five bucks each . . . I am cackling
silently, insanely, at the weird Zen ways of Fate, as I shamble along,
following Dinah. She frowns at me, thinking I am losing it.

But somehow a lingering question has been answered. I, who
wanted so badly to be an Indian, who worked so hard at it, who
put in dues, who found a blood connection, for God's sake, am
now suddenly noticing that we are, after all, just talking about another cultural metaprogram, another bureaucracy, another mind-
lock, another imaginary state, another theocracy, another oligarchy,
another systematized delusion, another control group, another . . .
myth: a myth of names and festivals and dances and costumes and
gifts and language.

There would be a downside to tribalism, of course! You would have the tribe, well and dandy, but then the tribe would have *you*, wouldn't it?

It is good that I have had my de-revelation, so to speak, early, because a scene of almost medieval horror awaits us at the airport, and there is no point being in a visionary mode. Better to pull into a shell and grunt, expecting the worst.

The roaring of the jets through the shimmering heatwaves of the airport parking lot is like chained dragons. We are about to try to cross the castle's drawbridge—and I have not been able to find my passport anywhere! This will not be good. I am going to suffer. But I have to try to get out of here. I have to go home. The trip is over. I am burned out. Let me go. But no. First the long lineup in the jungle heat. The whole process with the tickets, the credit card, and bad moment when the passport request comes up, and I start my explanation of why I don't have it, but how we don't have to worry, do we, because I am a Canadian, and Canadians don't have to show passports to get in and out of the U.S.A. or its protectorates. But, as feared, this does not work. The ticket agent is out to assert his power. I quickly start snarling. Dinah tries to intervene, but she doesn't have her passport either, so we are both shunted aside. I raise my voice, *something you must never do in airports*. I know this, but I am having another nervous breakdown, you see.

Dinah keeps me under control by a combination of kicking my ankles, elbowing me in the ribs, and slugging me on the shoulder. All I want to do now is howl like a thing in a trap.

It is looking like the end, one more time, when First Mate Angela Moore shows up out of nowhere and immediately takes over negotiations with the uniformed officials who have been summoned to keep Dinah and me isolated. The fact that our flight will be leaving shortly makes no impression on said officials. After much palavering in Spanish, Angela vanishes, and I think we'll never see her again, only to fall to my knees in thanks for salvation when she returns within half an hour with our passports, having miraculously found them somewhere. More than that, the Irish lass charms the main official into taking the unheard-of step of leading us through a maze of hallways and hangars at a gallop, taking a backroom shortcut to our departure bay, arriving at our jet with just seconds to spare, the hatchway already closed and the engines started. They halt everything and pop the door back open.

Angela confides: "They're actually very glad to be getting rid of us."

We hug our guardian angel goodbye, drag our bags up the ladder into the plane, the stewardesses (sorry, flight attendants) grabbing our stuff and stashing it for us and pushing us along. Like survivors crawling ashore, we collapse into our seats, sweating, gasping for air, lips dry and cracked, kneecaps wobbling, immediately buckling in, and seconds later feel the plane start rolling.

The next day, on the flight from Miami to Toronto, Dinah picks up an edition of *U.S.A. Today* and finds a story datelined San Juan, which mentions our little action. Just a couple of lines, ending with: "The protesters criticized the treatment of British Columbia's Indians by Christopher Columbus and his crew."

Not that the bastards ever came within three thousand miles of any such folk. And lucky for them, eh?

19

To the Powwow, with Expenses

There was a time when I longed for air travel. My earliest memories include a recurring dream of levitating just a couple of feet above the ground, which later grew into an ability to skim through the air above tree level, although it was always a strain to get started. *This*—being squeezed into an aisle seat on an Air Canada flight from Toronto to Edmonton—is a corruption of the very concept of flight. They shouldn't be allowed to advertise it as "flying." This isn't flying. This is being digested by a robot. I think the word "Help!" But there's no hope of an answer from God, and yelling it out loud wouldn't do me any good either. They'd just cut me off from the drinks, the bastards. The panic-darkness throbs under the canopy of my brain. I resort to yoga-breathing and reading *The Globe and Mail* right down to the editorials.

According to the editors, the land below (which I can't see because of the astonishing spread of pollution even across the pristine northern prairies) is writhing in the final contractions of the Great Constitutional Referendum. The fact that it is called the Charlottetown Accord gives me the heebie-jeebies, as though some ancient stratum had slipped loose from history and was tumbling around, smashing against different levels of our current society, threatening the whole thing with avalanche. Ah. Sigh. Apocalypse everywhere. Global warming. Constitutional discord. No cigs. *Help!*

I am hardly fit, it would seem, for the mighty deed I have presumably been called upon to perform; "presumably" because I don't really know what I'm expected to *do* when I arrive at my destination. It was all very vague over the phone—for security reasons, I gathered. At least, that's what Leonard Horse, the Medicine Man who called to invite me, implied when he said, "Don't wanna spill too much over the phone, eh?"

"Right on," I had correctly responded. But now I wish I'd asked a few more questions. Instead, as usual, I was a sucker for a Medicine Man. All I know is that it's a Sacred Powwow, and a "select group of white environmental types" have been asked to take part in an exchange of ideas, plotting a harmonious course with Red Power, etc. Common ground stuff.

"There won't be any speaking fee or anything like that," Horse added, testing me.

I fail, of course. "Well, it's an honour, but I don't have a personal budget for travel."

"No problem. We'll cover your plane tickets."

How could I refuse? Isn't this what I've almost always wanted to do: sit down with the leaders of the Red Power Movement and forge a coordinated strategy, just as we forged an alliance between conservationists and the anti-war movement so long ago? Grand geo-mystical thoughts.

But here I am, feeling like a piece of shit in a sardine can. Also, as usual, I haven't had any time to prepare, and I don't have a single coherent thought on the matter. I am certain there's a Teaching of some kind to be learned—this has become an itching in the back of my mind; and, naturally, I am hoping the itch will be soothed in the course of the powwow; just give me a revelation, a Path, a calling that will finally make sense out of the disjointed fragments of my chaotic life. That's a lot of burden to put on one little gathering of marginalized characters. I dunno.

It's also ego, of course. I was proud of that *Santa María* caper, but since getting back, I haven't had a single person remark on it, other than to have producers tell me it wasn't "as compelling television" as the drift-net trip, presumably because ships weren't actually smashing into one another. Somewhere out there, near Lillooet, B.C., I can tell myself by way of conciliation, there's a document signed by the official Spanish representative in San Juan apologizing for five hundred years of oppression, but since then, absolutely *nothing* in the world has changed one iota. All that happened, really, was that the professional diplomats smoothly dusted our little escapade into the black hole of minor media events.

We land in Edmonton in the midst of snow. At a place called Big Valley to the south, a major Bryan Adams rock concert is being wiped out by the snowstorm. I am wearing running shoes, with no long underwear or gloves, and only a light jacket. Where did sweet Southern Ontario September go? The closer I get to the Indians, it seems, the further away summer gets. I'm reading too much into things, aren't I?

There is a fine sense of emergency in the airport. Flights are delayed. Some are actually cancelled. It is a miracle we got in just ahead of the storm front ploughing down from the Yukon. I recognize a couple of faces—one is my old eco-war *compañero*, Rod Marining, who had once been the Non-Leader of the Northern Lunatic Fringe of Abbie Hoffman's Youth International Party. The former yippie had mellowed, of course. That is, instead of leading people's uprisings in threatened parkland in Vancouver or hitchhiking up to Alaska to jump onboard a protest ship en route to a nuke test, Rod had somehow landed a job as a civil servant working for the British Columbia government, and had stayed there—to the astonishment of his revolutionary buddies—for a couple of decades, monogamously married, raising a family, living in suburbia. His hair had been cropped, and while he still sported a full beard, it too had been trimmed. That was Rod, twenty years later: cropped and trimmed. Well, who was I to feel superior, reduced to being a mere reporter again? I had a dangerous (that is, debilitating) thought. Were Rod and I here for the same reason: to get back a sense of radicalism, which, for us, might equate with identity? This *could* turn out to be quite pathetic: old warriors stumping back to the field of glory, looking for the souls they lost somewhere along the way . . . *Now, Bob, it's been a rough ride, and it's snowing, and you're not dressed for it as you head up into the Rockies. But you've got cigarettes now. You can face anything.*

The other recognizable face belongs to Walrus Oakenbough (aka David Garrick, a geography graduate from Trent University), who retains both his long hair and his drooping, walruslike moustache. We served in the whale, anti-nuke, and seal campaigns together until having a political falling-out and almost coming to blows. That was a long time ago. I can scarcely remember the issue. It doesn't matter any longer. It is just good to see an old familiar face. We inquire about each other's kids. His are over in Japan, with their mother, and he hasn't seen them for years. So there is a certain bruised feel to Walrus. I introduced him to his ex-wife, so there is lots of subtext to our relationship.

I don't have to ask why *he's* here. Walrus has never lost his infatuation with things Native. He had travelled to Wounded Knee with Paul Watson, back in the early Seventies, and for his work under siege conditions had also been given an Indian name by the Sioux: Two Deer Lone Eagle. Walrus is, in fact, a walking encyclopaedia of aboriginal information, and while working the past few years as a research assistant for an NDP MP in Ottawa, he had never stopped trying to get the political Left, the eco-movement, and the Natives in step with each other. If anybody was responsible for the network that had arranged for this powwow, it was probably Walrus.

Rod and Walrus introduce me to five Native women, led by a New Age-style Métis lady named Alice, whose face reminds me vaguely of my mother's. The difference is that she's a hard-core feminist crazed-hippie Earth Mother cultist. She's quick to call me "Brother" and let me know that she is a Planet-Healer. These are some "Sisters" from her Circle, some of whom are also members of the Native Women's Association of Canada, which I know from my reading to be quite radical and opposed to the great Canuck Accord because it will perpetrate a male-dominance system on the reserves, leaving women as the second-class citizens they are today. Aha! This will not be lightweight. Political witches, I think nervously. They are attending the powwow to offer spiritual advice, Alice advises me, and to pray for guidance from the Great Mother. She's a splendid entity in her forties—Alice, that is—but she could also be much older and just in really good health.

Desperate to keep the chitter-chatter in the no-smoke zone to a minimum, I make a beeline for the nearest sliding doors to have a butt. Alice, apparently wanting a smoke almost as bad, is right beside me, digging a pack out of the folds of her gypsy-style gown. She wears a red bandana, an embroidered blouse, and a deerskin jacket, with lumberjack boots. As the doors are hissing open, she offers me a smoke, thus immediately becoming my nicotine bud. In unfamiliar surroundings, we junkies bond by the sacred death-pact exchange of tobacco.

"It's the revenge of the Indian," she says, holding a flaring wooden match under my chin. I cup her hands to ward off the wind, and bend for the flame, suddenly aware just how this little ritual could be interpreted by alien observers. ("Note how she offers the sacrament, how he clasps her hands in an embrace and bows to her, accepting the fire. Must be a religious thing.") I drag deep, saved! The smacklike rush.

"Pretty soon the body count should be about even, then," I wise-ass.

Alice takes a second to get it (such dark humour, after all), then laughs and gives me an appraising look.

"They thought your plane was gonna have to go to Calgary because of weather. But you got in just in time," she says. "Good Sign."

My reply sounds so much like a New Age pick-up line that I have to fight back a giggle:

"So what kind of Earth-Healing are you into?"

"The usual," she replies stiffly.

Oops, I'm behaving a little too casually, considering the historical significance of the occasion. I only had time for three beers, but it hits you harder up there. Gotta be more, um, something . . . I go conspirator-to-conspirator: "So what d'you think's going to happen in the next few days?"

She shrugs. "Maybe we'll get our shit together."

"Sounds good to me." But I am still a shade too flip. Her eyes narrow ever so slightly, and I realize she is not to be patronized.

"And then again," she drawls, blowing smoke, "maybe we won't."

"You can't tell with these things," I agree solemnly. That's good. Makes it sound like I go to powwows all the time. Gotta keep my footing here. Groan. Everybody's probably going to be hypersensitive about everything. Especially toward any hint of superiority tendencies on the part of visiting white pig-dogs.

"A lot of the Brothers have trouble dealing with Sisterhood issues," she says slowly.

"Not me," I am quick to reply. "I was raised by a single mother before it was fashionable. I sent my ex-wife to her first Women's Lib meeting, for God's sake."

A bark of laughter. "Not the brightest, eh?"

Whew! We're going to be okay, Alice and me.

It turns out she's the driver of the propane-powered, bent-bumpered, naked-hubcapped, rusting blue van which will be taking us up to a ranch high above the Athabasca River, three hours west of Edmonton. The voyage, I realize glumly, is far from over. And, indeed, soon I am looking back on the two previous three-hour ordeals (across half of Toronto and across half of Canada) as luxurious phases in a pilgrimage that is taking far too long. My back is starting to *really* hurt. Tendinitis throbs in my left foot. The good news is that there are blankets, sleeping bags, and cushions strewn about on a rug in the back of the van—magnificent mildew funkiness! Alas, the springs are nearly shot, the heater only serves the front passengers, and by the time we clear Edmonton, the snow has worked itself up into a froth of blizzard. Alice slows the van down to a crawl. Bald tires, of course. I can't tell if we're going uphill or down, although it *has* to be mostly up.

The engine splutters. It turns out there is a slight technical problem: we're almost out of propane. Somebody forgot to fill up. What? We could freeze to death! We are in the foothills, after all! Night has fallen. The blizzard is approaching white-out status. Where the fuck are we going to get propane at this time of night? We try two service stations, and the operators just shake their heads. A vanload of Indian chicks and aging hippies looking for propane in a snowstorm at night in oil-saturated redneck Alberta could certainly be described as quixotic, if not as a metaphor. No, don't think along those lines . . .

Walrus is sanguine, as ever. Bitter political experience and the ruination of the passionate love he once enjoyed have not corroded his inherent amusement at everything. While I am prone to articulating my discomfort and doubts, Walrus stays pretty much focused on the usefulness of what we are attempting to do. Somewhere back in Vancouver he has a stash of all his journals, going back to the Sixties, which will someday be displayed in an archives somewhere, and they will be deemed one of the great source material records of our time. He is, in fact, a scholar and a sage, but with a helluva temper if riled. At his peak, Walrus/David/Two Deer led a couple of thousand people onto a Trident nuclear submarine base. He was the first guy over the fence, and a mighty cheer went up and a rainbow came out. Ah, Walrus has had his Moment of Power. He is still a little crazy—some people would say a *lot* crazy!—all these many moons later, and the pouches under his eyes are puffier, and there are wrinkles, but he still radiates a palpable psychogravitational field emanating from some iron core of self: a candidate for eco-sainthood when these things are finally handed out.

As we bump along in the snow-blind night foothills, waiting for the engine to make its final propane fart, Walrus keeps our minds off our woes (we are starting to freeze in the back) by telling searing anecdotes, such as the time, during the siege of Wounded Knee, when somebody opened the church door at the end of a meeting of the Lakota Sioux and the American Indian Movement guys, and a U.S. Army bullet came flying straight down the aisle, shattering the plaster statue of Jesus with his bleeding heart exposed.

"And someone said: 'Hey, they shot their own guy!' "

This cracks up everyone in the van. Alice almost loses her grip on the wheel. The snow prompts Walrus to tell stories gleaned from his studies of how the first North American tribes survived the Ice Age by organizing themselves along the lines of a wolf pack, and by imitating the ways of the wolves. We howl, the whole van, for a while. Alice says this weather is Mother Earth testing our worthiness. But we'll be okay. Her Circle prayed.

Rod goes on in rather greater detail than I would like about the political undercurrents of the upcoming powpow, the legal background, even the Constitutional context. I find myself thinking "Help!" again. Rod's eyes dart from face to face in the reflected light of the headlights to see if anybody is following him. Hard to tell. I'm not, that's for sure.

There was a time when I was convinced Rod and I were in routine telepathic contact, and maybe we were, but we are no longer on a ship together. Our separate experiences since then have reshaped us. Then there is the fact, stark as a divorce, that Rod and I too turned on each other politically at a critical juncture, and I do believe the utter life-or-death trust of comradeship and brotherhood, once damaged, can never be completely repaired. But we are comfortable with each other—and I attach more value to that as the years go by. It is as though we mutually draw each other back into a familiar habit of behaviour at least well-known if not well-loved from the storied past. We know our roles so well there is no groping or probing or holding back or fencing. On top of that, we talk in the vernacular of characters from the same novel or movie, even though there have been all these other, seemingly separate subplots and adventures involving other people spliced between our encounters with one another. Yet we each remember exactly where the conversation left off. And, most importantly, we have all completely forgiven each other for our sins. For all our failings, each of us was present during the battles, and in retrospect that experience becomes redemption itself. I must remember this thought . . . it is hopeful.

The "Sisters" have said almost nothing, concentrating on rolling smokables in the dark and passing them along. My mood alters again. This is okay too.

Suddenly, we pull off to the side of the highway, wheels spinning in slush. I switch to full disgruntlement, griping aloud: "This is it, now we're going to have to struggle all night just to stay alive. Shit!"

Walrus shakes his head, sad for me. "Your faith is weak, Uncle Bob."

"Always was," I growl.

But Walrus is right—look to the big cosmic picture, wait, trust—and my pessimism is completely unfounded.

Alice, who has been steering by mystical Sisterhood antennae, has correctly sensed the presence behind dervishes of snow of a gas station and cafe that sells propane, as well as hot coffees and sandwiches. After this, I decide to stay as close to Alice as I can. She immediately gets the title of Earth Mother Figure Supreme, all my awe of womankind returns with a vengeance, and, of course, the good thing about having been raised by a single mom is that I learned how to suck up to women early. I make sure I squeeze in next to her when we return to the van.

"Can I hold that for you? Anything I can do to help? Smoke?"

It's shameless, but I remember Lloyd Austin's brilliant tactic of lying down behind a woman during the stick-up in San Juan. More than that, it's an instinct. Whenever you're in danger, find a woman to save you.

Alice is great. By the time you are forty years old, among aboriginals you are considered an Elder, she tells me. She says she's "just become" an Elder. Adroitly, I mumble that she can't possibly be *that* old. Witch or not, she laughs happily and I notice her knees part a few millimetres, one of those signs us cads learn to watch for. Ah, I'm going to fall in love, aren't I? Well, that'll make it an interesting weekend, for sure.

The last hour of the voyage goes almost smoothly, once you get past the tension of watching the snowflakes and the occasional set of slashing-by headlights coming like meteor storms, Alice handling the wheel deftly, like a star warrioress as we whip through hyperspace, and I recover just a whiff of that old Kerouacian "holy-boy road, madman road, rainbow road, guppy road, any road" feeling, and maybe even a residual trace of a Rainbow Warrior buzz, what with the Fate of the Sacred Earth hanging in the balance as we scurry like Tolkienesque characters along the ramparts of the glacier-damming mountains, unable to see a thing in the blackness and wind-drift.

I do have one genuine heart-stopping mystical moment—something that shakes my habit of cynical disbelief—when, peering at Alice's map with a flashlight, I realize that we are passing directly through the former territory of Michel Calihoo Reserve No. 132! I have been here before! Indeed, all around us must be the rolling sealike hills where Bob Calihoo (aka Royer) and I ventured nearly half a decade ago when we were researching *Occupied Canada*.

What had the size of the reserve been? Something like seven or eight thousand acres. Piece by piece, it had been broken off by Indian Agents and white politicians. As smallpox decimated the Calihoos, killing two out of three, the Canadian government kept revising the size of the reserve downward, according to a phoney formula based on population. On top of everything else, the survivors had to endure the chilling thought that each time someone died, the reserve shrank by another couple of hundred acres. It was a brilliant, if illegal manoeuvre by land-hungry authorities. At the same time, stonewalled by provisions of the Indian Act, the Calihoos were unable to buy the farm equipment they needed. The place was gamed out. Starvation set in. Finally, desperate to scrape together some cash, the last band chief sold off the remaining land. According to the treaties, it could not happen legally. But it did— it slipped through the cracks—and the disenfranchisement of the Calihoos was complete.

So out there in the whirling snow is a place that, when you can see it, looks like prosperous foothills cattle-grazing land, a free, peaceful place in a great liberal democracy. But the secret backstory is as dark as nearly every other story of clearances and occupations and displacements and invasions and refugees and ethnic cleansing everywhere throughout history. This just happens to be one of the Canadian dark places, where we drove people from their land, took it over, and left them destitute and starving, while our people grew rich and smug.

I had not counted on passing through *here*—the infamous place which I had written so passionately about years ago. And me being blind to it as I go along? Am I being told something? Is this intended to stiffen my resolve, make me take things seriously? I sense a metaphor traffic jam. A reminder, at the very least, that this is serious stuff, and I must remember not to be glib or arrogant. I'm going to be hanging with angry people. We have slipped, it occurs to me, into a former war zone, where the remnants of the Prairie tribes, cornered, with their backs to the wall of mountains, surrendered, and were herded off to the reserves. It was here, in these haunted hills, that an epoch of rambling freedom came to an end.

So I am back to brooding on the sadness of life by the time Alice steers us off the highway and down a narrow dirt road into an encampment where half a dozen huge teepees are lit from within by open-pit fires. They stand out in the snow-streaked darkness like fabulous jewels. In the middle, reflecting in gold off the teepee walls, a huge blaze leaps against the surging snowflakes.

Alice says softly: "The Sacred Fire. If it goes out, everything's lost."

Serotonin-deprived as I may be, I dimly perceive the primeval beauty of the scene: a human camp on the edge of the Ice Age. There should be soaring music playing now, lots of woodwinds. But these aren't goosebumps. Mainly I'm just cold. And instead of being thrilled to the marrow of my spirit, as I should be—isn't this the culmination of a nearly lifelong dream?—mostly I am thinking how I will die from exposure lying on the ground in one of those teepees, for sure. I can't believe I didn't bring a sleeping bag. What an ironic ending to my life! Saved as a young man from freezing to death by a Huron, killed off in middle age by pneumonia caught in a teepee surrounded by a whole mess of Indians. I am already coughing in broken-accordion wheezes.

The cough started shortly after I got back from San Juan. I promised the doctor I'd quit smoking if he'd give me some antibiotics. He was a new doctor and didn't realize what a liar I am when it comes to drugs. But it's coming back, the pain between the angel-wings that you want to scratch, but can't because it's coming from inside the rib cage, the attempt by your guts to turn inside out, the chisel-blows against the cracking plaster lining of your throat. Old Death, sitting on my shoulder. If there's work to be done, do it fast, I advise myself.

Fortunately, beyond the teepees is a huge two-storey log house, almost a mansion, blazing with electrical lights. It is the home of the wealthy parents of my beautiful Vegan shipmate from the *Sea Shepherd*, Suniva Bronson, who was apparently more impressed with the meat-eating brothers than she had seemed at the time of our voyage to Puerto Rico. So impressed, in fact, that she convinced her parents to make their ranch available as a location for the major Native/environmentalist powwow we're about to have. Suniva, who is as emaciated as ever, is waiting on the sprawling verandah and seems genuinely happy to see me, even if I was so malicious back on the boat when it came to her deeply held belief system. Seeing her in this context, it seems somehow wrong that she should be so anorexic, what with her folks being so rich. Some kind of Freudian rebellion going on here? Well, how could there not be?

She graciously insists, since I'm not equipped for camping, that I sleep in a room upstairs. A whole bedroom—to myself! Controlling my egalitarian instincts, I do not argue. Walrus and Rod seem to want to sit up and yak all night, but they've come from the West Coast. It's early for them. Besides, I'm older. I crash.

20

Passing the Eagle Feather

I awake to tinfoil light, ponderous flakes of snow marching down from the sky, the popping of firewood, doors thwacking shut, boots clomping, dishes clacking, the house filling up, and somewhere close by horses whinnying. Still jet-lagged, I make my way downstairs to discover that the house has indeed filled up with fifty or sixty people, mostly Native. Ah, but I also hear the familiar laughter of none other than Cap'n Watson himself, who is already spinning sea dog yarns by the fireplace in the main room. This is good reunion stuff. But wait, the captain is not alone. At his side stands his latest warrioress-*compañera*, a Southern belle named Lisa Distefano. They are a spectacular sight, my white-haired buddy in his black *Sea Shepherd* jacket, with his big boots, with a shit-eating grin on his face, and his eco-queen.

She is indeed lovely, with flowing ebony hair, looking smartly military in her own *Sea Shepherd* jacket, with tight black slacks and cowboy boots. She greets me like a long-lost brother. I don't know exactly how old she is, but she is young enough to tell us that when she was a kid she had a picture she'd clipped from a magazine framed on her wall, a somewhat famous photo of Paul and me standing on the ice blocking the path of a sealing ship. She worshipped us, she announces, and had set her mind as early as that on connecting with one of us. The clear implication is that, had I lived my life righteously, I *could* have been the lucky one to be with her as readily as Paul, if, like him, I had abandoned Canada and moved down to Los Angeles, or if I had stuck with fulltime eco-activism and carried on with the battle. Fate? Or brutal karma? With a languid toss of her hair, she indicates I lost, Paul won.

The happy pair are at that early stage in a relationship where the conversation is almost entirely about sex, and about what each other just did or said. She tells us half a dozen times "how incredible this guy is," as if we didn't know. Comrades-in-arms are always taken aback, I guess, when an old buddy's new girlfriend shows up and dominates the conversation, full of herself for having caught his attention, but since none of the rest of us is going to get to make out with her, do we really have to listen to so much ribald witticism or witness so much touching, squeezing, feeling, groping, pinching, pecking, nibbling, and hugging of Paul? For his part, the good captain seems addled by satiation. Nothing wrong with that. It's an animal thing, love. But maybe they should be off somewhere humping while we stern warriors ponder the fate of the planet, undistracted.

The moment the lady is out of earshot—actually physically letting go of him for a minute, to my astonishment—Watson explains that she once appeared in a *Playboy* magazine spread, not as an actual staple-in-the-navel foldout, mind, but still butt-naked as the day she was born. Great! I finally meet an ex-*Playboy* model who once longed for me, but too late. She's already mated with the other guy, and moreover, I notice she quickly shakes off any vestigial hero-worship notions she had about me.

This is the trouble with being a hero. You can never measure up, unless you're willing to get a hernia. Although I suspect she is also trying to subtly depose me as a contender for the captain's ear. She calls Paul "baby" a lot. Hard not to get the feeling that the rest of us are just nuisances in the way of keeping Paul's attention focused entirely on *her*. Walrus, Rod, and I exchange weary seen-it-all-before-with-other-chicks, old-crony looks. How long can this one last?

Wii Seeks is here! We greet each other with firm Revolutionary Handshakes followed by a hug. His return home with the document signed by the official Spanish representative was a triumph, he reports, solidifying his position as a radical Elder. Even the boys on the province-wide Union of Chiefs expressed offhand praise. Big deal for them to say anything.

"Did you ever find that press release?" I blurt, referring to my masterpiece.

He and Paula and Suniva and I all laugh, but the others, who weren't onboard for the expedition, don't know what we're laughing about. There is a bond forever between people who voyage together because they alone will speak the memory-language of the trip. But the bond excludes everyone else. Lisa, I notice, does not like being outside of the loop. Stories about the *Santa María* caper are quickly chopped off.

"Baby, shouldn't we-all be gettin' goin'?" she asks Paul.

"An android!" Rod whispers, as soon as they're gone.

I see it immediately: the battery-pack buttocks, the circuitry under the plasto-flesh, the positronic brain; sent from the future either to keep Watson alive because of some presumably useful impact he will have on history, or to subtly trip him up so that he doesn't do something that's supposed to happen. Depends on which side she's with . . .

While we are having our happy little reunion and getting to know (or become suspicious of) each other in the main living-room in front of the fireplace, there are knots of people all around us drinking coffee, smoking, and talking intensely among themselves, and I sense some sort of slow-motion energy vortex building up. We are preparing to move. For once, I am content to just shuffle along. The group gestalt is completely out of my hands. I'm a visitor here. Except for Suniva and her parents and a couple of ranch workers and one other guy, a bald young lawyer from B.C., we are the only whites here. The rest are Native or Métis, Wii Seeks explains, from as far away as Manitoulin Island, with representatives of the Cree, Saulteaux, Shuswap, Gitksan, Carrier, Ojibway, Blackfoot, and Assiniboine people.

Without me hearing anyone actually give an order or even directions, we find ourselves gently shooed out onto the verandah, looking out over a tableau of gold and red and yellow autumn leaves softened by the veil of falling snow, formlessness in the distance everywhere, the white-cowled shoulder of the barn barely visible across a small field of stippled snow, the teepees speckled with ice, the Sacred Fire still leaping, although there is no one around it. Suniva fixes me up with a jacket and a scarf and woollen mitts, and off we trudge, boots and running shoes making satisfying crunching noises, along a path knee-deep through the piled-up snow, clutching steaming coffees in Styrofoam cups with plastic lids. There is a hint of burnished light gleaming three-dimensionally beyond the incoming crystallized squall. When I focus on a single flake, the whole plunging universe lurches and slows down, although only until the flake enters the nullification zone of the snow on the ground; and for lack of a singular object on which to concentrate, the whole sky goes back to rushing downward until I can find another flake to focus on.

Entering the barn, we climb up a ladder into the loft. I'd forgotten how head-swimmingly glorious is the smell of fresh hay! We settle, easily sixty of us, onto bales that have been pushed onto their sides in a rough circle. Dust motes tremble in the cold grey-white light. We can see our breath. We wrap ourselves in blankets and sleeping bags. Horses are clunking around downstairs while the wind rattles the windows and dogs bark. Two guys carry in a black pot filled with glowing coals and set it down carefully on its three legs in the middle of the loft where the hay has been swept away.

Taking this as a hopeful sign that I might be allowed to smoke, I dig out a cigarette, but several people glare at me immediately, frowning and shaking their heads, not leaving me much room to pretend I don't understand. I fold, avoiding everyone's eyes but Rod's. He has watched my entire humiliation, saddened to see me so reduced in stature by my low-class addiction to cigs. But even though he doesn't do nicotine, he empathizes. I can *feel* a wave of his empathy absorbing a microscopic but welcome-relief bit of my torment. Maybe, once you've shared telepathic rapport, the channel can be reopened no matter how firmly it seems closed. Anyway, I am starting to see things a bit through Rod's eyes, so it all becomes a bit more exaggerated, more animated, enhanced, you might say. I think Rod has a better grasp of the gestalt of a scene than I, who am always striving to record, to memorize, to immortalize, using up too much of my limited attention span on details. He also sees this, I am starting to remember, in some sort of historic context. This is post-Oka, after all, and the environmental movement is perceived by Native activists as being a force not necessarily on the Aboriginal side when the crunch comes. I think that's how it went. Somehow, *we* are going to mend this feeling of alienation. It starts to come back to me from when Rod was babbling about politics in the van when we were looking for propane last night, how important this gathering could be. How we four old-timers—mainly Paul of course, but also Rod himself, Walrus, and I—had been selected, somehow or other (it wasn't clear by whom, except that Leonard Horse, the Medicine Man, and Suniva were involved), to represent honky eco-radicalism at this otherwise fundamentally all-Native and Métis summit.

Hmm. I should have paid more attention to what Rod was saying, but in the depths of my suffering, didn't. And now I am sitting here dumbly trying to follow the intricacies of a political chess game being played out around me by people who have lived on the board all their lives. Just because I wrote a book about their struggle doesn't mean I know anything at all. Everything I wrote might have been wrong. Probably was. Probably?

The Medicine Man and chief organizer, Leonard Horse, stands in the middle of the circle holding an eagle feather between his fingers. He has a great modern Plains Indian look, complete with stitched snakeskin boots, deerskin vest, a crimson silk shirt with flared sleeves, fabulous big rings on all his fingers, hand-wrought metal bracelets and wristbands, a beaded throat necklace, long black hair like folded wings pouring out from under his leather cowboy hat, a large tasselled pouch at his waist, and a small medicine bag tied by thong around his neck. His eyes look out from hiding places above the high cheekbones and his jaw moves under a drooping overhang of moustache, his voice coming from a cavern that provides its own echo: a natural orator, with all the dramatic gestures, the sweeping movements, the graceful pacing, the body language. In addition, he holds onto a huge black Talking Stick, which he is not afraid to use to emphasize a point. I admire his style but settle resignedly into my bale of hay, pulling the blanket tight, psyching myself for the long haul.

Leonard starts us off on a positive note. The Sacred Fire almost burned out last night, he reports, but one of the young white guys who works on the Bronson ranch noticed the coals going out there in the blizzard, ran and got some kindling, put it in the coals, got down on his knees in the snow, blew on the kindling, and got the Sacred Fire going again. If it had gone out, all the work that went into this gathering would have been in vain.

There is a general round of nodding and a murmur of approval. Good for the white boy!

A couple of Elders carry a woven cord of smouldering sweetgrass around the circle. The men remove their hats before fanning the fumes toward their bowed heads with their hands. A sacramental ritual. A purification. Something. I really don't know. When in doubt, imitate. Try not to feel self-conscious. Get into the group mind-space. Like I used to be able to do as a kid in church. Harder now.

Loading up the peace pipe with lovely dark brown tobacco, Leonard tells us: "For those of you who may not smoke, you don't need to inhale. Just take a little puff, blow it out, pass it on. It's the sharing of the pipe that counts. But you got to remember, tobacco is a sacred herb. Its use by our people as a sacrament was corrupted by the Europeans, who synthesized it and made it into a deadly addicting narcotic, hundreds of times stronger than it should be. Like any sacrament, if it's abused it becomes a tool of evil. It becomes cancer. None of our people ever used to get cancer, yet they grew tobacco and smoked it for thousands of years. The cancer is the evil that came out of the White Man's excesses and perversion of a sacred herb."

It seems that, as he speaks, the Medicine Man is looking directly at me, although it might be somebody behind me. I feel a trifle edgy. Certainly, all this talk about tobacco, Leonard Horse fiddling with his lighter, the joyous whiff that drifts across the loft, has got me wanting a smoke real bad. The pipe, in due course, solemnly and very slowly gets passed around. *Finally* it reaches me. Never mind the niceties of a laid-back non-junkie puff to be exhaled in cloud form, I suck it back, deep and hard, slamdunking my lungs with a shock of nearly pure tobacco, yes! But, God, it's strong! Can you O.D. on this? I have to fight back a coughing fit. Spots explode in the air. I am suddenly almost weightless. Gotta be careful not to just sort of drift over onto my side on the floor.

The Medicine Man's eyes, from their hiding places, are zeroed right in on me. He's holding back a grin, if not outright laughter. Did I see a glimpse of a sorcerer in there, mocking me? I am a perfect ex-ample, after all, of the results of the White Man's corruption, abuses, excesses, and perversion. After a long while, I let out a pencil-thin stream of sacred smoke. Not much left. Most of it has been absorbed into my blood system already. Bad form, no doubt. Whiteboy nic-smackhead taking a grossly huge hit of the communal tobacco sup-ply in front of everyone. But I feel a lot better, if giddy.

Next, the Sacred Eagle Feather is passed around. Each person who is handed it stands and speaks—for as long as they like, appar-ently. I note that Leonard Horse hangs on to the big Talking Stick, however, which could presumably be used to bring closure if some-one got into a blathering jag that went on for days and nights.

Pretty much everybody speaks. I worry a bit when the feather reaches Wii Seeks, for I remember him as an orator who enjoyed the art form and tended to stretch his monologues out. This is, after all, an excellent captive audience, something between a trained cadre of Sunday churchgoers—obedient, orderly, familiar with the rituals—and a gang of very hard-core political types. These are not the Gucci Indian lawyers I'd met in Ottawa while in pursuit of the Calihoo claim. No, these are the traditionalists like Leonard, the healers like Alice, the hereditary clan chiefs like Wii Seeks, pipe-carriers, Longhouse People. Most of their clothing is old and worn and used and repaired, and gives off the smell of wood smoke. Although, among them, I notice, there are younger men with a harder look, stylishly attired in bandanas and guerrilla fatigues. Have to keep in mind that at a gathering like this there are bound to be members of the Warriors Society present, maybe even some veterans from Oka.

They have set up a kitchen under heavily patched canvas awnings where food is being cooked (entirely by women) in huge pots and frying pans left simmering while we gather here. The smells waft up into the barn through opening and shutting doors: venison, pemmican, beets, rhubarb, corn.

A Saulteaux man accepts the Sacred Feather and tells of not being able to get a passport because the bureaucrats in the Indian Affairs Department insist his bloodline ran out a long time ago. My ears perk up. So it is not just the Hurons who failed to really go extinct. It didn't matter what his grandmother said. It didn't matter what his father and mother said. And certainly none of them enjoyed any of the rights guaranteed in the treaties signed with their ancestors, since the Saulteaux were so conveniently "extinct." He has no choice: every time he crosses the border between Canada and the United States, he has to get out of whatever car he's riding in and sneak across a field or along a ravine, rejoining his friends a mile or so on the other side; a stateless man, the creation of some nest of civil servants ensconced behind their desks in Ottawa.

While some orators inevitably go on rather longer than a jaded television interviewer, accustomed to digging for twenty-second clips, can stand to hear, most speakers, it turns out, have little more to say than their name and what band and reserve they are from, so the ritual of speaking goes fairly smoothly. Wii Seeks himself sets a good example by only going on for half an hour. I am surreptitiously timing him on my watch.

There are at least a dozen hereditary Chiefs, three Wing-Chiefs, an apprenticing Medicine Man, and an herbalist. It is the older men who speak the longest, with the younger men hardly offering anything at all. Are they as restless as me? This would be real democracy at work, I guess. God, what a laborious process! I should have brought some Valiums. The women are generally even more circumspect, except for one of the young ladies who was in the van with us. She identifies herself as a staff member of the Parliament Hill office of the Native Women's Association, and talks animatedly for a few minutes about the Constitution, ending up saying, "Native women and children need a safeguard against the abuse of power by male leaders."

"Save it for Ottawa," one of the Chiefs quips. There is a light sprinkle of chuckling in the otherwise resounding silence. Embarrassed, the young lady hands the Feather along.

Mostly there is talk about the reserves that people came from, and the problems they confront there: housing shortages, shenanigans by Indian Affairs officials, scams being worked by area politicians and businessmen, police meddling; what you'd expect. But not excessively long-winded.

Things bog down a bit when we get to a youngster who is peddling wild rice grown and harvested by a Native co-op. He is a favourite of the crowd because he is so humble and shy at first, but brightens in the warm backwash of laughter at his first few self-deprecating comments, and goes on to tell us in numbingly encyclopaedic detail everything we could ever possibly want to know about the history and cultivation of wild rice, its impact on aboriginal cultures, role in the ecosystem, et cetera.

Captain Watson makes an efficient, professional speech about how he has seen the oceans dying with his own eyes, how he has done everything in his power to prevent their destruction, how we all have to be more radical, how he served at Wounded Knee, how he made his ship available to go after the *Niña*, *Pinta*, and *Santa María*, and how he is standing by, ready as ever to help his Brothers and Sisters. He is in his element, for this is a scene worthy of a great director: a secret meeting of the eco-underground and Native Medicine People and Warriors, in the mountains, no less, in a barn, with real horses around, a scene from *Battle to Save Planet Earth*, *Episode 235*. I see Robert Redford in the lead, as Paul, and Lisa played by . . . well, Lisa, I'm sure.

When he's orating, Paul always seems on the edge of a blush, as though he was really just a shy little kid up there because he *has* to do it, no choice. I'm not sure I believe any longer we can do what he says—seriously change anything. But maybe somebody's gotta say it. Over and over again. I have, of course, heard all this before, and am starting to glaze over.

When it's his turn, Rod starts off bravely, talking about how government and industry work hand-in-glove, how the best hope to save the endangered forests is for the Native people to join with conservationists at every opportunity, but his words seem to be soaking into the hay. Rod is kind of speedy, used to getting reactions, jumping on them, rolling along. Barely a dozen sentences into what was shaping up as a ten- or twenty-minute lecture, he suddenly decides he doesn't have much to say, and mumbles, "I'm proud to be here. Thanks."

Walrus shuffles his feet for a moment, and then talks slowly, and at considerable length, about the alienation of the political and mystical sides of things, how he felt when he first held a seal pup in his arms and the time he witnessed a whale being killed, which in both cases he saw with his own eyes as direct assaults upon Mother Nature. Yet he has always felt in accord with the ways of the Native people, who also kill animals for their pelts, but not in an industrial way. In his travels he has taken part in many a traditional Sweat Lodge ceremony, and was adopted by the Oglala Sioux. He has been guided at various moments by rainbows and eagles and dolphins. He knows that this mystical relationship between humans and the natural world is real. Yet as he works in his office on Parliament Hill, he never sees *any* sign that a single politician is even aware of this, so it is like being a sighted man walking among the blind. And that's what we're up against, a powerful industrial-mindset oligarchy that only views Mother Earth as a commodity to be exploited. And they will never stop unless they are *stopped*.

Lisa tries to play humble, talking about how she knows things are different down in L.A., and she's American, "but I can't help that, just like I can't help that I'm a woman," and how she always carries Mace and a stun-gun in her boots back home.

Alice, in striking contrast, closes her eyes as she speaks, holding the feather like a supplicant with both hands. "Before coming here, I had a vision. Rainbow Woman came to me and said that the Earth is in trouble, the land is in trouble, and what needs to happen here on Turtle Island is a balancing. The aggressive, making-it-happen, building-it, analyzing-it intellectual energy must be balanced by the receptive, allowing, surrendering energy of the Feminine Principle . . ." Hippie talk, if you ask me, but pleasant to listen to.

She goes on for a while, and I notice the Medicine Man's Talking

Stick is starting to churn a small hole in the hay on the floor. For a guy who may be a sorcerer, he's getting impatient awfully fast. Finally, he coughs. Loudly and artificially.

Alice's eyes blink open, and her serene expression writhes into a new configuration: steel blazes in her eyes. She pauses, mouth pointedly open.

"Those who want to learn more about feminist issues can attend the workshops," Leonard Horse says brusquely. "Let's move along."

Thank Christ it isn't me Alice hands the Sacred Feather to, because it would burn the fingers, I'm sure. I'm afraid to look at her.

When it does come to me, it feels like I am standing in a huge, echoing confessional booth, with all these sombre priests around me. I am tempted to do a shtick, to lighten the mood. But the Altar Boy Within prevails, and as I stare at the feather, I am reminded of birds and flying, which brings to mind yesterday's ghastly flight and the evil colour of the air over Western Canada. So I ad-lib a nice little sermon about the contradiction between knowing that the forests of the Northern Hemisphere are soon going to be burning, thanks to global warming, and flying on a jetliner spewing greenhouse gases to come here to try to do something about it. Every time I fly I stoke the global fire. I know that. Yet I do it. I feel guilty because I don't act on my knowledge. And I think I'm very typical.

"So partially I'm here to learn how to resolve these contradictions in myself."

One of the Sisters whispers to me, after I have passed the Sacred Feather along: "Catholic background, eh?"

The bald young lawyer from Vancouver, who introduces himself as Bruce Clark, makes for a change of pace. Holding the eagle feather he radiates anger. In fact he can hardly move his jaw for all the muscles bunched up in his neck. He doesn't look at any of his fellow white guys.

"What I have to say isn't what everybody wants to hear," he grates ominously. "So I'm going to save it for our discussion this afternoon."

I don't know the lawyer from a hole in the ground, but he obviously has a reputation. I can tell from the uneasy shuffling of at least half the people sitting on the bales of hay, and a few outright groans, that they have heard him say whatever it is he's going to say before. But there are also several grunts of approval: a big response from this crowd. He has support.

Shit. A trouble-maker. And a white guy. Wouldn't you know?

2 1

"Willing to Pick Up a Gun Right Now"

As he sits by the fireplace, brooding like Rodin's *The Thinker* while waiting for the main room to fill up, the intense young lawyer reminds me of the Vegan leader on the *Sea Shepherd*, Ian Bamfield, Suniva's former squeeze. Ian was passionate about not allowing honey in the galley because it exploited the labour of bees. The big difference, at a glance, between the skinny Vegan and this new contender for title of Chief Fanatic is that the lawyer has more meat on him than the Vegan zealot had. A carnivore, I am sure. He'll be a Black Robe in reverse, is my bet.

But as we wait, Rod and Walrus take turns briefing me on what they have picked up about Clark: he might look a bit bizarre with his shaved head, and his chic jumpsuit, but he has interesting credentials. He spent time when he was a kid living in an Indian residential school in Whitehorse and has an Indian name from the Lil'Wat people, meaning a mountain sheep that looks out, a guard, to make noise if there's a threat. Something to do with walking along precipices. He got started doing criminal law in Northern Ontario, which meant mainly cases involving Natives. "He's one of those guys thinks it's a structural problem," Walrus whispers.

Some people squat on the floor, others stand. The younger, hip Native guys are mostly leaning against the walls, which gives them a good vantage point to watch all of us, not just the speaker.

Finally, asserting leadership, Leonard Horse takes a seat and drags it directly opposite the fire, facing the lawyer. The Medicine Man taps on the floor with his Talking Stick to quiet everyone down. He introduces the lawyer as a White Brother who has fought the good fight on the people's side, and whose analysis "may be hard for some of you to take," but must be considered. Hardly a screaming endorsement. There is in fact a deep wariness in the Medicine Man's voice. The image comes to mind of a cowboy about to let a particularly ornery bull out of the gate. I don't think he knows exactly which way this is going to go. Some kind of backroom struggle preceded this, I can see by the tension in other people's faces: Suniva's, her parents, several of the younger Natives. But there is an excitement, too.

The lawyer remains motionless, seemingly oblivious to us all, for nearly a minute before he suddenly jumps to his feet, looking us over coldly, like a Field Marshal inspecting the troops, and declares:

"Anybody who isn't willing to pick up a gun right now should get up and leave this place."

Not missing a beat (she must have expected this), Alice can be heard to mutter: "Oh great, and give them an excuse to blow us away!"

The Medicine Man glares at her, but Clark shrugs it off and launches into a non-stop harangue.

His stance is one of withering scorn for anyone so stupid as to fail to grasp his every allusion. He clenches his fists, shakes them, writhes with vein-throbbing anger. This guy is a spit-flyer. I have not seen anything like it, up close, since having to cover political rallies as a young reporter, trying to take notes as one demagogue or another gave his best shot at stirring the masses. As an old peacenik, I know I should have got up and walked out already, but nobody else has moved a muscle, and do I really want to lead the opposition at somebody else's party? Besides, this guy, loonie or not, is mesmerizing. A true something-opath. As long as you accept his fundamental assertion—the need to pick up weapons now, or everything will be lost—it all flows logically and inexorably to his foregone conclusion: the need for an immediate act of insurrection against the civil authority. When he says "everything" will be lost, he means all future claims on land that is rightfully Native, including virtually all of British Columbia, of course. Recent rulings by supreme courts at the provincial and federal level have been secretly but methodically moving toward a point where Aboriginal rights will be de facto extinguished entirely through bilateral side-deals with individual bands. It all goes back to the British North America Act, which a series of honky judges have improperly fortified on the basis of the "given superiority" of the White Race, especially its judiciary. He asserts this as though it is one of those things that everybody knows. An absolute given.

The Charlottetown Accord is a total crock, he continues, the final nail in the coffin built for Native cultures by neo-colonialism. Ovide Mercredi, Grand Chief of the Assembly of First Nations, is an Uncle Tom. A suit! A Judas! So is the President of the Native Council of Canada—hey, wait a minute, that would be my old shipmate, Ron George, aka Tsaskiy! Paul and Wii Seeks and Suniva and I exchange outraged looks. He can't say that about an old buddy of ours! For that matter, I have listened to Ovide Mercredi speaking to a crowd of businessmen in Toronto's Royal York Hotel. He'd said: "As soon as our land claims are settled, you will have to do business with us. So get used to it." I had joined the self-flagellating applause. Give us tough love, Chief! I was impressed by his chutzpah and intelligence. But no, *he's* part of the conspiracy to entrench the White Man's control over every last inch of Canadian soil through the false promise of self-government, which simply means the final co-opting of the elected tribal councils—a constitutional coup to be etched in stone for all time. Beware the fine print! Watch out for all the asterisks in the consensus version dealing with First Peoples. It adds up to one last giant fraud to strip the Aboriginal of what little he has left. And somewhere in there, the multinationals are set loose upon the land.

God knows, should the Charlottetown Accord be passed on October 26, the Native people of Canada could very well be screwed forever and the last tracts of intact biosystems razed. With the Canadian elite behind the Accord, the lawyer argues, it is unstoppable unless there is another Oka. Here. Now. *After* the Referendum will be futile. The takeover will be a done deal. (If you would make history, first you must set deadlines. Is there some great truth here?)

It is hard for me to imagine the entire jurisdictional mountain of statutes, regulations, and directives involving Aboriginals in Canada shifting quite so apocalyptically overnight. But who am I to stand up here and try to tell *anybody* how the Indian Affairs Department works? Or why the Apocalypse *isn't* at hand. Never mind the crowd probably not appreciating me pooh-poohing their champion, I would as soon debate the mad lawyer *mano a mano* as wrestle with a wolverine. Nor am I quite so dumb as to let myself get trapped into assuming the public persona of the liberal apologist urban honky eco-faggot, getting ripped to intellectual pieces in front of everybody. Oh no! See Bob keep his big fat mouth shut. See how *others* handle things. This is cowardice, eh? Great! I am enormously pleased with myself, staying out of the fray. This is much more Zen than jumping up and yelling: "You psycho! Here's a gun! Why don't you just shoot yourself and get it over with, and nobody else will have to die as a result of your madness!" No! Stay close to the ground. Listen.

The ancient admonition, "Beware the man with one book," echoes through my head. Yet everything he says has a ring to it. I may not like his style or his agenda, but he's a convincing bugger, I have to say, and what he has to say fits squarely with my own reading of the dark side of Canada's history.

Slamming fist into hand, the lawyer tells us that in order to address the law you have to look at the whole law, the same as when you look at the facts, you have to look at the whole truth. Now the whole law consists of the constitutional law and the criminal law. The constitutional law upon which this country was founded since the eighteenth century says that where judges assume jurisdiction in unsurrendered Indian territory, by definition they are guilty of treason and fraud. The fact is, that occurred in British Columbia, notably in 1864 when Judge Begbie hanged a group of Chilcotin Indians. In hard constitutional law that was an act of murder by the judge. He goes on: "Now when my colleagues say we must look at the law and follow these judicial processes, that is exactly my point. The difficulty is when I go into our courts and ask the courts to address this constitutional law, the words of which are absolutely plain and clear, they read those words but they won't address them publicly. They become hysterical. They cite inferior law, that is the law of the Criminal Code, which is a law inferior in status to the Constitution. That is, they wilfully blind themselves to the Constitution in order to silence the messenger."

His main point is that jurisdiction was assumed illegally by the colony of Canada over sovereign Aboriginal nations, their lands and resources, so an Aboriginal or supporter who defends himself against the Canadian state has the "Colour of Right" on his side, which has standing in international law. What the Canadian courts deem illegal on unsurrendered Aboriginal land doesn't matter; it is the Canadian courts which are illegal in the first place.

Whew! I don't like him, but he has hit the nail on the head!

Paul, who has been down in Los Angeles long enough to have grown somewhat accustomed to the presence of guns, and who is used to taking command of wobbly situations, respectfully waits for the Medicine Man to break the silence when the lawyer is finished, then says calmly: "Can I suggest that the question you raised at the beginning be deferred to the end, which will make it possible for some of us who may be under surveillance to take part in a discussion which we might otherwise have to exempt ourselves from? You can't be sure there aren't provocateurs or agents present." Paul has obviously attended a few powwows over the years. This gets the tree-hugging, bunny-loving, old-style Gandhian non-violence wimps, like Walrus, Rod, and me, off the hook long enough to stick around for the main show. Mind, we're not quite alone. Alice and the ladies from the Native Women's Association of Canada look like they're about ready to get up and walk, too.

The lawyer gnashes his teeth, but the Medicine Man quickly accepts deferral of the question of taking up arms until the last day "when we gather around the Sacred Fire" as a pretty good compromise. He is obviously relieved. There is no actual vote on the matter, one cannot help noticing. The Medicine Man—who is becoming, methinks, more imperial by the hour as the drama of the powwow unfolds—simply thunks his Talking Stick on the hardwood floor. The ante has certainly been raised. We have gone straight from Sacred-Eagle-Feather pleasantries to the question of armed revolution, and we are only halfway through the first day.

I have followed along this line of thought before, thanks. When

I was young and vastly underestimated the power of the state, I too thought a single, highly individualistic raised fist scooped up some kind of media time-share—and if that fist contained a gun, well! Exponentially more power: automatically! Although what "power" meant, well, that depended on who you talked to. Still, a gun ratcheted everything up. No denying that.

Out of the stunned silence, it is Rod who finally speaks up.

The lawyer had pointed to the famous *Sparrow* land claims case involving the Gitksan and Wet'suwet'en as a major trap laid by the honky land-grab conspirators, with Aboriginals being hoodwinked this time by a nefarious running-dog double-agent establishment lawyer named Marvin Storrow (also from Vancouver) who, while appearing to have won serious ground for Natives, had in fact set them up for a fall. Everywhere else, so far as I had read, that particular decision had been held up as a milestone in the advancement of Native rights—and one that enraged the entire right flank of Canadian public opinion: the hunters, farmers, trappers, furriers (an ancient layer of the Canuck zeitgeist, still alive and busy slaughtering). For years, Marvin Storrow has been (at least figuratively) in the gunsights of every redneck in the land. To listen to him being pilloried by this arrogant young intellectual is almost more than I can take. But I don't want to overstep the bounds of my acceptance here by becoming the pro-establishment asshole.

Rod doesn't seem to care. As sweetly as an angel of brotherhood, Rod affixes the lawyer with his most innocent bushy-tailed expression. "I happen to know Marvin Storrow, and as far as I can see, what he's done is terrific. It helps the Native cause no end."

Boom! Down comes the intellectual hammer! The lawyer is pitiless. He couldn't have been much happier if the personal bum-boy of some supreme-court honcho had showed up to plead for sanctuary. Rod is his meat. He has listened to a lot of brain-dead hippie shit in his time, Clark assures us, but this drivel is the worst. With implacable legal logic, he eviscerates Rod's "naivety," turns several good phrases in a row that make Rod look like a slack-jawed mental Neanderthal, and spits on his very ability to conceptualize at the most fundamental level of cognition. He puts the boots to him. Jackboots. Ouch! Ouch! It is such a trashing that we, Rod's old buddies, sit silent, just wishing it would end, that Rod wouldn't have to take any more rhetorical whip-lashes on his poor shredded ego. I have never seen anyone intellectually humiliated like this in public before.

Several of us are actually blushing. Observing Rod's suffering, I think: Man, I know I'm not going to tackle this guy if I don't have to! Come on, cowardice, stay the course! Mouth—shut your face!

After Rod has been chopped up into legalistic/moral/existential/ political sheep droppings, there is a collective letting-out of breath. Nobody wants to look at him, so simple-minded and anti-revolutionary has he been made to sound. I even find myself sub-consciously shifting a couple of inches away from him.

The lone dissenter having been clobbered embarrassingly into speechlessness, and the rest of us too intimidated to clear our throats, there is another stunned silence.

But once again, like the Paul Newman character in *Cool Hand Luke* getting up from the prison yard floor after having been beaten to a pulp by the main bad guy/sadist, it is Rod who speaks. *Oh no, I plead, trying to get through to him telepathically, don't do it. He'll just make you look like a peasant, an LSD victim or something, all over again.*

It takes a mountain of ego, I suddenly realize, to be able to risk great loss of face. If that is somehow the case, then Rod is way ahead of me. For, no sooner has he been swatted down by our resident Che Guevara than he coughs delicately, and adds a supplemental to his previous question, displaying some familiarity with parliamentary debate, which goads the lawyer into paroxysms of denigration.

Yet when he runs out of breath and has to pause (like a seal hunter who can't quite kill the seal, I muse), Rod, unbowed, takes one more polite, gentle run at him. Astounded that the retired yippie has sprung back up one more time, the lawyer pummels him with re-newed verbal fury—so much so that Rod is beginning to look like the underdog. And, of course, the underdog position is *the one to have* around here. The lawyers may think that his crunching-to-the-marrow of Rod's intellectual bones has ended the matter. Wrong en-tirely in a subcult! He retains enough of a sense of an audience to dimly perceive he has hammered Rod too long, kicked him in the temples too hard when too many people were watching. He is now the bully, while Rod is the brave, mentally handicapped victim, fighting softly back.

Despite the lawyer's eloquent rhetoric, at the end of the debate there is a delicate standoff. Rod has given voice to resistance, not by opposing the idea of using guns directly, but by defending a white lawyer, a competitor of Clark's, not what you would consider a obvious line of argument with a mainly Native group, yet it strikes a chord. They see the hidden white-guy power struggle there. Nothing is pure, eh? At least, I presume they see it. They must also surely see the cold logic of not rising up, ill-equipped, against superior firepower. Now the lawyer is appealing to the Ghost-Shirt community. We will be saved by magic! A fabulous appeal. I have gone there myself in the past to ask for help, although now, listening to someone else do it—appeal to the crazed romantic in people—I can't help but be appalled. Whatever you're going to do, do it yourself! Quit trying to get other people to fight the battle, you bastard! If you're going to lead, lead from the front lines only.

But I'm silent now for another reason: everything the guy has said, I believe, sadly, is true. Unbearably, miserably, historically true. We are another South Africa, except that here, the oppressors are the majority. God, what a dismal thought! Who wants to hear it?

Alice has been trying to catch the Medicine Man's eye so she can speak, but he has been ignoring her. Now that the exchange with Rod seems to be over, she grows impatient, knocks on the floor with her knuckles. The Medicine Man shakes his head, refusing to look her in the eye, bangs the Talking Stick on the floor, and declares: "Meeting adjourned." When he stands, he turns his back on her and the cluster of Sisters squatting on the floor, and walks out of the room.

Am I being oversensitive to "women's issues"? Maybe I've been too long in Toronto . . . Or is our host being rather stunningly rude to the ladies, whom I hadn't really thought of as a fem-faction before, just as neat, stoned older chicks? Rod and I, shocked, put our ears to Walrus's moustache as he points out: "This isn't good for solidarity."

"How do we get out of here?" I want to know.

Rod is serious: "We should run for the van now."

Alice is so pissed she doesn't even look at us, her friends, as she stands up with dignity. The women stamp out of the room en masse onto the verandah where they yank on boots and jackets and stomp off to the teepees. In the confusion, Paul and Lisa do a fade, tiptoeing away, holding hands.

The snow has almost stopped falling. Late afternoon sun fizzles between the pines, and for the first time I can see mountains, blue and dim. Looking weirdly triumphant, for a guy whose big powwow is melting away like the snow around him, the Medicine Man has marched over to his trailer, which he enters, still not once looking back at anyone, and slams the door.

I offer my condolences to Suniva, when I bump into her, for the twist things have taken. But she looks oddly elated. For me, the revelation that the True North Strong and Free's very existence as a geopolitical unit is based on raw conquest rather than any legitimate rule of law comes as no great shock; the lawyer's speech has been more of a depressing reminder. For Suniva, this is news, shocking news—but, rather than being devastated, she has this peculiar glow about her. As though she has *found something*. A new belief system! Something conceivably as pure as Veganism. I can see it in her eyes: she is being radicalized. I feel a pang of envy. If only I could work that juice up again!

"So the country is built on lies, tricks, fraud, deceit, ripoffs. What's new? What does he expect us to do about it?" I ask. "Throw ourselves in human waves on Parliament Hill?"

But she doesn't notice my wit, just my cynicism. Too bad. We are not exactly in synch, Suniva and I, but she is a nice, idealistic kid.

Seeing that the rest of the afternoon is unexpectedly free, Suniva comes up with the brilliant idea that those of us who want to go horseback riding might grab the moment. Great! I have been riding horses—not often, but enough to know basically what to do—since I was sixteen, and a couple of buddies and I used to rent pintos for a day at a time and race them around the edge of an abandoned quarry. Climbing on a horse has always filled me with great alarm, but the fear seems to ignite some kind of euphoria. The big effort is

not to let my hands shake, revealing to the horse and my compan-
ions alike that I am scared almost to the point of nausea. The only
hope is to fake firmness mixed with genuine interest in the horse, as
though all you do at nights is worry about horses' rights. *Horseshoes
okay, big fella? Haven't ridden for a while, have I?*

My horse, a glistening golden palomino with a white mane, seems
like a no-nonsense character, not entirely pleased with the bit. How
many tons, I wonder. Looking up at its face, I think: Is it seriously
being proposed that I attempt to control this behemoth *from on its
back* by pulling on those little leather thongs? Even if they are connected to mechanical devices that do cruel leverage things to the
inside of its mouth. How can men and horses ever deal with each
other as equals with a situation like this? Horseback riding is inher-
ently cruel. I want to raise the issue with Suniva, to see what the
Vegan position is on exploiting the labour of horses. I don't want to
revert to my old mischievous anti-Vegan behaviour. I just wonder:
Where does forcing a horse to run, carrying you on its back, or you'll
torture its tender mouth or whip its neck or naked flanks, fit in with
any coherent moral system? When you think about it, it's fundamentally perverse.

As a kid, of course, I thought nothing of forcing the animal to gallop until it was staggering. And it was all so easy. You just hung on
to the saddle horn with both hands and ducked the branches lashing back at you. It helped to stand up in the stirrups whenever you
could so the tail of your spine wouldn't get fused, nor your balls
smacked. I remember all this, and I am determined not to do anything immature, especially up here in mountain country. As the
snow coagulates into scabs and wet meadows emerge, spiky scrubs
shake themselves dry. Hooves clatter on mashed slate. The mountains, although still distant, are *above* us now. The ranch was on the
very upper limits of the woodland foothills, so as we leave it behind
we are quickly up on the lower alpine slopes. The tricks of riding
come back to me: basically, to make the horse go forward, you kick
him in the ribs. To make him stop, pull on reins. To make him go
sideways, kick the appropriate flank. Ride with one hand on the
reins, the other on the saddle horn. When in doubt, grab the horse

by the hair on its neck. Only put the balls of your feet in the stirrups, in case you get dumped, so you won't get dragged along on the ground and killed in a horrendous fashion.

The presence of Lisa makes us older dudes probably just a touch more hormonally imbalanced than usual, because we have barely trotted clear of the gate at the end of the pasture before Rod, Paul, Walrus, and I are torturing our four-legged slave-species into a race. Rod rides a horse like he drives: no caution whatsoever, right at the edge of disaster, seemingly oblivious to any danger, as though he were charmed. Walrus looks so much like a psychedelic cowboy anyway, that it only seems natural that he should be riding, intense but grinning, eyes glinting. Paul isn't quite as much in his element out here as he is at sea. He had a bit of trouble getting up in the saddle, and his horse seemed to want to be arrogant. But now he's flushed with adrenaline and rides like a guy in a movie, almost recklessly, determined to win. Lisa seems to know how to talk to her horse, cooing noises with lots of "pal" stuff, and quickly catches up, and even takes the lead.

Suniva and one of the ranch hands take up positions, I notice, riding herd on us in case anything goes wrong. At full gallop, hooves blurring, the seven of us charge along a line of pines, quartz glittering in the trail, saddles thwapping sweatily, striking sparks as we clatter along the gigantically slanting vista of the Rockies, squinting in the wind, getting into that miraculously non-violent wave action of loping, which permits us to finally settle into the saddle and go with the motion—even though we have reached the lip of the mile-wide valley plunging down maybe another mile to the Athabasca River, jagged with rapids, a mountain-slicer sawing away at the titanic gap in the otherwise surely impenetrable plates of granite and ice. And we are hurtling along the edge of all this, concentrating madly on what is directly ahead, even if it is entirely up to the horse not to make any mistakes—and what by the way is the maximum speed one should push a horse on a loose rock trail along the edge of a gargantuan gorge? After all, he's being tortured into doing this. What is our excuse? The high dramatic point comes when Rod's horse stumbles. He saves himself from crashing to the ground and maybe bouncing over the side to his certain death by the un-dignified yet effective tactic of clutching the beast around the neck.

Great vistas are debilitating in the same way as Zen is. You shrink to ant size. Perspective leaps at you, overwhelms you. Scale comes crunching down. Having stopped our wild dash, we resume the trek, more sensibly, by letting the horses amble along the trail while we soak in the sound of rapids far below. Saddles squeak. The bits make tinkling sounds like Tibetan monastery bells. Hooves squeak on bro-ken slate. We hear the occasional thud of a horseloaf hitting the trail, and the wind blowing down on us from vast mountain basil-icas. Paul shouts to hear his echo, but his voice simply vanishes. The void before us is too immense for an echo. The sky is like something that has been torn open, clouds rushing silently upward. We are strung out single file, gnats upon ants, crawling through the debris where the continental tectonic plates have mashed together, riding up on top of each other like ice floes.

Is this what they mean by "Indian country"? We are silenced. I start to hallucinate, actually. It seems like my time-sense has accel-erated, and I am watching the passage of eons instead of seconds. I hang on to my saddle horn as though it were the control stick of my time machine. Suddenly, the Secret of the Rockies is revealed to me: these mountains are only pretending to sit still. In fact, they are *sneaking along*. Their secret is that they move, you see. They are the heaviest, most densely packed objects in the universe, the epitome of eternal motionlessness, and supposedly not animate in any way (stone cold dead!), yet they *slouch by*: just the most infinitesimal fraction of an inch every thousand years. Collars pulled up, hands in pockets. Infinite slow fade. A Marching of Elephant Buddha Fountainheads, faces turned away, shaking the whole planet for bil-lions of years. Yet totally invisible to you and me because we buzz by so lightning-bug-like, while they crunch secretly along in super-slow motion.

When we pause to turn and look back towards the east, we are high enough to see the cowl of particulate and hybrid molecules hovering above the plain so far below us. Was it just yesterday I'd been in the middle of all that—thousands of miles away across the prairies? And now I'm climbing onto the rocky shore on the far edge of the great photochemical sea. That is, if it *has* an edge!

From here, I can see the phenomenon in cross-section. You blink your eyes, but it won't go away. More like a dirty window than a cloud. Its size alone is harrowing. It stretches all the way to the Alberta horizon. *You can see it. It is no longer in the future. It is here.*

Suniva remarks, with fear in her voice, "This is the first summer I've ever been able to see it from here. It never used to come any higher than the foothills, except for fires."

"The world is already changed," Walrus observes in full meditative prophet mode. "Different air, different planet. The air changes, everything else starts to change."

"Is it too late to stop it?" asks Suniva.

"Probably," says Paul, when no one else will presume to answer. He slumps in the saddle under the weight of the thought.

"Doesn't give you licence to quit trying, though," he adds, ever the leader of men, looking around at us with barely masked disappointment: his old buddies, the front-line dropouts.

Ever the junkie, I pull out a package of smokes, offer one to Walrus. We light up in the wind like seasoned cowboys. Marlboro Men at the end of the world as we know it. I cough sorely.

"Y'-all gotta cut that shit out," Lisa advises me, just a touch unnecessarily. "I wish I could *help* you!"

But, of course, the planetary death-cloud out there is an extension of the one inside my lungs. It's not just that there is a connection, it's that they are fallout from the same dark alchemy. As without, so within. So, finally, with mine own eyes, I have come face to face with it: I have seen doom actually looming.

22

The Talking Stick Descends

Back at the ranch we eat outside under canvas strung from poles. There's moose meat, venison, rabbit, quail. Dumplings, too. And pea soup. I detect a French influence here. One moment the angle of the light from the setting sun ripples blindingly through the steam over the big pots, then the radiance is gone, snuffed behind a mountain. The plume from the Sacred Fire flares like a nimbus, then is also gone, leaving ghostly ribbons. I offer anybody who looks older than me a cigarette (the all-important offering of tobacco to an Elder to get him or her to speak), but half of them don't seem to understand English, and after we've smiled and nodded at each other a few times, I move along. Finally getting one conversation going, I make the mistake of suggesting to a fellow about my age, who looks every inch the weathered ranch cowboy except for the pigtails, that there should be more parklands, both provincially and federally.

He fixes me with direct eye contact for the first time, blows smoke dismissively. "Just another way of taking our land," he drawls.

Ah, yes. Of course. Well, haven't I been revealed as the village idiot? Actually, I knew that . . . just didn't see it . . . in . . . context . . .

Since his big revolutionary speech, the bald lawyer has been elusive, to say the least, so far as the rest of us honkies are concerned. Of course, we're perceived as Rod's allies, and therefore some kind of liberal mush. But not once have I seen him smile at anybody, not even his numerous Native comrades from various blockades and courtrooms. He has a great cliff of forehead collapsing backwards under the sheer mass of excess neocortex, swollen, of course, by higher evolution. He exchanges clenched-fist salutes with his Brothers, assuming the Warrior stance, but once he starts talking, he seems to hunch forward under the weight of some towering burden. I have met lawyers like him: usually Marxists or Trotskyites, high on some uncut cocaine of abstract thought, eyes paranormally bright from an incandescent inner vision of razor-sharp, unadulterated, history-rectifying Truth in action.

We are briefly introduced. Obviously he views me as some kind of running-dog corporate media scum cum mushpot whaleloving tree-hugging peacenik McLuhanite cultist. We shake hands stiffly and non-revolutionarily. He has a steel grip, and knows it. His upper lip automatically curls into an expectant sneer, waiting to hear what drivel I will offer up.

"I just don't see the point of advocating starting something you can't possibly win," I blurt lamely.

"When you're dealing with legal chicanery and genocide," he snaps back, "what have you got to lose?"

"They've got F15-AS, y'know."

"Strictly speaking, we've got the law."

"People can get hurt."

"If you're already hurting, it's a matter of degree. Of course if you're part of the elite, it's a risk"—withering look—"indeed."

A smirk. I give him a sickly smile back. It's over. I didn't land a glove. He hardly had to lift a finger.

We both become busy in other conversations. What did I think? That I could beat this guy? He's a charismatic. There's not a line I could utter that he couldn't run circles around. Bright? Probably some sort of genius level. Mad? That's certainly the way he strikes this layman.

We Green White Guys party that night in Paul and Lisa's cabin, which tourists normally pay a small fortune to enjoy. We call it a "strategy session." Somehow or other, despite the dry-camp designation for the powwow, wine and spirits have been smuggled in. This is good. I feel guilty, naturally, because I should be mingling further with the Brothers and Sisters up at the lodge or the teepees or the cluster of trailers or around the Sacred Fire. Instead, I am down here hidden among the pines in a luxury dude-ranch suite with my old cronies, secretly boozing it up. If nothing else, we've found *our* tribe.

This is just great! Haven't had a reunion, the four of us old Seventies-era veterans together, for over ten years. Laughter is the name of the game. Poison gas may have swallowed the Great Plains, maybe even the whole of the planet, but this is a moment to burble and gurble.

And to strut our stuff for Lisa's benefit, let's admit! It is a mystery, but even I, who should know better, tend to perform just a tad more enthusiastically when there is a beautiful young female watching and listening attentively. My cruel secret goal, of course, is to make young Lisa rue her misfortune at having landed Paul instead of me. Look what *you* missed! Older. A little more French, shall we say? A blacker sense of humour. In any event, I'm not the only cock-shocked idiot there. Rod and Walrus are every bit as caught up in the libidinous excitement as me. How can we three adult males, with all the experiences we've been through with women and wives and mothers and daughters, still be so easily wound up by the mere presence of a good-looking wenchling? Of course, by now we have, each of us, had a peek at the copy of *Playboy* Paul has brought with him, featuring his beloved, and so the level of titillation has been ratcheted up. Still, it must be our nature as beasts to dance for these female creatures. Maybe that's all we were really intended for. As the sauce flows, so flow the hormones, and for a long time, instead of analyzing the geopolitics of ecology, we talk about sex, with Lisa leading the discussion. "I revel in my sexuality," she advises us, risking obviousness. Paul blushes a lot, but he looks generally as pleased with life as I have ever seen him, so why be critical? Am I envious? Of course!

We are eventually ejected from the lovebirds' nest into the chill mountain night. Bristles of hoarfrost glitter in the moonlight. Our breath pours out in silver clouds. Starlight from billions of years ago infuses the sky. The cosmos, right at hand. Just open a door and there you are: infinity.

* * *

The next day at breakfast in the dining room in the lodge is not good, and the crowd has thinned out. Wii Seeks is gone. Had to get back to Lillooet. He'd looked for us last night to say goodbye. Couldn't find us. Right. That would be because we were having a, yes, a strategy meeting. Of course. Guilty, guilty, guilty.

Leonard Horse stands after breakfast to inform us in a darkened voice that "in view of the divisions that have developed, it has been decided to caucus." My breath is shocked out of my body for a moment. Wait a second! Here we are, up on the mountains, above the death-cloud, near the end of the world, probably: a band of good-guy Rainbow Warriors, the fulfilment of an ancient Native North American prophecy, no less! And all we can *do* with such an incredible situation is *caucus?* Split up into little bitching separate groups, right? Oh no! Not *here!* Where's the purity? I had been waiting for the secret to be revealed: the age-old Red Man's path, maybe even the Way of doing guerrilla battle. Sure, the old tactics were useless against a certain kind of cannon-and-cross invasion by psychos, but if there is a guerrilla spirit that bides its time, sooner or later the secret Red Man's Army will fall upon the sleeping European and Asian conquerors—seven generations later!—and take their whole heads! All this meant figuratively and symbolically, of course. And, of course, it's crazy. But this is what I think I'm here to help do: foster the adoption of some kind of nature-worshipping Native mindset on a mass scale; bring the great supertanker of Western thought around just a couple of inches so that it might not inevitably smash on the rocks ahead. Some such fantasy! Yet now it looks as if I might as well be back with the Indian lawyers in Ottawa, making careers out of manoeuvring over land claims. Or even worse: back among environmentalists at a board meeting, shoving their halos in each other's faces. What do we need to caucus about? If the goal is to stitch together a joint vision, let's just get started. Let's not (there it is again, the honky word) dither. If, on the other hand, the big question is actually whether or not to pick up a gun (and that's how it's been defined for us so far), I'm attending a whole different powwow.

Paul raises his arm slowly to make a point, and Leonard nods out of deference to the world-famous eco-radical.

"Before we do this, I've just got one thing to say, and I am very respectfully aware that many of you will know this from your own experience—Oka, Wounded Knee, name it!—the moment you declare open war on the state, which only has one abiding interest, which is its own strategic interests, nothing more, nothing less— like Kissinger said, it has no soul or heart—the state will come down on you like a hammer. It'll stop at nothing to destroy you. They'll throw you in jail, they'll fire at you, and if that doesn't work, ultimately they'll bring in the warplanes. Jumping in front of them and waving a gun around may feel good for a while, but unless you've got a brilliant strategy, you're dead meat."

There are a few harrumphs and a few nods, but mainly everyone in the room remains impassive. Except for my buddies, I can't read anybody. Paul sits down, a bit flushed, unaccustomed to having his words vanish so completely into the air.

What I'm wondering is, who needs to caucus at this stage? As I recall, Leonard Horse invited me on the grounds that we were going to "get it together," and here is our very own Medicine Chairman telling us to split up into factions to determine the rather fundamental question of whether or not we should go running around shooting people. That tiny despairing voice deep inside says, once again: "Help!"

"Just how many caucuses are there?" Walrus wants to know. He is every bit as unhappy as Paul and I are with this turn of events. I don't know what his experience at Wounded Knee was like, when there were real bullets being fired in his direction, but he rigorously practised non-violence with me during our years together as eco-activists, and he is working, happily and radically enough, in an office in Ottawa for a Member of Parliament. Crazy though he may still secretly be, I have to assume he continues to embrace some kind of Gandhianism, and, therefore, like me, he doesn't see a need to resort to caucusing on such a basic issue.

It seems, Leonard intones, that there is a Native People's Caucus, a Women's Caucus. And a caucus for the Green White Guys.

Alice cannot contain herself: "That's sexist and racist bullshit!"

Leonard turns on her furiously. "And I don't want to hear any more feminist crap from the dykes sitting over there!"

With that, he hammers the Talking Stick on the floor, rises with the dignity of a thousand generations of patriarchs making their final stand. He looks around the room with almost Moses-like contempt and pride. He has chastised the whores and defined the politics of the day. Thus and thus. It is done. Live with it.

"I guess," Rod whispers to me in the stunned silence, "it's over."

I nod bitterly. Paul, Lisa, Walrus, Suniva—their jaws have all gone slack.

Alice's now-very-white face hardens as she clambers to her feet, followed in a shocked sleepwalk, like people drawing back from a fatal accident, by her Sisters. Their faces are tight-muscled, eyes hard, their nostrils are flared, as if smelling fly-buzzed meat three days gone bad. I have seen guys piss women off before—done it myself a few times, ashamed to admit—but nothing on quite this scale. It is awesome. There is a time warp here, I see. Here is a man who wants to play the role of a great chieftain of the past, uniting the tribes, and in two short days he has already managed to shatter the tiny band that he had to begin with into unrepairable fragments.

I look around for the bald lawyer. By definition, he's part of our caucus, which should be fun. But he has melted away. Can't say I blame him. Hey, it's mutual, buddy!

The Natives slowly but surely drift out toward their campers and pickups. Suniva's parents and the staff, including Suniva, fade into the background. Alice and the Sisters disappear into the teepees. Paul and Lisa head off to do a bit of caucusing on their own, leaving Rod and Walrus and me staring at each other.

"Hike, anybody?" asks Walrus.

We head out past the barn. Once we've climbed the last barb-wired horse-pasture fence, the mountain high kicks in, and soon the three of us are flashing in and out of tongue-tied awe at the Rocky Mountain spectacle unfolding around us (as though we are in the centre of a Brobdingnagian flower of rock that keeps opening) and laughing wildly at our own and each other's brilliant lines. Some of it is just relief at getting away from the bleak group mind-twisting going on back there. Rod is inspired to lie flat on his back on a slope with his head a good two feet lower than his boots and lets out a "Whoaaaaaa-yahhh!" that has Walrus and me doing the same im-

mediately. *Yesss!* I am walking on sky, with the crenellated mountains themselves overhanging the blue infinitude beneath my shoes.
Staring *downnnnnnnnnn*. I can feel the planet I am glued to moving
through space. Great stuff!

That night, we three rogues—Walrus, Rod, and I—accept Alice's
invitation to join the Sisters in one of the teepees. I can't help wondering if we aren't repeating some historical pattern here: mellow
hippie-type white guys show up, score with Native chicks sick to
death of macho crap from the hometown boys. Certainly, there is a
delicious feeling that we have slipped out of our century. This could
be any night, almost, in the last couple of hundred years in this part
of the world: coals are smouldering in the fire pit in the middle, with
the smoke neatly being sucked up through the opening at the top of
the poles. We are huddled in a circle around the pit, wrapped in
blankets and borrowed sweaters, hay and pine branches and sleeping
bags underneath, three Green White Guys and eight Earth-Mother-
and-Daughter angels, smoking our faces off, while tiny diamond-
points of ice gather on the outside canvas.

The discussion is all fulminating politics for the first few hours. It
takes a while for Alice to come down from her rage. But as the moon
glides over the armoured mountain shoulders, spreading silver fire
on the frosted grass, the conversation turns mystical, as it should,
and she talks of magical herbs and healing and the Great Mother.
Even Walrus, who is a lay expert on mushrooms, is impressed by the
depth of her knowledge.

We are all in agreement that the powwow has been a complete
bust. Although we try not to dwell on it, the subject keeps coming
up, and each time we are reduced to brooding again. History being
the pitiless grinding machine that it is, what might have been a
unique moment has been squandered. Most likely it was slated to be
nothing anyway, but it had the potential of being at least a minor
catalyst. Hard not to regret its collapse.

Still! Looking around at the shadows thrown by the coals, illu-
minating people's features, glowing in their eyes, knowing that the
mountains are all around, listening to an owl, the sleepy flubbering
of horses, seeing the smoke twirl upward, showering sparks among
the stars, the smell of pine and hay, the thrilling murmur of women's

voices, their laughter: this is a good scene. Had we males been
younger and less burdened by the twists and turns of our lives,
and ditto for the women, it might have turned into some kind of ec-
static group sexual bonding ritual, but alas . . . it remains entirely
platonic—which is okay too. After all, I can talk to Alice as if I have
known her all my life. Moreover, she knows more than I do. About
nature. About the cosmos. About the planet. A voyeuristic journalism vampire as ever, I curse myself for not having a tape recorder.
The reality is, I am snuggled into a warm teepee on the rim of the
Great Plains, talking to a woman whose knowledge has been handed
down through generations, going as far back as the last Ice Age . . .
no, further! In some mysterious way, that knowledge goes all the
way back in an unbroken thread to the African Mother, the first real
human . . . and back further, at least in terms of information passed
on through gestures and squawks and pointing . . . and down, in a
swoop, it goes through the stages of phylum to the primeval ooze.
Alice's eyes glint redly as she reminds me that all life is part of the
one Life Force, grown from the same shift in chemistry during the
planet's infancy. This is a good conversation for Alice, too. How
often does she run into an older white guy from the city who whole-
heartedly agrees that the rocks are alive? Yes! We have got to the
point where we can *feel* them hulking and bulking up around us. If
we follow the teachings, Alice assures us, we can learn to soak up energy from them. We grew out of them. We are Brother Rock come
alive. We can tap into his essence. And I think of how my Huron
saviour showed me how to put my sleeping bag down in the ashes of
a fire on the glacial moraine, and that's what kept me alive as the
temperature dropped. And that's why I am here. Somehow, there is
a connection between that moment—on the other side of the
prairies, so many years—lifetimes!—ago, and this. But strain as I
may to make sense of it, I can't. I try to explain the connection between these two events to Alice.

"It's *all* connected!" she exclaims.

I know. I know. But I forget.

And later, she adds: "No matter how alone you feel, through your
mother you are connected to the Great Mother."

That's what I wanted to hear! That sends a sigh of relief not just through me, but through Walrus and Rod. Rod, in fact, flops backwards, crying: "Wow!"

Somewhere during the night, a wolf howls, and the howl goes echoing along cliffs and among gorges, so pure—wild nature, Mother Earth's own clear voice—we are all left silent, shivering with ecstasy for a long time afterward, there being nothing more to say. Brother Wolf has spoken. What he said, God knows.

By dawn, I am well on my way to a case of bronchitis. Too much smoking and talking. Not properly dressed. Not enough cushion between me and the winter-hardening ground. It got cold in the teepee eventually. Just by itself, babbling all night is hard on the throat. Much as I would have happily and non-lustfully climbed into the sleeping bag with Alice, I wasn't invited, so I had to settle for wrapping myself in a couple of blankets, which weren't enough to keep me warm. How strange, I think when I wake up shivering, if I have come some kind of full circle from the day I was saved trying to winter camp without proper equipment.

I crawl out of the teepee in the first light, constipated, ravenously hungry, bladder about to burst, shuddering from cold, hacking and spitting phlegm, my back killing me, my buttocks sore, shoulder muscles aching, lungs searing, chest rattling horribly, throat raw, hideously thirsty, head pulsing, eyes gunked, a crink in my neck, stitch in my side, itching all over, mouth tasting of tobacco shit, wishing I *had* died. Oh God, I just w-w-w-want to be w-w-warm!

Why couldn't one of these Great Experiences just be relatively painless for once?

23

The Fall of the Medicine Man

The bald lawyer is gone. What this means is anybody's guess, but it has to be significant. If he was a happy camper, I'm sure he'd still be here. His advocacy must not have been universally approved of. Either that or he's won and it's over, and everybody remaining is under instructions to keep us out of the loop. Paranoia would be easy in a situation like this.

Whatever the outcome of the secret backroom caucusing amongst the only group that matters, it has not left our Medicine Man in a cheery state. Through breakfast, he broods mightily, sipping coffee, ignoring his food. The ranch staff have already eaten and found work to do to keep themselves busy. Suniva looks like she's been doing too much yoga: here and not-here. Her parents look plain stressed. There are only half as many Natives as at the beginning.

Not a talkative lot at best, today they are utterly silent. As though waiting. It dawns on me that these are the ones who have been the most impassive, most tight-lipped of all, with the least to say when the Sacred Feather was being passed around, the ones I would have guessed were bored or fundamentally uninterested. They are also, generally speaking, the younger ones. Which is another surprise. From them all I hear are the sounds of utensils being used, chairs moving, boots squeaking.

Alice and the Sisters sit at two separate tables in the furthest corner of the dining room, and they might as well be on another planet. They would seem to have tuned the rest of us out completely.

Walrus and Rod are as groggy and numb as me. The only two people who look like they have been having a good time are Paul and

Lisa, both with radioactively glowing auras. Lisa has to restrain her giggling several times, at Paul's embarrassed hushing.

Leonard winces when Lisa giggles, but absolutely refuses to look in the direction of the Green White Guy Caucus. Obviously we were spotted emerging from the Women's Caucus teepee. In the old days, at this point, we'd pretty likely have been tortured to death. As it is, I realize belatedly, we appear to have signalled our political allegiance as clearly as possible, and for the Medicine-Man-As-Leader, that makes us running-dogs of the Lesbian Conspiracy.

I am beginning to see the beauty of caucusing. Surely this isn't intended, but we have become three parties, with the two smaller opposition factions—Green Whites and Native Women's Association—driven into each other's, um, political embrace. The numbers have shifted dramatically, too. With half the Native caucus, plus the lawyer, having vanished overnight, the greenies-and-women's coalition has become a significant force . . . even if the bottom line is that there has been hardly any public debate at all—about anything! I've heard of confused, nebulous meetings, but this is insane! One would hope that the man charged with responsibility for the Talking Stick had been manoeuvring adroitly in the back rooms, building bridges between the factions—but since he didn't show up in the teepee where *two* of the factions were huddled in solemn enclave, he must have spent all his time with the *third* faction. And not manoeuvring so adroitly, by the looks of it. Half of those people didn't leave overnight by coincidence. Sure, maybe they left because it was clear that nothing was going to be decided. Maybe that's what you do at a powwow: stay until you're not interested any more. Vote with your feet. But then, I could have it all wrong, and maybe the real business of the powwow has been quietly done, and the people who have departed are off zealously fulfilling their revolutionary missions. They might have walked because they didn't like the direction in which Leonard was letting things drift, or they might have walked because they agreed with the lawyer, and already thought the profile here was too high, things were being talked about too openly. Either way, the Medicine Man has come out of the backroom power struggle severely weakened; hard for him to rule absolutely, as a real leader should, with half his biggest caucus gone and the opposition, which he has totally alienated, in bed with each other. Yet because he appointed himself, who is to throw him out? There's no apparatus.

Or so it seems to me. Until I see the Native gestalt at work, moving with unnerving swiftness.

The tension finally breaks when Leonard Horse digs a tobacco pouch out of his vest and starts absentmindedly rolling a smoke. He has been so steadfastly ignoring nearly half the room that he is totally unaware just how intensely we are focused on those busy, bony fingers of his. He is just about to strike a match when Alice's voice comes lancing across the room:

"I thought this was a no-smoking area."

Nearly everyone reflexively looks at the beautifully embroidered and prominently displayed NO SMOKING sign.

You wouldn't think an irritatingly banal comment like that could be so charged with icy malevolence. She hasn't just told him to stop smoking. She's told him to *shut his stupid face and do a complete fade.* Maybe I'm too accustomed to subtext—seen too many Woody Allen films—but it is crystal clear to me that Alice has fundamentally challenged the Medicine Man's rule. It is a frontal assault. Whatever he says next, she's going to hammer him with a tough question, followed by a tougher question until she kicks him off his throne, and she ain't interested in being nice any longer. Leonard has gone from being a holy Medicine Man to being just plain The Man. She will be remorseless. I saw last night how far she can take every argument. She is deploying. Leonard's goose is cooked. Should *not* have crossed her.

The Medicine Man's lips draw back so his face becomes wolfish, and his eyes snap up to meet his nemesis, but she's already *there*, waiting for him, the Evil Eye aimed. Slowly, he rises, as though fighting his way to his feet against enormous gravitational drag. Or is he being *pulled* from his seat, very much against his will? Alice's eyes narrow to pencil-lines. She sits as implacably as Brother Rock. I can feel these two force fields rushing across the room at each other, and it suddenly becomes overwhelmingly obvious to me: what I have been witnessing is nothing less than a clash between a shaman and a witch. I have only been seeing things in urban Eastern Canadian terms, hearing the charges and counter-charges of sexism and feminism, seeing the same weary old struggles that infect mainstream society. But that's only the surface, as perceived through the filter of my slightly postmodernist senses. This is older, deeper, deadlier. Of course, he calls himself a Medicine Man and she calls herself an Earth-Healer, but it's shamanism and witchcraft they seek to practise, all right. How good or bad they are isn't for me to measure, but they can both throw around some kind of psychic fire, I'm sure. In a perfect Aboriginal world, he would be the patriarch and she would be the matriarch; teamed up, they would rule. But they hate each other's guts. In his vision, he leads the tribes in a historic uprising, emulating his ancestors. In hers, she brings the power of nature to bear to heal the world, emulating hers. Whose side am I on?

Somebody, turning in his chair to watch the action, knocks a coffee cup off the table. Rod jerks as though a shot has been fired. We exchange knowing looks. My old buddy's eyes are haunted. Rod is very sensitive to this kind of higher psychic stuff. Who really made that coffee cup fall? Brother Leonard or Sister Alice?

Leonard's chair squeaks backwards as he steps away from the table, grasping the Talking Stick, and I think: *Shit, we're going to have to tackle him*, because it seems he is starting toward Alice with the intention of hammering her brains in. On the other hand, the stick might easily break on Sister Rock's sculpted head. She doesn't flinch. Her Evil Eye gleams in a shaft of morning light.

The Medicine Man stops as though he's hit an invisible wall. His focus shifts to some point in the air dead ahead. He is in a trap, isn't he? You can see the lightbulb coming on. And like a smart animal, he instantly goes dead. With just the smallest flicker of his eyes he takes in the whole room, reading the situation with newfound clarity. He can see perfectly well that there's *nothing he can do*. He can't bash in Alice's head in front of everybody. He might even be realizing he's made all the wrong political decisions so far. He's been dysfunctional as a facilitator. He has allowed the agenda to be dominated by one over-the-top white legal fruitcake. He's acted the sexist pig, and calamitously underestimated the power of the Sisterhood. He lorded it over us Green White Guys, ordering us around like underlings, or worse—liberals. Maybe there is something in the

Native way of letting leaders emerge that dooms them, the game going to the guys who are the most self-absorbed. But then that would have doomed the Europeans too, wouldn't it? Still, what I see on Leonard's face, as he looks at his world crumbling around him, is awful. It is a peculiar kind of man-pain, a dying of the hard-won ego. And then I remember: there's tradition for this. In the ancient golden era of the great Iroquois Confederacy, it was the women who picked the chiefs, and when the chiefs blew their gig, it was the women who impeached them.

Rod's head has been twisting back and forth like a spectator at a Ping-Pong match. "She's got him," he whispers after a minute.

Indeed, Leonard suddenly breaks eye contact with Alice, turns awkwardly, very much as though spirits were fighting for control of his muscles, and lurches in the opposite direction, Talking Stick clacking on the flagstones as he marches, mustering all his dignity, somehow under compulsion, toward the French doors leading out onto the verandah. As he jerks past the last table, his hip smacks against it, knocking another coffee cup flying. *Crash*. Rod twitches again. As Leonard's hand seizes the doorknob, I see that he is trembling. And then he's gone, clambering stiffly, almost staggering, toward the Sacred Fire.

Alice and the Sisters burst out in merciless laughter.

At first, it is all I can do not to join them. Yay, Sisters! The guy has, after all, been behaving abominably toward them. Just because I've romanticized him in my own head doesn't mean he should be allowed to get away with anything less than treating women with full egalitarian respect. Harrumph! Of *course* I'm on their side; a mama's boy is always going to want to go play dolls with the girls rather than full-contact football with the guys. I take a certain amount of pride in the fact that I am rather seldom consumed by the urge to hurt or, much worse, *be* physically hurt. One thing: Leonard Horse doesn't like getting hurt either, and he's hurting badly.

So instead of laughing, I get up as unobtrusively as possible, and while pretending to take my dishes to the kitchen, I slip out the back door and trudge away along the gravel road lined with pines, opposite the open field with the Sacred Fire and the teepees; blue peaks and clouds melding together way beyond the barn. Several crows burst into conversation, their *caws* echoing away.

Leonard is standing, alone, staring into the Sacred Fire, which has burned low. Smoke swirls around him. He unties his ponytail so that his hair plumes dark and huge in the gusting wind. He leans for support on the Talking Stick like someone who has just committed seppuku, or a general at the end of a long losing battle where he has thrown thousands of lives away. In defeat, he is a more dramatic figure than ever. And I remember something Paul told me about the Oglala Sioux: in times of crisis, the Medicine Men would try to lead. And if that failed, the Warriors took over. Lacking in consensus-building skills as Leonard may be, he at least *tried*. I have a horrible feeling that we *all* blew something here. We weren't worthy. We came to the pass on the Sacred Mountain, a place where we were supposed to meet our destinies, and there was nothing there except new and ancient struggles for power, strategic interests, egos, ideologies, cabals, decadence, lust.

Man, am I *down*!

I want to go over and commiserate with Leonard, give him some advice. I know what it's like to be a fallen leader. But I also know he needs to be alone right now. So do I.

24

Discussion by the Sacred Fire

Nothing gets resolved. There is no final session. The powwow just dissolves. Might as well head home.

By the time we have packed and loaded our stuff into Alice's van, Paul's and Lisa's bags into their rental, it is mid-afternoon. The teepees are down, bare poles left standing, a skeleton encampment. Truck engines are revving. A cold front has come in. The clouds are dark, heavy with snow. Everyone is anxious to get going. But a Native guy in his thirties, one of the most non-communicative of all, comes over, surprisingly, and invites us, as a group—"You folks from the city" (pointedly excluding Alice and the Sisters)—to come say a few words over at the Sacred Fire.

"I'll wait," Alice says icily, shaking her head in disgust.

The Medicine Man is nowhere in sight. There are about a dozen Natives, all guys, standing around the fire. They are hard-muscled, stern-faced, athletic, with traditional braids, headbands, and medicine pouches. Several are wearing camouflage tankpants and jackets, the kind that hunters favour—these guys must hunt a lot, I assure myself—and then I notice that their boots are all rather military. It hits me: *Gong!* The Warriors Society has finally revealed itself.

"You guys've got connections," the oldest-looking warrior says. "How can you help us?"

That boils it down nicely. We take turns dancing artfully. Paul first, since he is the famous one with all the Hollywood contacts, the big-name stars as supporters, rich American backers. He delivers a really good speech about Sun Tzu, author of the ancient Chinese text, *The Art of War.* "You guys have to read this if you expect to win *any* campaign. Napoleon used it. General Giap used it in Vietnam."

But when he's finished, the question comes back: "What millionaire superstars can you put us in touch with?"

Paul, I'm sure, is not about to throw open his contact list with the names and private numbers of his benefactors and supporters, never mind his membership list. These are the survival lynchpins of a small organization. You give those away and you've got nothing left. It takes decades to build a list such as Paul must possess. He is insistent, at any rate, that what's important is not the question of money, or of getting Brigitte Bardot onboard, but of strategy and tactics. But sure, he'll ask a couple of stars he knows if there's any way they could back anybody here.

Lisa's southern drawl and her good looks work against her. She manages to sound like the ultimate American super-organizer, as though she has been running Paul's organization for years, instead of having just arrived in the good captain's bunk. She uses lines like "You've got to get your shit together," as though she was talking to a bunch of raw whale-saving recruits. But nobody seems to mind. They just enjoy looking at her.

Rod hasn't got too much to offer. He works as a bureaucrat in a government ministry. It's been a lifetime since he charged the barricades at People's Park. But he *does* know a lot of people in the West Coast environmental movement and on the political scene, and he'll certainly talk to all of them, trying to get them mobilized. Absolutely.

Walrus is the practical, realistic presenter. He works on Parliament Hill, after all. He can channel information back and forth. He can stir the pot a little in the House of Commons by getting his MP to ask the right questions. "Consider us networked," he assures them.

And now my turn. Well, I can talk to people in TV back in Toronto, although the truth is, I can't promise much. I can write columns in a weekly on the West Coast which gets read by other local media, at least. So that's something. But mainly what I can try to do for them is get them hooked up with fax machines and e-mail. Just as I finish saying this, my cigarette burns down to the filter, and

I flick it into the fire, thinking nothing of it. Ah! For a moment, I seem to have everyone's attention. Certainly they are all looking at me intently. Thinking this must be due to the brilliance of my suggestion, I give a little la-de-da lecture about modern news communications systems. The attention drifts away. I can tell by the looks on their faces they were hoping for something more tangible. I'm not giving my all here, am I? The truth is, I am bone-tired, disillusioned, feeling abused. And I don't know what this is about any more. "It would help if I knew what kind of situations we're talking about," I venture.

The Warriors exchange looks, shrug. One at a time, minimalistically, they cite the issues they're facing: a smelter wanting to build another dam after nearly wiping out the salmon runs with the first one; plans for logging on traditional hunting lands by a Japanese multinational; low-flying NATO military jets on training flights, freaking out the caribou; mine tailings leaking into upstream water supply; the usual battlefronts. Ho-hum unless it's *you* being poisoned or starved out. Oh, and almost a light one, a final throwaway: some Sun Dancers wanting to hold traditional religious ceremonies on land owned by a white cattle rancher in a place called Gusta-Something Lake. I am relieved. Nobody is talking about taking hostages.

Finally, the Warrior who spoke in the first place blurts out:

"Don't *any* of you guys have any money you can kick in?"

We all look at each other. Paul laughs first, followed by the rest of us. Me a little more nervously than the others since I'm getting paid a Toronto television reporter's salary, which must look pretty good compared to anyone else's here, and I do have a swimming pool, but hey, my mortgage is a fuck of a lot bigger than the pool. . . .

Paul points out he doesn't even pay himself, just lives off his lecture and teaching fees.

Lisa, cheerfully: "I'm a volunteer."

Walrus shakes his head, grins wanly: "I work for the NDP."

This actually elicits a round of chuckling.

Rod: "And I work for the B.C. government." Even more wanly.

Again, miraculously: laughter!

It ends with a friendly but somewhat desultory round of Revolutionary Handshakes. Nothing very specific seems to have been dealt with. The burning issue of guns has not been publicly addressed—but maybe this is the Indian Way: if something is uncomfortable to talk about, nobody talks about it. Subjects just get dropped. If there *is* a Plan, damned if I know what it is. Certainly nobody has scribbled an Alternative Magna Carta. We have networked, that's about it. And we are still Brothers, somehow. But our Green White Guy input hasn't been sought too systematically. This reminds me, unfortunately, of my days as the flack for the Kwakiutl. They'd listen to me, then carry on doing exactly what they wanted to do all along. It comes down to strategic interests, indeed. In this case: *theirs.* What of the giant death-cloud spreading over Turtle Island? Oughtn't *that* to be a fit subject for tactical discussion? What we have here is a failure to connect.

To which I offer the great Canadian response: Oh well.

The first few flakes of snow are coming down. Hey, who's cueing the symbolism? All along the weather has been perfectly scripted, now that I think about it: the near white-out coming in, the beauty of the snow once fallen, its sudden melting, the reincarnation of autumn, the nighttime clamping-on of chains of ice, now this: softly, silently, erasing the mountains, the true end of Indian Summer.

Suniva's goodbye hug to Watson is effusive. How can you *not* love your former captain if he got you back alive? But she is reserved with us Three Rogues. Although we have not debated the Great Issue of the Day at all, I sense she is disappointed in me, in particular, as an old crewmate, for having supported the limp-dick option of not leaping into the cauldron of civil war. She's still glowing with some kind of New Understanding; a skinny, fanatical little blonde, young enough to be my daughter, oozing love for humanity and All Living Things from every pore.

As we are clambering into Alice's van, Walrus confides to me: "I guess nobody told you, but absolutely the worst single thing you can do at a powwow is throw *anything* into the Sacred Fire. Especially something as grossly low-level as a cigarette butt. If anybody does, it's total bad luck. Poison. Wipes out all the good hard-earned accumulated karma at a blow."

"Why the hell didn't somebody say something to me?" I protest.

He grins. "I guess they just couldn't believe anybody would do anything as sacrilegiously fucked-up as *that*. It's like shitting on an altar during mass, okay?"

Lovely. In the final minutes of the Great Gathering I have managed to soil the Sacred Fire itself, violating one of the most fundamental taboos, dooming *everything* to failure.

"So it's all *my* fault, after all," I mutter under the burden of old Catholic guilt reflexes.

But Alice is in a sagacious mood. As she aims the van toward the highway, flicking on the wipers against the thickening snowflakes, she says with a shrug: "It was fucked anyway."

25

Good Hunting at Gustafsen Lake

Fastforward two years to September 1995:
I am sitting on my desk in the newsroom studio safely back at my job in Toronto, watching the images fleeting across the myriad screens, waiting to do my live pop for the *Six O'Clock News*, when the anchor comes on to announce that the RCMP have just held a press conference at 100 Mile House in British Columbia, where the biggest, most expensive armed standoff in Canadian history is happening—a group of some two dozen Native "cult followers," as the media keeps calling them, versus a seventy-man army of Mounties. Although the police are already backed up by choppers and armoured personnel carriers, they have additionally equipped themselves with twenty-four-hour Westcam surveillance, night vision, heat sensing, trip-wire booby traps, on-ground cameras, and early detection devices. Surely, nothing can move without being instantly targeted. What foolish creature would dare? The Mounties have spent five million dollars so far and fired maybe fifty thousand rounds of ammunition into the camp, leaving holes fifty feet up in the trees. The slaughter at Waco, Texas, has just happened.

Miraculously, so far, no one has been killed. It turns out the sun dance is really the legendary ghost dance. The ghosts are called forward to block the bullets. The great Spirit is said to be onside. And so far, regardless of the murderous barrage aimed at the camp, nobody has been reported injured. The sun dance was banned in the nineteenth century because it made the Natives a more viable military force, convinced that they seemed to be impervious to invading European armies. These guys in revolt near 100 Mile House were armed with more than fantasies, though, having managed to fire a couple of hundred volleys back at the Mounties.

Amid reports, our anchorman intones, that the RCMP have asked for military assistance from troops deployed in Kamloops on "training exercises," more violence is reported from the camp where the summer-long armed standoff continues. There has been a "firefight," it seems, between Mounties and occupants of a red truck on a road close to the Sundance Defenders camp at Gustafsen Lake. A stern, clipped corporal tells the cameras that *thousands* of rounds were fired, managing to make it sound like some kind of tit-for-tat exchange of bullets, army-to-army.

"The officers were actively pursued by persons from the armed camp and only great restraint on the part of the officers prevented what could have been a very serious incident."

Bison armoured personnel carriers were used, yes, four of them, yes, but "strictly in the defensive posture" to extract the officers to safety.

The red truck was "disabled" on the road just outside the camp. Several people fled the truck and were pursued by the police, who halted when they were shot at, but "returned fire, wounding three. One of the casualties, a woman, was seriously hurt."

I close my eyes. I know who it has to be. Jesus, I hope it's not her. Not Suniva.

In the days to come, we will learn—mainly via the Net—that the instant the red pickup truck, occupied by three Ts'Peten Defenders on their way to get water, had been "disabled" by a command mine, a fourteen-ton bulldozer-equipped armoured personnel carrier came crashing out of the bush with camouflaged, flak-jacketed Emergency Response Team members on board, rifles aimed. As the APC came charging straight toward them, Wolverine, the driver of the crippled pickup, leapt free, hoisted his rifle, and tried to shoot out the onrushing APC's tires, while the other two Defenders, and the camp's pet dog, jumped out the passenger door and fled for their lives toward the bush. Overhead a surveillance chopper plunged hideously low, its Westcam eye swivelling like a turtle's to take everything in . . . McLuhan and Bradbury and Orwell, it's all coming true!

Big Brother controlling the medium! The RCMP have it all on tape, available on VCRs with a court order: the blowing up of the truck, Wolverine leaping away at the last minute before the APC rammed him; quite possibly the only reason he survives is because the APC, on its second run at him, snagged on a stump . . . Except, mysteriously, there *is* one piece of videotape missing from the court evidence: the couple of moments when we should have seen Suniva Bronson down below, the quarry, running like a deer, the camp dog holding loyally back to stay beside her. She is, we'd note, unarmed. A sinewy waif, her skinny arms darkly tanned, blonde hair sunburned almost white, this young lady is seriously trying to get away as the APC and the chopper and the guerrilla-fatigue guys with machine guns close in, firing, with every intent, as far as she can see, to kill her . . . The Hunt! This is exhilarating, no? They *do* have footage of the instant, just before the moments that are missing, when an RCMP sniper—one of sixty officers in the field that day!— picked off the dog. It went tumbling, back legs thrashing, in a mist of blood, and Suniva, the gentle Vegan, staggered and paused in anguish, watching it die. Then started to run again, scrambling desperately. But the next sequence, when a .223 slug found the tender flesh of her skinny little arm, and shattered it, is gone. No record. It was just one bullet, after all, in the hail of twenty thousand rounds of ammo fired by the Mounties in a two-hour period that day.

Somehow they got her back to the camp. God knows what kind of pain she was in, but when the RCMP radiophoned an offer to come in with an ambulance and take her away, she refused. It was only later, after all the twisted politics had worked their way through the media nervous system, that she allowed herself to be taken to hospital, where she was charged, of course, and eventually sentenced to six months in jail.

The worst moment, emotionally, came after she had been released when she went down to the police station with her mother to retrieve her driver's licence, and a cop dragged them both into a room and forced them to watch the Westcam tape of the dog being shot. Tumbling. The blood. Try a little psychology on the Veggie. She has borne her terrible pain and mutilation stoically, maintained her dignity in front of the media and juries and judges, but now she screams.

Days passed after the first news of the shooting before her name was released to the media. By then, Bruce Clark had made his appearance on the stage, described as a "controversial legal superstar." Wow! The Mounties try to keep him out of the camp, but he is indomitable, and is finally grudgingly let through. When he emerges, it is to declare in a chanting voice that "the camp is requesting third-party adjudication, as per the 1704 Instrument of Remedy set up by Queen Anne between the Colony of Connecticut and the Mohegan Indians, which was ratified in the Royal Proclamation of 1763, which stated that the making of land grants by Crown officials on land for which the Crown could produce no deed of sale from the Indians occupying it was henceforth to be considered the crime of fraud. Both the federal and provincial governments in Canada are guilty of fraud as per this Proclamation, which was renewed in Article 35 of the 1982 Repatriation of the Canadian Constitution from Britain." Et cetera. He has advised his clients that "as a matter of strict law, you are acting within your existing legal rights by resisting the invasion." Meaning the RCMP invasion of *their* land.

Ah yes, it comes back. I am familiar, indeed, with those arguments, doctor. They are good arguments. Righteous arguments. Legally iron-clad arguments, even. But, along with a fellow sentient being, sweet, sensitive, loving Suniva has been shot.

It had begun peacefully enough when a Shuswap Elder named Percy Rosette had approached Cariboo rancher Lyle James and asked if he could use the camping site at Gustafsen Lake, a popular local fishing and partying hangout, for a sun-dance ceremony. He'd seen the place in a vision. James did what I had done in a roughly similar situation years ago back in Anmore: "Sure, fella." When the Sun-dancers decided not to move away in the fall, the rancher got edgy. At one point he went down to the camp with about fifteen of his hands to serve an eviction notice. Bad move. Bad vibes. A day later, two fisheries officers encountered six men who said they were from the camp. A shot was fired in the air. The fisheries guys beat it. Things escalated. Fisheries officers moved in and charged two Natives with illegal gill-netting during a closed period. Searching their truck, Fisheries claimed to have found a stash of AK-47s, Glock 9-mm semi-automatic pistols loaded with Black Talon bullets designed to inflict maximum damage on human tissue, not to mention knives, machetes, camouflage gear, and a garrote made of piano wire.

Despite the arms seizure, more shots are fired. Ovide Mercredi arrives to mediate, but won't support Clark's demand that his clients' petition for third-party adjudication, as per the aforementioned proclamations and remedies and articles and renewals. It would commit the entire Native community to a non-starter of an issue, constitutional angels dancing on pins. He is a disappointment to the camp. Still, Mercredi tells reporters unflinchingly that the RCMP are advancing plans to invade the camp. "They told me that they have to go ahead for two reasons—one, they don't want to set a precedent. And two, they are saying white public opinion demands it."

With the exit of the Grand Chief, things quickly deteriorate. Two bruised and burned Mounties display their bullet-riddled flak-jackets after being caught in machine-gun crossfire during an ambush near the camp. They say. Only the jackets saved them. They say. Not everyone buys this story, especially after the manufacturer announces that the light-duty vests the officers were wearing were only designed to withstand small-arms fire, and if they'd really been hit by machine-gun fire, they'd be dead meat.

What is most amazing about the standoff is the political impact on the provincial NDP, which has been languishing in the polls. Premier Mike Harcourt, himself a lawyer, takes a hard line with the "Clark Thesis" that, constitutionally speaking, the province still belongs to the Indians. Taking time out from a power-luncheon meeting of premiers in St. John's, the normally laconic West Coast archliberal metamorphoses into a flagwaver. Maybe he has enough constitutional shit on his plate already, but he waves aside the entire argument about the proclamations and articles. This is clearly and simply a criminal matter. Illegal occupation. Police being shot at. Harcourt ends up demonizing the Sundance Defenders as being "seized by a cult mentality." (The NDP isn't?) Anyway, under his support-your-local-rancher banner, the NDP has soared in the polls throughout cowboy country. With the rural vote in his pocket, Harcourt is said to be considering a snap fall election.

It becomes a very weird story after that. Bruce Clark is dismissed from the case by the judge, but sneaks back into court through a side door and throws a sheaf of documents on the clerk's table, while yelling at the judge, whereupon he is "restrained." *Attacked!* he howls. He is finally led out in shackles and cuffs, with tape over his mouth. A not altogether displeasing image, I have to admit. Once released, he flies into exile in Amsterdam, saying awful things in radio interviews back home about Canadian judges and their complicity in genocide. He wants the Queen to look at the petition from his clients. He's delusional, the cops say. "A wing-nut," another authority growls. His rants make good clips, but what he's saying—somehow charging the average Canadian with genocide—seems over the top, except to a hard core of legal purists and, well, Natives. By the time Clark gets to the vital legal link—his allegation that Canada has violated Articles 2A and B of the Covenant for the Prevention and Punishment of the Crime of Genocide, 1948—the cameras turn away and the microphones are withdrawn. His "rant" is not technically as outrageous as it sounds, presented in a shouted voice in the midst of a scrum. Article One of the Convention makes genocide a crime under international law. Article Two defines genocide as any of the following: a) arbitrarily killing members of another community or ethnic group, b) inflicting serious bodily or mental harm, c) deliberately inflicting conditions meant to destroy a racial or ethnic group in whole or in part, d) forcibly removing children from their families or communities.

And yes, there *was* legislation forbidding Natives from speaking their mother tongue or holding religious ceremonies, the smallpox-infected blankets stories are probably true, and the residential schools certainly were. There's dirty linen there in Canada's past, no doubt about it. But we are talking about Canada *today*, where we spend millions of dollars on negotiations rather than just shoot it out, like at Waco. The mainstream Canuck media does not buy Clark's contention. Come off it! *Genocide*—being committed by gay-loving, gun-hating Mr. Nice Guy Canadian governments acting in collusion? You mean the feds and the provinces successfully conspiring together? Next item.

The last of the Gustafsen Lake camp defenders finally surrenders, and everyone is hustled off to jail in irons. The longest criminal trial in Canadian history will follow, with the third-party adjudication issue consistently being ruled out of order. Sentences, based on criminal charges of illegal firearms use, mischief, and, in Wolverine's case, attempted murder, range from three years to six months.

The big media eye turns elsewhere in search of food.

It occurs to me, staring at the grim reflection of myself in a barroom mirror, after learning it was Suniva who got shot, that I should have spoken up when we were sitting around the fireplace in her parents' lodge by the Athabasca, back when the lawyer made his passionate and oh-so-irrefutable case about the Colour of Right. I *should* have stood up and said something strong about the limitations of certain forms of redress, especially when the risk is sky-high. I *should* have said something about the tricks of exerting political influence without triggering a deadly response from the state. I could have made the point that sometimes your friends are your worst enemies. This should all have been said in a fatherly and mature fashion. But I sat back, didn't I? Content to observe. And I let Rod take the heat. I didn't feel like a fight with the whiz-bang lawyer. I wimped. If I *had* stood up in public, and spoken some veteran activist commonsense stuff about the insanity of going up against vastly greater firepower, playing their game, maybe impressionable people like Suniva wouldn't have gone along with the gig and got hurt. Of course I'm not my Sister's keeper, we're all consenting adults here, and I no doubt enjoy too high an opinion of my skills at persuading younger people. Especially brave strong-willed younger people. As for people who have visions, who can argue? Half of history at least was made by people acting out their dreams. All technically mad.

Every non-action is an action, didn't some Zen type say? If so, I helped set events in motion that led to Suniva being shot by not acting and I might have set a different wave of probability, or whatever it is, in motion, by acting. I had thought, craftily, that I could side-step my karma by remaining disengaged from the struggle. But no. Not that simple. My inaction, by leaving other actions to roll on unimpeded, clears the decks for mayhem. You can't escape your responsibility.

My cellphone rings, pulling me out of the morbid stupor into which I have slumped. It's Watson from Seattle.

"Looks like I've got a new campaign issue. Get this, a West Coast Indian tribe wants to start up whaling. Can you believe it?"

Oh no. Not *that*!

26

What Side Are You On?

It took until October of 1998 before I found myself on the deck of Watson's converted Coast Guard cutter, the *Serenian*, cruising in pouring rain into the mouth of the harbour at the Makah Indian Nation village of Neah Bay, just a few miles east of Cape Flattery on the Olympic Peninsula. I was not at all happy to be pitted against Brothers who wanted to take up whaling after seventy years of not bothering.

If karma is involved, an awful wheel seemed to have turned here. The renewed killing of Pacific grey whales was to be done, the Makah insisted, in the name of cultural revival, in order to get in touch with the spiritual experiences of the ancestors, preserve their identity "as a people." But documents came out showing deals had been cut behind closed doors with Japanese and Norwegian whaling interests that had nothing to do with tradition, and everything to do with money and political interests. The Makah Elders were *said* to be all in favour of renewed whaling, but not all of them *were*. Said one: "I remember when my grandfather went whaling. He went whaling because he *had* to."

Still, the Tribal Council was all in favour, and the U.S. Government, mysteriously, had given the Makah permission to make a "subsistence" kill, even though the International Whaling Commission had failed to recognize the Makah as living a subsistence existence . . . A snake pit!

And things were a little tricky when Dinah, the trusty camera-person, and I went to a sort of media reception at the Neah village community hall where our cover as just regular media types ("Paul

Who?") was almost blown. It seemed possible that some of the hefty paddlers trained for this vital traditional hunt to help out Japanese merchants (bow, wink) would be more than happy to corner us in a parking lot. But we got away. Or I did. Dinah stayed behind to help Watson and the whales.

By November, a full moon after I'd come and gone, a mob of Makah on the beach started hurling rocks at Watson and his crew, sending four people to hospital, and doing it, significantly, with blissful PR indifference to the surrounding horde of media. It was clear the Makah weren't going to be any more passive about asserting *their* strategic interests and pushing their national policies than the Japanese, Icelanders, Inuit, or Norwegians.

But then, they *are* a nation, the Makah, even though only eight thousand strong; one of the more-than-five-hundred little quasi nation-states strung like beads across North America, with border disputes flaring everywhere. This was a key point to remember whenever anyone started pontificating about "the Natives" wanting this and that. In fact this was something of an ancient story, retold: the foreigners come and make deals with different tribes, alliances form, and then shift. For a strategic reason, to preserve their forest, for instance, a tribe cooperates with conservationists, but sees nothing contradictory in also working with sealers and whalers or even becoming loggers themselves. Machiavelli would shrug, of course, seeing the American reservations and Canadian reserves as fifteenth-century-style Italian principalities, each with its internal power struggles, jockeying for independence and control. Evoke tradition! Run up the flag! Chant the songs! Revere the ancestors! The Scots would do the same. What people wouldn't?

Nevertheless, I curse, watching the harrowing footage of some three hundred rocks being hurled at my old *Sea Shepherd* buddies, and I cringe at the primeval anger of the crowd of Makah stone-throwers. Are we getting "traditional" here or what, stoning people?

Getting a case of them ol' Green White Guy blues. Maybe it's time I took a walk in the bush and went looking for that Huron.

Acknowledgments

Without Roberta, this book would not only have died completely at least twice, it would never have been extricated from the guts of the computer. Without Steve Hurlbut, I would never have gotten out on the ocean like I did. Without Moses Znaimer generously cutting me slack to write, I'd have never gotten it down. And without Doug Gibson seeing through the excess, it would all be in vain anyway. Hey!

About the Author

ROBERT HUNTER was born in St. Boniface, Manitoba, became a reporter in Winnepeg, then moved to British Columbia, where he was a columnist for the *Vancouver Sun*. He holds the first Greenpeace membership card ever issued, and was the first president and chairman of the board of the Greenpeace Foundation. Adopted as an honorary Brother of the Kwakiutl, his involvement with Native causes deepened over the years, including his work as an adviser to the Nimpkish Band Council in British Columbia. In recent years, he has lived with his family in Toronto, working as the environmental specialist for City-TV.